CONTENTS

KU-038-762

A NOTE ON REFERENCING AND ENDNOTES

Throughout *Filmish* you will find quotes from various theoretical works, each followed by a page number in brackets. This number is the page within the source text where the quote can be found. Every text referred to in *Filmish* is fully referenced in the endnotes, which start on page 178. The endnotes also reveal and explain the references and allusions found in the text and artwork, as well as providing recommendations for further reading and viewing, and supplementary notes on the subjects explored in this book.

FOR CAITLIN

FILMISH

-A GRAPHIC JOURNEY THROUGH FILM-

BY EDWARD ROSS

SELF MADE HERO

ALBA | CHRUTHACHAIL

The publisher acknowledges support from
Creative Scotland towards the publication of this title.

First published 2015
by SelfMadeHero
139-141 Pancras Road
London NW1 1UN
www.selfmadehero.com

Copyright © 2015 Edward Ross

Written & Illustrated by: Edward Ross
Edited by: Dan Lockwood

Publishing Assistant: Guillaume Rater
Sales & Marketing Manager: Sam Humphrey
UK Publicist: Paul Smith
US Publicist: Maya Bradford
Publishing Director: Emma Hayley
Designer: Kate McLauchlan

A CIP record for this book is available from the British Library

ISBN: 978-1-910593-03-5

10 9 8 7 6 5 4 3 2

Printed and bound in Slovenia

If you watched my life in flashback, you'd see I've always been in love with film. As a kid, we'd cycle to the cinema every Friday after school to watch whatever was showing. Seeing **Jurassic Park** for the first time blew my 7-year-old mind. Shoes sticking to the tacky, popcorn-covered cinema floor, every moment was a joy to my eyes and I knew I wanted more.

Soon I was consuming everything I could. I was only 8 years old when I first saw **The Terminator**, sneaking in to watch the last twenty minutes of it on the family's small black and white TV. I was enthralled – film stoked my imagination, and my passion for the medium grew as I did.

As a teenager, I had stacks of VHS tapes that I rewatched endlessly – **Robocop, 2001: A Space Odyssey, Fargo, Pulp Fiction** and hundreds more. When the VHS recorder broke, I remember staying up till two in the morning watching **Dawn of the Dead** on TV, bleary-eyed and hypnotised by its slow-burning horror.

Film-nerd status took hold. By the end of high school, I was volunteering every summer at the Edinburgh International Film Festival, one year watching so many films I was left dazed and unable to recall a single one of them by the end of it. During term time, I was studying film at university, discovering a whole host of weird and wonderful concepts at work in the movies.

It was out of this fascination that the idea for *Filmish* was born. If a life watching films has taught me anything, it's that the movies can offer us so much more than simple entertainment. They are a place we can go to learn more about ourselves, our culture and the world we live in.

Over the next seven chapters, *Filmish* will take you on a journey through film, exploring an eclectic mix of more than 300 movies from across film history, to shed new light on some of your favourite movies and answer a number of intriguing questions along the way. What is it about horror movies that shocks and repels us? Why is **Die Hard** the greatest architectural film of the last three decades? What makes Disney films dangerous?

The movies are more than just entertainment – they're a thrilling treasure trove for the cinematic adventurer willing to take a step off the beaten track. In this exhaustively researched book, brimming with movie references, even the most weatherworn film fan is bound to find something new.

I hope you enjoy the journey!

Edward Ross

THE EYE

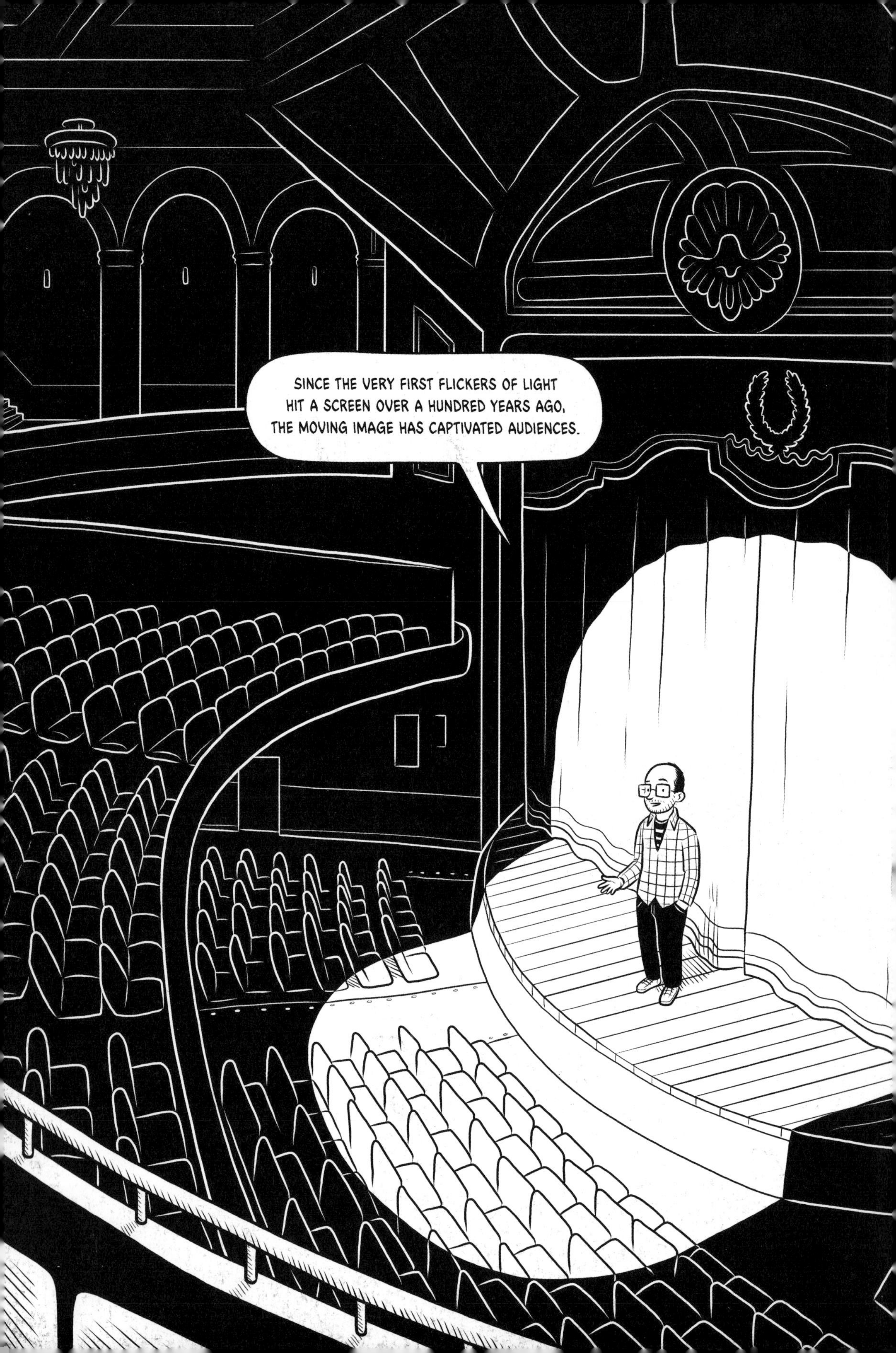
SINCE THE VERY FIRST FLICKERS OF LIGHT HIT A SCREEN OVER A HUNDRED YEARS AGO, THE MOVING IMAGE HAS CAPTIVATED AUDIENCES.

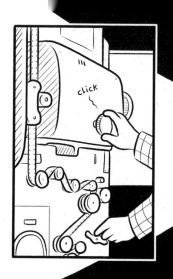

WE WATCH, TRANSFIXED, AS THE PROJECTOR'S LIGHT CUTS THROUGH THE DARKNESS AND MOVING PICTURES DANCE BEFORE OUR EYES.

A GROUNDBREAKING INVENTION, THE MOVIES **REVOLUTIONISED** THE WAY WE SAW THE WORLD, BREAKING DOWN BARRIERS OF TIME AND SPACE TO BRING NEW POSSIBILITIES INTO VIEW.

FROM THE SIMPLE SPECTACLE OF **ARRIVAL OF A TRAIN AT LA CIOTAT** (1896) TO THE 3D IMMERSION OF MODERN BLOCKBUSTERS, FILM HAS DELIGHTED AUDIENCES FOR MORE THAN A CENTURY, OFFERING US ENDLESS WAYS TO SEE THE WORLD ANEW.

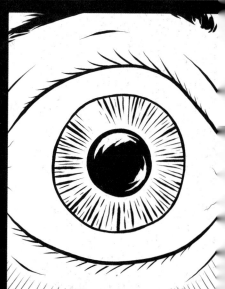

AS ITALIAN FILM THEORIST FRANCESCO CASETTI PUTS IT, "FILM SET OUR VISION FREE, RESTORING IT TO US WITH AN INVIGORATING POTENTIAL." (p7

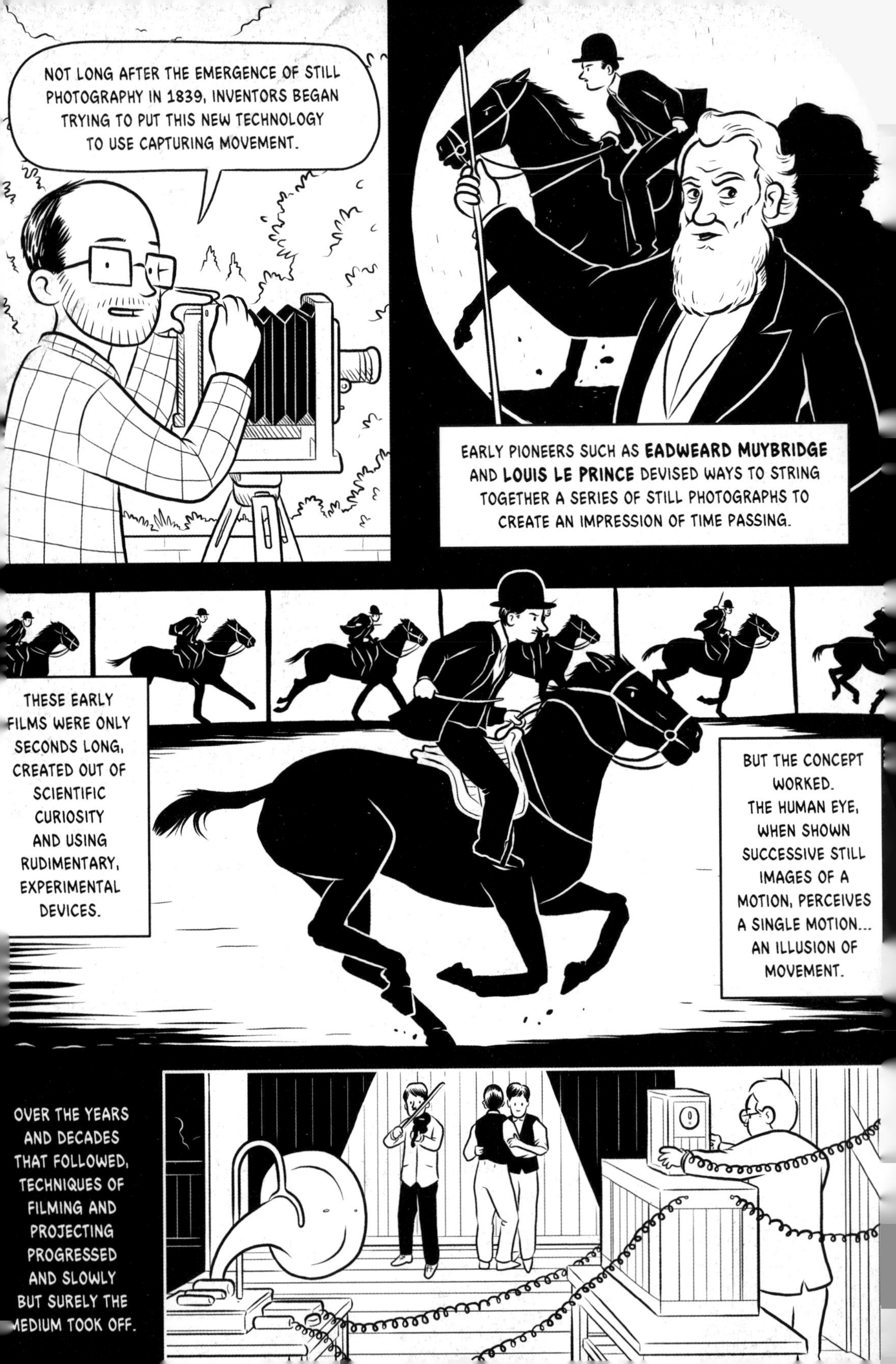
NOT LONG AFTER THE EMERGENCE OF STILL PHOTOGRAPHY IN 1839, INVENTORS BEGAN TRYING TO PUT THIS NEW TECHNOLOGY TO USE CAPTURING MOVEMENT.
EARLY PIONEERS SUCH AS **EADWEARD MUYBRIDGE** AND **LOUIS LE PRINCE** DEVISED WAYS TO STRING TOGETHER A SERIES OF STILL PHOTOGRAPHS TO CREATE AN IMPRESSION OF TIME PASSING.
THESE EARLY FILMS WERE ONLY SECONDS LONG, CREATED OUT OF SCIENTIFIC CURIOSITY AND USING RUDIMENTARY, EXPERIMENTAL DEVICES.
BUT THE CONCEPT WORKED. THE HUMAN EYE, WHEN SHOWN SUCCESSIVE STILL IMAGES OF A MOTION, PERCEIVES A SINGLE MOTION... AN ILLUSION OF MOVEMENT.
OVER THE YEARS AND DECADES THAT FOLLOWED, TECHNIQUES OF FILMING AND PROJECTING PROGRESSED AND SLOWLY BUT SURELY THE MEDIUM TOOK OFF.

PUBLIC PERFORMANCES BEGAN TO TAKE PLACE ACROSS THE WORLD, TENTATIVELY AT FIRST IN THE FORM OF **THOMAS EDISON'S** PEEPBOX-STYLE EXHIBITS AND LATER WITH THE **LUMIÈRE BROTHERS'** PUBLIC PROJECTIONS.

MERELY DOCUMENTS OF EVERYDAY EVENTS, THESE FILMS BORE WITNESS TO LIFE IN THE LATE 19TH CENTURY.

THEY MAY SEEM QUAINT NOW, EVEN MUNDANE, BUT TO THE EYES OF THOSE EARLY AUDIENCES THE SHEER EXISTENCE OF THESE MOVIES WAS SPECTACLE ENOUGH.

SOON, CINEMA'S PIONEERS WERE USING THEIR CAMERAS TO FILM IN FAR-FLUNG LOCATIONS AND DOCUMENT IMPORTANT HISTORICAL EVENTS, OFFERING AUDIENCES WHAT FILM HISTORIAN TOM GUNNING CALLS A "CINEMA OF ATTRACTIONS". (p39)

A FASCINATION WAS GROWING FOR THIS AMAZING **SUBSTITUTE** TO THE HUMAN EYE, WHICH COULD BEAR WITNESS TO HISTORY ON OUR BEHALF.

UNLIKE A HISTORICAL PAINTING, A BATTLEFIELD SKETCH OR A NEWSPAPER STORY, THESE IMAGES COULD BE TRUSTED IMPLICITLY. YOU COULD **SEE** IT WAS REAL AND **KNOW** IT WAS TRUE.

THE POWER OF CINEMA WAS ASSURED.

FOR SOVIET FILM-MAKER **DZIGA VERTOV**, THE CAMERA WAS MORE THAN A MERE SUBSTITUTE FOR THE EYE: IT WAS AN INSTRUMENT THAT COULD **OVERCOME** THE FLAWS OF HUMAN VISION.

WE CANNOT IMPROVE THE MAKING OF OUR EYES, BUT WE CAN ENDLESSLY PERFECT THE CAMERA. (p15)

FOR VERTOV, THE MOVIE CAMERA HAD THE CAPACITY NOT JUST TO RECORD REALITY BUT TO REVEAL AN UNSEEN WORLD TO THE AUDIENCE, MAKING "THE INVISIBLE VISIBLE, THE UNCLEAR CLEAR, THE HIDDEN MANIFEST, THE DISGUISED OVERT". (p41)

HIS DIZZYING MASTERPIECE **MAN WITH A MOVIE CAMERA** (1929) TAKES THIS IDEA AND RUNS WITH IT, USING AN ASTONISHING NUMBER OF TECHNIQUES TO REVEAL THE VIBRANT HUMANITY OF SOVIET LIFE.

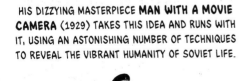

DISSOLVES, SPLIT SCREENS, MULTIPLE EXPOSURES, SLOW MOTION, REVERSE MOTION AND NUMEROUS ILLUSIONS ARE DEPLOYED TO CAPTURE THE DYNAMISM OF THE SOVIET PEOPLE AT WORK AND PLAY.

HOWEVER, AS THEORIST MALCOLM TURVEY POINTS OUT, THE STAR OF THE SHOW IS NEITHER THE 'MAN' OF THE FILM'S TITLE NOR HIS HUMAN SUBJECTS, BUT THE **MOVIE CAMERA** ITSELF.

IN VERTOV'S FILM, THE CAMERA IS PRESENTED AS AN ONSCREEN CHARACTER, SHOWN WATCHING, SEARCHING, EVEN BLINKING ITS IRIS. AT THE END, IT PERFORMS AN ENCORE TO A DELIGHTED AUDIENCE, DANCING AND BOWING ONSTAGE AS IF ALIVE.

AS TURVEY ARGUES, FOR VERTOV THE CAMERA WAS "AN OBJECT FOR REVERENCE, FAR MORE POWERFUL THAN WE ARE, AS IF ENCHANTED, AS IF POSSESSED OF A POWER INDEPENDENT OF US." (p33)

THIS WAS A COMMON SENTIMENT AMONG EARLY FILM-MAKERS, WHO SAW THE CAMERA AS A POWERFUL NEW TECHNOLOGY CAPABLE OF ILLUMINATING REALITY AND SHOWING US THE UNVARNISHED TRUTH.

THE LENS OF THE CAMERA IS AN EYE WITHOUT PREJUDICE, WITHOUT MORALS, UNTOUCHED BY ANY INFLUENCE.

DIRECTOR JEAN EPSTEIN (p8, QUOTED IN CASETTI)

IT'S A NAÏVE ASSERTION. WHILE THE CAMERA CAN CERTAINLY REVEAL THE WORLD TO US ANEW, IT CAN ALSO BE A POWERFUL TOOL OF DECEPTION...

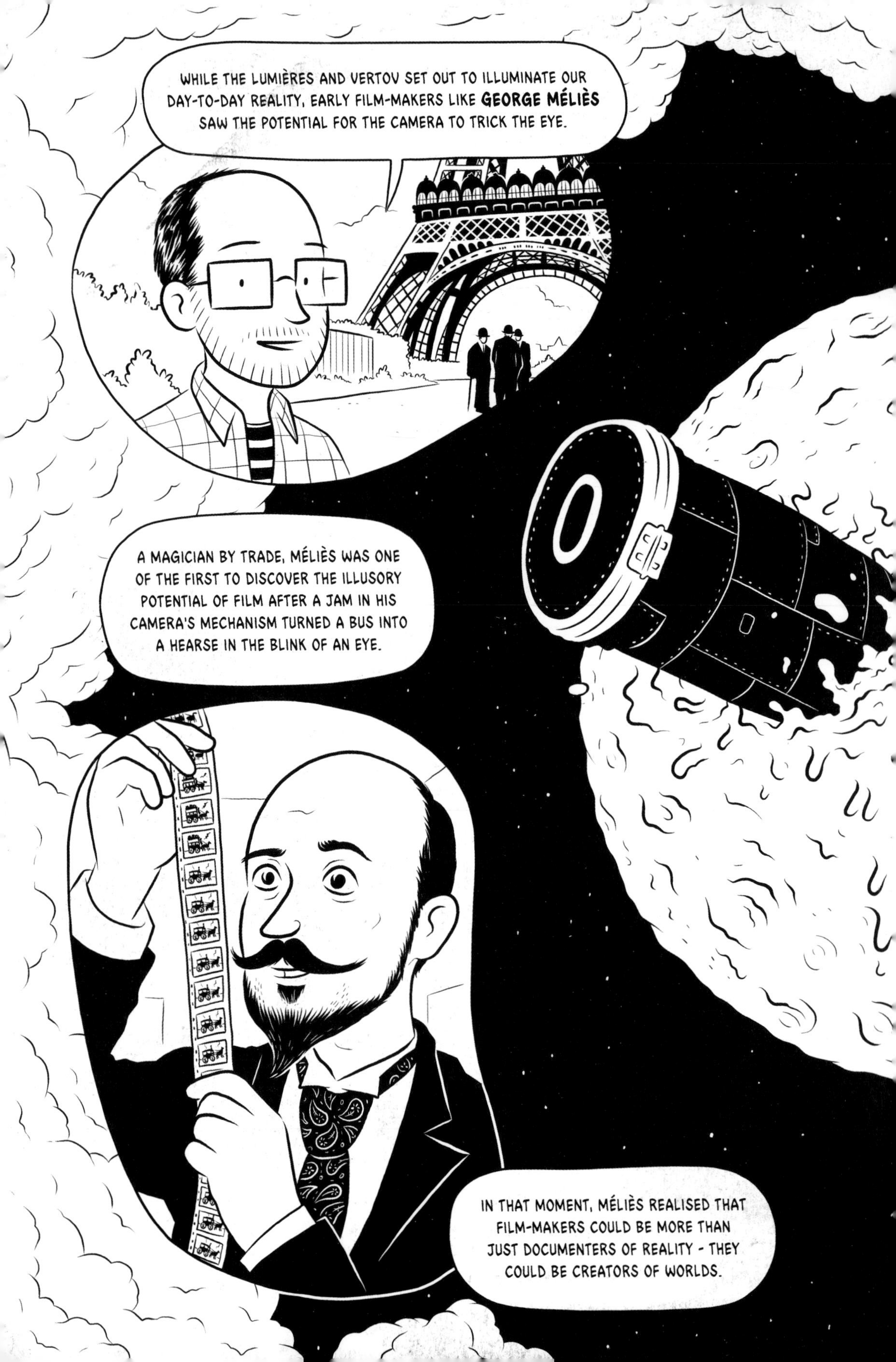
WHILE THE LUMIÈRES AND VERTOV SET OUT TO ILLUMINATE OUR DAY-TO-DAY REALITY, EARLY FILM-MAKERS LIKE **GEORGE MÉLIÈS** SAW THE POTENTIAL FOR THE CAMERA TO TRICK THE EYE.
A MAGICIAN BY TRADE, MÉLIÈS WAS ONE OF THE FIRST TO DISCOVER THE ILLUSORY POTENTIAL OF FILM AFTER A JAM IN HIS CAMERA'S MECHANISM TURNED A BUS INTO A HEARSE IN THE BLINK OF AN EYE.
IN THAT MOMENT, MÉLIÈS REALISED THAT FILM-MAKERS COULD BE MORE THAN JUST DOCUMENTERS OF REALITY - THEY COULD BE CREATORS OF WORLDS.

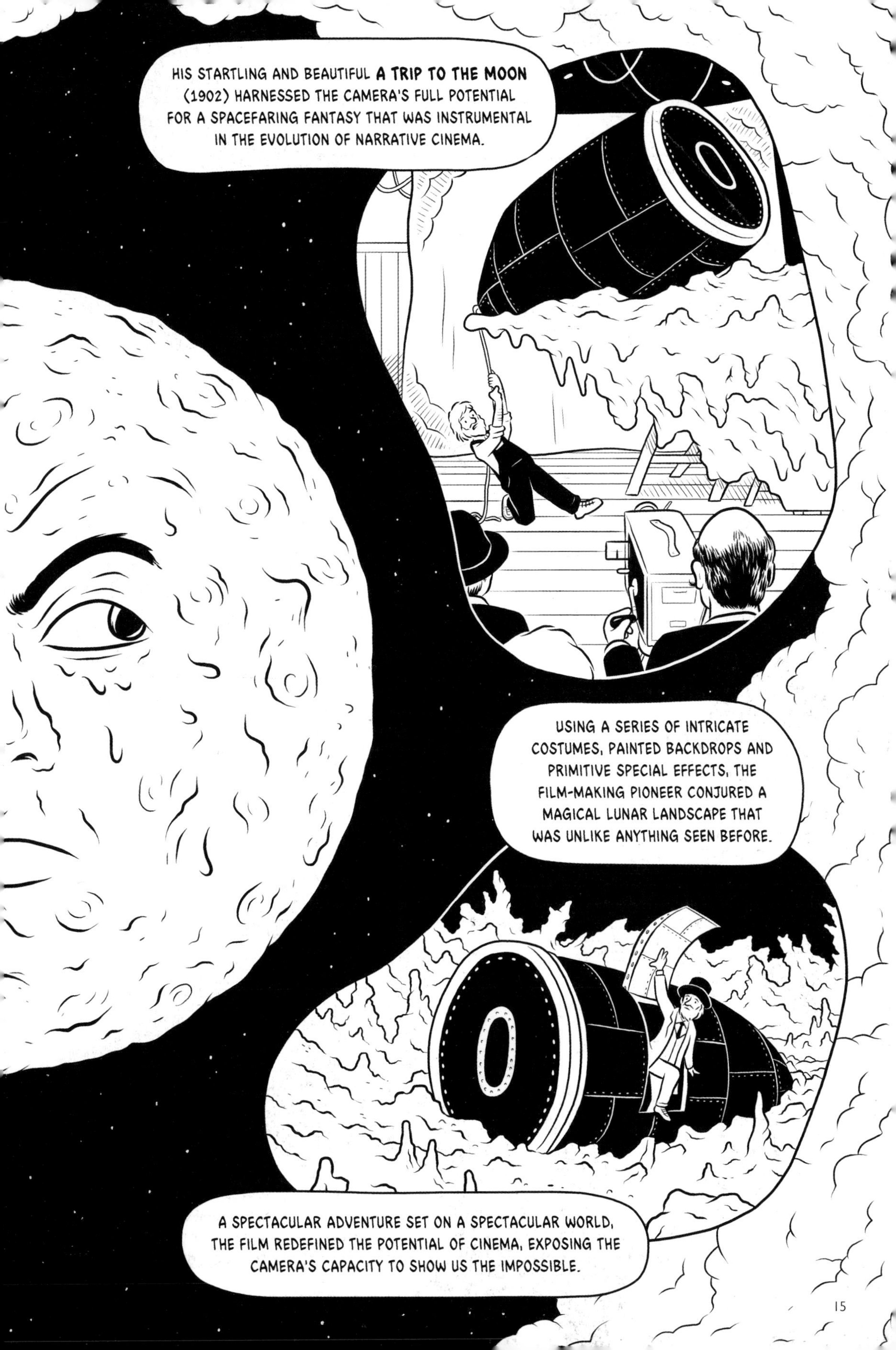
HIS STARTLING AND BEAUTIFUL **A TRIP TO THE MOON** (1902) HARNESSED THE CAMERA'S FULL POTENTIAL FOR A SPACEFARING FANTASY THAT WAS INSTRUMENTAL IN THE EVOLUTION OF NARRATIVE CINEMA.
USING A SERIES OF INTRICATE COSTUMES, PAINTED BACKDROPS AND PRIMITIVE SPECIAL EFFECTS, THE FILM-MAKING PIONEER CONJURED A MAGICAL LUNAR LANDSCAPE THAT WAS UNLIKE ANYTHING SEEN BEFORE.
A SPECTACULAR ADVENTURE SET ON A SPECTACULAR WORLD, THE FILM REDEFINED THE POTENTIAL OF CINEMA, EXPOSING THE CAMERA'S CAPACITY TO SHOW US THE IMPOSSIBLE.

WHILE THERE IS A CERTAIN INNOCENCE TO MÉLIÈS' ILLUSIONS, NOT ALL CINEMATIC TRICKERY IS QUITE SO UNPROBLEMATIC.

THE PIONEERING DOCUMENTARY **NANOOK OF THE NORTH** (1922) ATTEMPTED TO SHOW AUDIENCES THE REAL LIVES OF INUIT PEOPLE LIVING IN THE CANADIAN ARCTIC.

YET DESPITE ITS CLAIMS TO VERACITY, A NUMBER OF SCENES IN THE FILM WERE STAGED FOR THE CAMERA.

IGLOO SETS WERE BUILT WITH OPEN SIDES TO ALLOW FOR FILMING, NANOOK WAS SHOWN HUNTING WITH A TRADITIONAL SPEAR RATHER THAN HIS GUN AND EVEN HIS ONSCREEN FAMILY WAS NOT HIS OWN.

A CONSEQUENCE OF BOTH NECESSITY AND ROMANTICISM, THE RESULT IS AN INEXTRICABLE MIX OF ACTUALITY AND FICTION, WHICH AUDIENCES WERE SOLD AS FACT.

THE FILM RAISES SERIOUS QUESTIONS ABOUT THE TRUST WE PLACE IN A CAMERA'S OBJECTIVITY. FAR FROM BEING "AN EYE WITHOUT PREJUDICE", THE CAMERA IS ONLY AS RELIABLE AS THE FILM-MAKER HOLDING IT.

THE THINGS A FILM-MAKER CHOOSES TO SHOW OR HIDE, AND THE CAMERA ANGLES AND PERSPECTIVES THEY PROVIDE US WITH, HAVE A HUGE IMPACT ON HOW WE PERCEIVE THE WORLD.

DURING HOLLYWOOD'S **GOLDEN AGE** BETWEEN THE 1930s AND THE 1960s, FILM-MAKERS WORKED DILIGENTLY TO MAINTAIN THE CINEMATIC ILLUSION AND IMMERSE THEIR AUDIENCES IN THE SPECTACLE OF THE CINEMA.

CONCERNED THAT VIEWERS WOULD BE SHAKEN OUT OF THEIR EXPERIENCE BY TOO MUCH OVERT STYLE AND WOULD QUESTION WHAT THEY WERE SEEING, A NUMBER OF CONVENTIONS EMERGED THAT WORKED TO IMPERSONATE HOW THE HUMAN EYE SEES THE WORLD.

THIS IS ACHIEVED THROUGH DEPTH THAT APPROXIMATES THAT OF THE HUMAN EYE, CAMERA ANGLES AND CUTS THAT APPEAR NATURAL AND MOTIVATED AND AN ONSCREEN WORLD THAT DOESN'T ACKNOWLEDGE THE PRESENCE OF THE AUDIENCE.

THIS **INVISIBLE STYLE**, WHICH STILL FORMS THE FOUNDATIONS OF HOW MAINSTREAM FILMS ARE MADE, NATURALISES THE IMAGES WE SEE, MAKING THEM FEEL REAL AND OBJECTIVE TO OUR EYES.

THESE TECHNIQUES ALLOW THE VIEWER TO GET WRAPPED UP IN THE MOVIE BY PUTTING THE NARRATIVE FRONT AND CENTRE AND CREATING "A HERMETICALLY SEALED WORLD WHICH UNWINDS MAGICALLY, INDIFFERENT TO THE PRESENCE OF THE AUDIENCE". (p17, MULVEY)

HERE'S LOOKIN' AT YOU, KID.

MADE AT THE HEIGHT OF THE GOLDEN AGE, ALFRED HITCHCOCK'S **REAR WINDOW** (1954) DEPLOYS MANY OF THESE CLASSIC TECHNIQUES TO IMMERSE US IN ITS TALE OF VOYEURISM AND VIOLENCE.

IN THE FILM, THE WHEELCHAIR-BOUND REPORTER JEFF SPIES ON HIS NEIGHBOURS' APARTMENTS FROM HIS WINDOW AS HE INVESTIGATES A POTENTIAL MURDER.

FOR FILM-MAKER FRANÇOIS TRUFFAUT, THE FILM IS THE PERFECT ANALOGY FOR THE CINEMA: "THE COURTYARD IS THE WORLD, THE REPORTER/PHOTOGRAPHER IS THE FILM-MAKER, THE BINOCULARS STAND FOR THE CAMERA AND ITS LENSES." (p79)

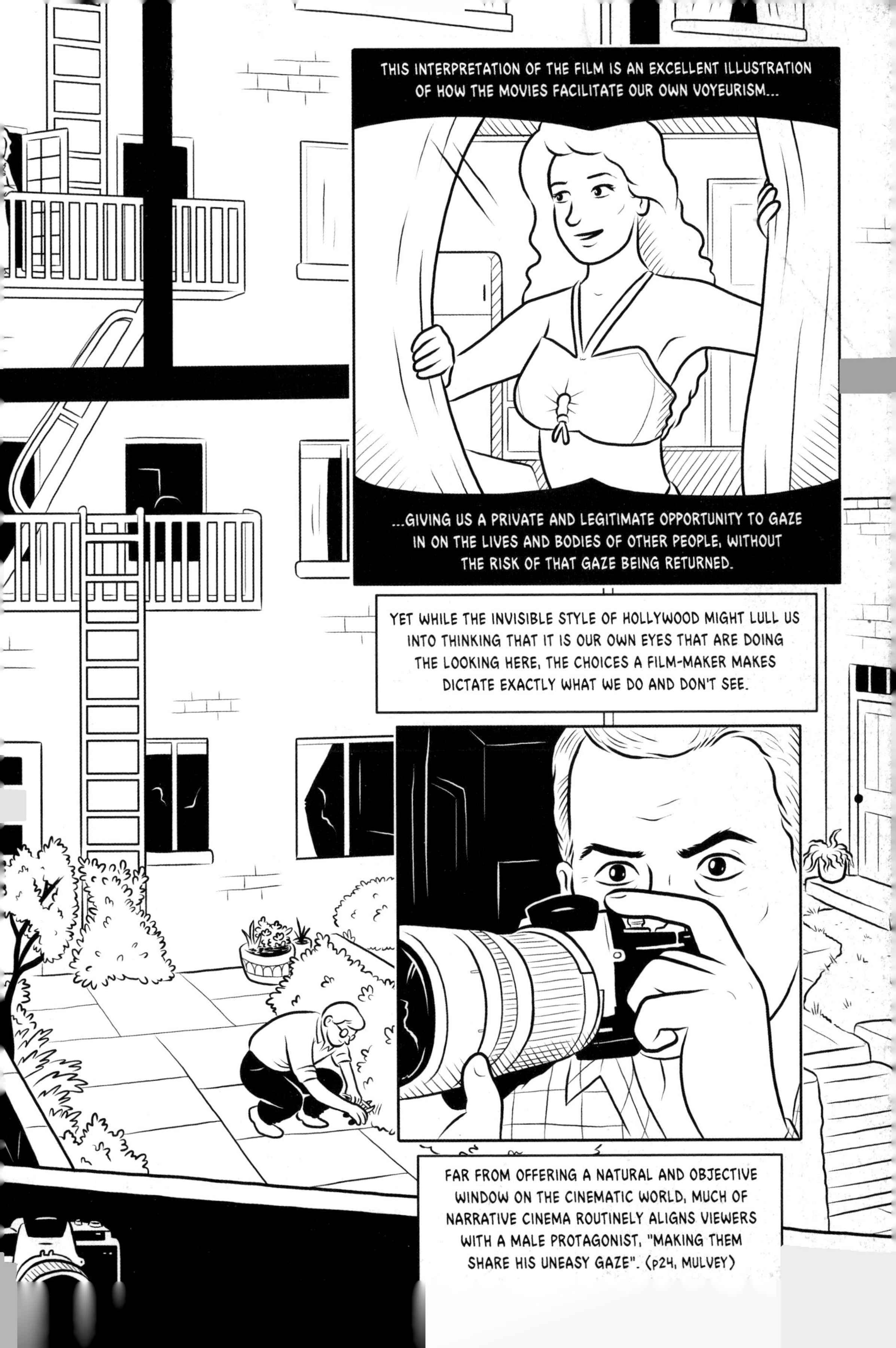
THIS INTERPRETATION OF THE FILM IS AN EXCELLENT ILLUSTRATION OF HOW THE MOVIES FACILITATE OUR OWN VOYEURISM...
...GIVING US A PRIVATE AND LEGITIMATE OPPORTUNITY TO GAZE IN ON THE LIVES AND BODIES OF OTHER PEOPLE, WITHOUT THE RISK OF THAT GAZE BEING RETURNED.
YET WHILE THE INVISIBLE STYLE OF HOLLYWOOD MIGHT LULL US INTO THINKING THAT IT IS OUR OWN EYES THAT ARE DOING THE LOOKING HERE, THE CHOICES A FILM-MAKER MAKES DICTATE EXACTLY WHAT WE DO AND DON'T SEE.
FAR FROM OFFERING A NATURAL AND OBJECTIVE WINDOW ON THE CINEMATIC WORLD, MUCH OF NARRATIVE CINEMA ROUTINELY ALIGNS VIEWERS WITH A MALE PROTAGONIST, "MAKING THEM SHARE HIS UNEASY GAZE". (p24, MULVEY)

A RESULT OF THE DOMINANCE OF MEN BOTH IN FRONT OF AND BEHIND THE CAMERA, HOLLYWOOD CINEMA'S PREDILECTION FOR MALE PROTAGONISTS HAS LED TO A CAMERA WHOSE VIEWPOINT IS TYPICALLY DICTATED BY THE **ACTIONS** AND **LOOKS** OF MEN.

IN THIS SITUATION, FEMALE CHARACTERS BECOME "AN INDISPENSABLE ELEMENT OF SPECTACLE" (p19, MULVEY), ONSCREEN LESS AS ACTIVE AGENTS AND MORE AS **OBJECTS** TO BE GAZED UPON OR CLAIMED AS A PRIZE.

THIS IS WHAT INFLUENTIAL FILM THEORIST LAURA MULVEY CALLS THE **MALE GAZE**, A SET OF CONVENTIONS THAT FORCES THE AUDIENCE TO LOOK AT THE WORLD FROM A ROUTINELY WHITE, MALE, HETEROSEXUAL PERSPECTIVE.

THE RESULTS OF THIS ARE **ENORMOUSLY PROBLEMATIC**, AS THE CAMERA ESSENTIALLY TAKES OVER FROM THE AUDIENCE'S EYES, OBLIGING THEM "TO SEE WHAT IT SEES" REGARDLESS OF THEIR OWN PERSPECTIVE. (p45, BAUDRY)

AS FEMINIST FILM CRITIC BELL HOOKS ARGUES, "THERE IS POWER IN LOOKING" (p510). WITH THE POWER OF THE GAZE SO OFTEN ACCORDED TO THE MALE PROTAGONIST, THESE FILMS HELP TO **REINFORCE MALE POWER** IN BOTH THE FICTIONAL AND THE REAL WORLD.

MICHAEL POWELL'S CREEPY AND COMPELLING **PEEPING TOM** (1960) IS A FILM WELL AWARE OF THE POTENT AND PROBLEMATIC POWER OF THE MALE GAZE.

THE MOVIE FOLLOWS ASPIRING FILM-MAKER MARK, A SERIAL KILLER WHO FILMS HIS VICTIMS SO THAT HE CAN WATCH THEM DIE AGAIN LATER FROM HIS HOME THEATRE.

WE SEE THESE MURDERS THROUGH THE LENS OF MARK'S CAMERA, A LITERAL INTERPRETATION OF THE MALE GAZE THAT LEAVES US **COMPLICIT** IN HIS CRIMES.

BUT WHILE MARK'S VIOLENCE AGAINST THESE WOMEN IS REAL, THE FILM STRESSES THAT THE MALE GAZE IS ITSELF A SOURCE OF **SYMBOLIC VIOLENCE** THAT SUBJUGATES AND OBJECTIFIES WOMEN.

A PROSTITUTE, A NUDE MODEL, AN ACTRESS - MARK'S VICTIMS ARE WOMEN ROUTINELY SUBJECT TO THE MALE GAZE, ALREADY WOUNDED EITHER PHYSICALLY OR PSYCHOLOGICALLY BY MEN'S EROTIC INTEREST IN THEIR BODIES.

THUS, MARK'S HOMICIDAL HOME MOVIES BECOME THE LOGICAL CONCLUSION OF THE SYMBOLIC VIOLENCE OF THE MALE GAZE, A CONTINUATION OF THE VIOLENCE THESE WOMEN HAVE ALREADY MET WITH.

SO ENGRAINED ARE VOYEURISM AND THE MALE GAZE IN FILM LANGUAGE THAT THE IDEA OF CHALLENGING THEM WOULD MEAN TEARING DOWN THE MOST FUNDAMENTAL CONVENTIONS OF CINEMATIC STORYTELLING.

THIS IS JUST WHAT LAURA MULVEY HERSELF DID FOR HER INNOVATIVE FILM **RIDDLES OF THE SPHINX** (1977), A PIECE OF CINEMA THAT KNOWINGLY BROKE EVERY RULE IN THE HOLLYWOOD HANDBOOK.

PART OF THE FILM FOLLOWS LOUISE, A YOUNG MOTHER STRUGGLING TO CARE FOR HER DAUGHTER IN A PATRIARCHAL SOCIETY INDIFFERENT TO HER PLIGHT.

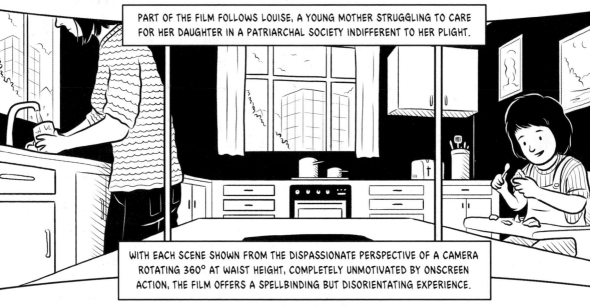

WITH EACH SCENE SHOWN FROM THE DISPASSIONATE PERSPECTIVE OF A CAMERA ROTATING 360° AT WAIST HEIGHT, COMPLETELY UNMOTIVATED BY ONSCREEN ACTION, THE FILM OFFERS A SPELLBINDING BUT DISORIENTATING EXPERIENCE.

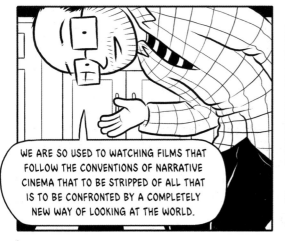

WE ARE SO USED TO WATCHING FILMS THAT FOLLOW THE CONVENTIONS OF NARRATIVE CINEMA THAT TO BE STRIPPED OF ALL THAT IS TO BE CONFRONTED BY A COMPLETELY NEW WAY OF LOOKING AT THE WORLD.

DELIBERATELY AVOIDING THE IMMERSION THAT MOST FILMS SEEK, **RIDDLES OF THE SPHINX** OFFERS A PERSPECTIVE THAT RE-ENGAGES THE VIEWER, RESULTING IN A FILM THAT "NEEDS TO BE STUDIED, NOT MERELY EXPERIENCED". (p92, MCDONALD)

ALTHOUGH EXPERIMENTAL CINEMA LIKE MULVEY'S HAS PROVED THE MOST CAPABLE AT TEARING DOWN THE CONVENTIONS THAT SUPPORT THE MALE GAZE, MAINSTREAM CINEMA HAS OFFERED ITS OWN KINDS OF RESISTANCE.

DISSATISFIED WITH THE CONCEPT OF A SINGULAR MALE PROTAGONIST, A NUMBER OF FILMS SUCH AS **MAGNOLIA** (1999), **AMORES PERROS** (2000) AND **BABEL** (2006) FOLLOW INTERTWINING LIVES, OFFERING US MULTIPLE POINTS OF VIEW ON THE SAME EVENTS.

EQUALLY COMPELLING, SOME FILM-MAKERS HAVE USED **UNRELIABLE NARRATORS** TO FOREGROUND THE SUBJECTIVITY INHERENT IN A SINGULAR PERSPECTIVE.

CITIZEN KANE (1941) TELLS THE LIFE STORY OF A NEWSPAPER TYCOON THROUGH THE RECOLLECTIONS OF THOSE WHO KNEW HIM.

DESCRIBED AS EVERYTHING FROM AN AMBITIOUS NEWSMAN TO A MONSTROUS MILLIONAIRE, THESE ARE VISIONS OF KANE SKEWED BY SUBJECTIVITY, WHICH TOGETHER PAINT A COMPLEX PICTURE OF THE MAN.

IN AKIRA KUROSAWA'S SAMURAI DRAMA **RASHOMON** (1950), FOUR PERSPECTIVES ARE GIVEN BY WITNESSES OF THE SAME CRIME.

WITH EACH ACCOUNT CONTRADICTING THE OTHERS, KUROSAWA'S INFLUENTIAL CLASSIC QUESTIONS THE RELIABILITY OF SUBJECTIVE TESTIMONY AND THE **LIMITATIONS** OF SEEING THE WORLD FROM A SINGLE VIEWPOINT.

SUBJECTIVE POINT OF VIEW IS A KEY COMPONENT OF THE HORROR MOVIE AND, AS PETER HUTCHINGS ARGUES, "THE EYE IS THE PRINCIPAL ORGAN FOR HORROR CINEMA". (p112)

ABOUNDING WITH IMAGES OF ALL SORTS OF OCULAR TRAUMA, FROM THE EYE-POPPING GORE OF **EVIL DEAD 2** (1987) TO THE UNWANTED OCULAR ACUPUNCTURE OF **AUDITION** (1999), HORROR FILMS SEEM TO RELISH THE GRISLY FATE THAT MIGHT MEET THE EYE.

KIRI... KIRI... KIRI...

BUT MORE IMPORTANTLY, THE EYE IS SHOWN TO BE AN ORGAN THAT CAN'T BE **TRUSTED**. THROUGHOUT THE GENRE, VISION IS REGULARLY TEASED, CONFUSED AND BLOCKED.

LIGHTS FLICKER AND FAIL, KILLERS LURK JUST OUT OF SIGHT OR APPEAR IN THE BLINK OF AN EYE AND CHARACTERS OFTEN CAN'T TELL IF WHAT THEY ARE SEEING IS REAL.

HORROR TOYS WITH OUR VISION TO ELICIT FEAR, PLAYING ON THE ANXIETIES ASSOCIATED WITH SEEING TOO MUCH OR SEEING TOO LITTLE, AS OUR DESIRE TO LOOK DOES BATTLE WITH OUR INSTINCT TO TURN AWAY.

IN SLASHER FILMS LIKE **HALLOWEEN** (1978) AND **FRIDAY THE 13TH** (1980), THIS OBSESSION OVER VISION BECOMES A KEY THEME, AS WE ARE REPEATEDLY THRUST INTO THE POINT OF VIEW OF THEIR MURDEROUS ANTAGONISTS.

INITIALLY FIXATED ON THIS STALKING MALE GAZE, A TWIST IN PERSPECTIVE OCCURS IN THESE FILMS AS THE FEMALE HERO, OR **FINAL GIRL**, IS BROUGHT CENTRE STAGE, TURNING THE TABLES ON HER TORMENTOR BY DARING TO **LOOK BACK**.

AS HORROR THEORIST CAROL CLOVER EXPLAINS, "THE FINAL GIRL LOOKS **FOR** THE KILLER, EVEN TRACKING HIM TO HIS FOREST HUT OR HIS UNDERGROUND LABYRINTH, AND THEN **AT** HIM, THEREWITH BRINGING HIM, OFTEN FOR THE FIRST TIME, INTO OUR VISION AS WELL." (p48)

A NEAT REVERSAL OF THE MALE GAZE, THIS MOVE RETURNS NARRATIVE POWER, AND THE POWER TO LOOK, TO THE FEMALE HERO, REQUIRING AUDIENCES TO ADOPT A POINT OF FEMALE IDENTIFICATION – SOMETHING SADLY RARE IN MAINSTREAM CINEMA.

AS CLOVER PUTS IT, "IF, DURING THE FILM'S COURSE, WE SHIFTED OUR SYMPATHIES BACK AND FORTH AND DEALT THEM OUT TO OTHER CHARACTERS ALONG THE WAY, WE BELONG IN THE END TO THE FINAL GIRL; THERE IS NO ALTERNATIVE." (p45)

THIS NOTION OF **GAZING BACK** IS AN IMPORTANT ONE. THE IMPLICIT POWER OF THE RETURNED GAZE IS PARTICULARLY EVIDENT IN FILMS WHERE ONSCREEN CHARACTERS LOOK DIRECTLY INTO THE CAMERA'S LENS, OSTENSIBLY AT THE AUDIENCE THEMSELVES.

A STRIKING EFFECT, THE EYES STARING BACK AT US ACKNOWLEDGE OUR GAZE, BREAKING THROUGH THE INVISIBLE '**FOURTH WALL**' THAT EXISTS BETWEEN THE REAL WORLD AND THE CINEMATIC ONE.

IN MAINSTREAM CINEMA'S "HERMETICALLY SEALED WORLD", THIS WAS LONG CONSIDERED A NO-NO. AS THE EARLY FILM CRITIC AND SCREENWRITER FRANK WOODS PUT IT:

IMMEDIATELY, THE SENSE OF REALITY IS DESTROYED AND THE HYPNOTIC ILLUSION THAT HAS TAKEN POSSESSION OF THE SPECTATOR'S MIND, HOLDING HIM BY THE POWER OF VISUAL SUGGESTION, IS GONE.

YET POWERFUL EXAMPLES OF DIRECT ADDRESS CAN BE SEEN THROUGHOUT CINEMA HISTORY, FROM THE SHOCKING GUNSHOTS FIRED AT THE CAMERA IN **THE GREAT TRAIN ROBBERY** (1903) TO THE SELF-REFERENTIAL AUDIENCE ADDRESS OF **FUNNY GAMES** (1997).

WHAT DO YOU THINK? DO YOU THINK THEY HAVE A CHANCE OF WINNING? YOU ARE ON THEIR SIDE, AREN'T YOU?

AN EXAMINATION OF RACIAL TENSIONS IN A NEW YORK NEIGHBOURHOOD DURING A SWELTERING SUMMER'S DAY, SPIKE LEE'S **DO THE RIGHT THING** (1989) OFFERS A PARTICULARLY POTENT EXAMPLE OF DIRECT ADDRESS.

IN ONE AUDACIOUS SEQUENCE, A SERIES OF CHARACTERS GIVE MONOLOGUES DIRECTLY TO CAMERA, EACH SPOUTING A STREAM OF RACIAL ABUSE ABOUT ANOTHER RACE.

DAGO, WOP, GUINEA, GARLIC-BREATH, PIZZA-SLINGIN', SPAGHETTI-BENDIN', VIC DAMONE, PERRY COMO, LUCIANO PAVAROTTI, SOLE MIO, NON-SINGIN' MOTHERFUCKER.

WITH BLACK AND ETHNIC MINORITY CHARACTERS SO OFTEN RELEGATED TO THE BACKGROUND, AND SO OFTEN SUBJECT TO THE WHITE MALE GAZE THAT DOMINATES HOLLYWOOD CINEMA, HERE THEY STARE BACK ACCUSATIVELY - UNFLINCHINGLY MEETING THE AUDIENCE'S GAZE.

IT'S A STRIKING, UNFORGETTABLE SEQUENCE. BY RETURNING OUR NORMALLY UNCHALLENGED GAZE, THESE CHARACTERS FORCE US TO ACKNOWLEDGE OUR OWN COMPLICITY WITH RACIST POWER STRUCTURES AND CHALLENGE OUR CASUAL ACCEPTANCE OF THE RACIAL STEREOTYPES FOUND THROUGHOUT CINEMA.

SINCE MULVEY'S SPIRITED ATTACK ON THE MALE GAZE IN NARRATIVE CINEMA, THE WAY THAT THE MOVIES POSITION US AS AN AUDIENCE HAS RADICALLY CHANGED.

ALTHOUGH THE INVISIBLE STYLE STILL DOMINATES, WE ARE NOW MORE CONSCIOUS THAN EVER OF THE MEDIATED NATURE OF WHAT WE SEE AND THE SUBJECTIVE VIEWPOINTS THE MOVIES OFFER.

LIKE THE CHARACTERS IN **DO THE RIGHT THING**, INSTEAD OF BLINDLY SUBMITTING TO THE CAMERA'S MALE, IMPERIAL OR HOMOPHOBIC GAZE, AUDIENCES ARE LEARNING TO RETURN THESE GAZES WITH THEIR OWN CRITICAL, ANALYTICAL 'OPPOSITIONAL GAZE'.

THE MOVIES HAVE KEPT PACE BY OFFERING US INCREASINGLY COMPLEX VISIONS THAT NO LONGER WORK TO UPHOLD THE ILLUSION OF A HERMETICALLY SEALED WORLD AND INSTEAD PUSH THE BOUNDARIES OF FILM STYLE TO "SET OUR VISION FREE".
(p7, CASETTI)

TODAY, JUMP CUTS, ZOOMS, SPLIT SCREENS AND MANY OTHER VISIBLE TECHNIQUES CAN BE USED WITHOUT THE AUDIENCE BLINKING, WHILE TECHNOLOGIES SUCH AS CGI AND 3D ARE REDEFINING NARRATIVE CINEMA AS "SOMETHING TO INHABIT RATHER THAN WATCH".
(p266, BUKATMAN)

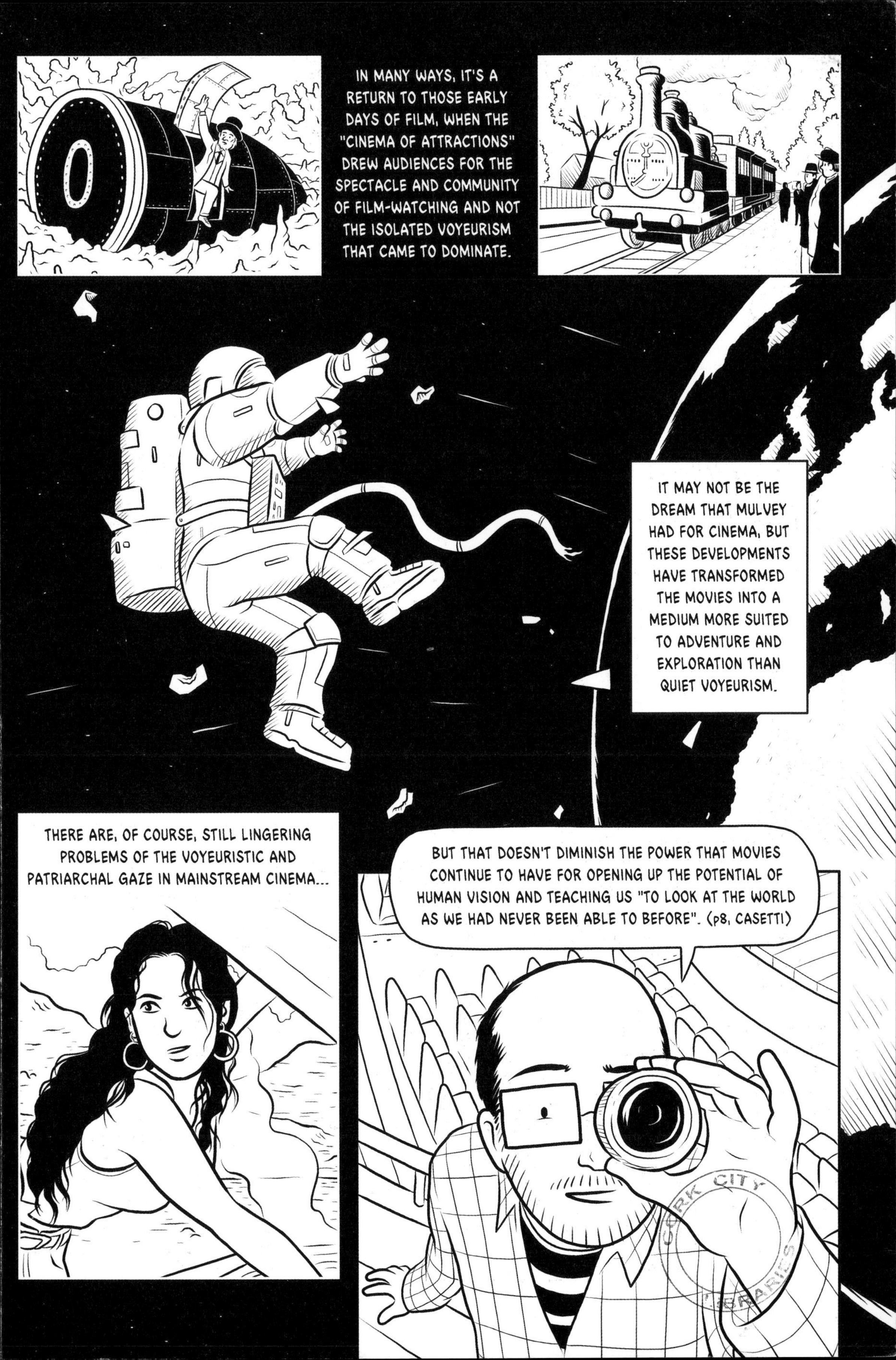
IN MANY WAYS, IT'S A RETURN TO THOSE EARLY DAYS OF FILM, WHEN THE "CINEMA OF ATTRACTIONS" DREW AUDIENCES FOR THE SPECTACLE AND COMMUNITY OF FILM-WATCHING AND NOT THE ISOLATED VOYEURISM THAT CAME TO DOMINATE.
IT MAY NOT BE THE DREAM THAT MULVEY HAD FOR CINEMA, BUT THESE DEVELOPMENTS HAVE TRANSFORMED THE MOVIES INTO A MEDIUM MORE SUITED TO ADVENTURE AND EXPLORATION THAN QUIET VOYEURISM.
THERE ARE, OF COURSE, STILL LINGERING PROBLEMS OF THE VOYEURISTIC AND PATRIARCHAL GAZE IN MAINSTREAM CINEMA...
BUT THAT DOESN'T DIMINISH THE POWER THAT MOVIES CONTINUE TO HAVE FOR OPENING UP THE POTENTIAL OF HUMAN VISION AND TEACHING US "TO LOOK AT THE WORLD AS WE HAD NEVER BEEN ABLE TO BEFORE". (p8, CASETTI)

THE BODY

THROUGHOUT ITS LONG HISTORY, CINEMA HAS TRAINED ITS EYE MOST PROMINENTLY ON THE **HUMAN BODY**.

WE ARE A SPECIES "FASCINATED WITH LIKENESS AND RECOGNITION" (p18, MULVEY), AND THE CINEMA OFFERS US A MEANS TO EXPLORE THE BODY, IN ALL ITS FORMS.

THE HUMAN BODY IS AN ENDLESSLY FASCINATING THING. FLESH, BLOOD AND BONE MADE ANIMATE, THE BODY IS THE ESSENTIAL **MATTER** TO OUR INTANGIBLE **MIND**, WITHOUT WHICH WE COULD NOT EXIST.

BUT MORE THAN MERE ORGANIC MATTER, THE BODY IS A POWERFUL SYMBOLIC FORCE SHAPED BY CULTURE AND SOCIETY.

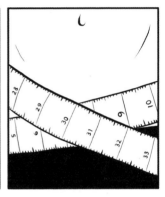

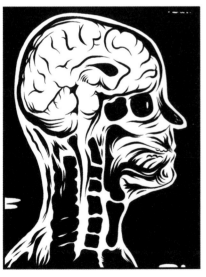

YET, "DISTRESSINGLY SUBJECT TO DISINTEGRATION AND DECAY" (p21, ELDER), OUR BODIES ARE A BATTLEGROUND FOR ANXIETIES OVER LIFE AND DEATH, INSIDE AND OUTSIDE, THE SELF AND THE OTHER.

AND SO, FROM THE GLAMOROUS BODIES OF MOVIE STARS TO THE MONSTROUS HUMAN FORMS FOUND IN HORROR AND SCIENCE FICTION, THE HUMAN BODY HAS BEEN BROUGHT TO LIFE AND MOTION ONSCREEN IN COUNTLESS WAYS.

THIS APPEAL WAS AT THE HEART OF EARLY CINEMATIC PERFORMANCE, WHERE EXAGGERATED MOTIONS AND EXPRESSIONS CLEARLY REFLECTED THE THEATRICAL AND VAUDEVILLE TRADITIONS FROM WHICH SCREEN ACTING EMERGED.

AS JAMES NAREMORE POSITS, PART OF THE BASIC APPEAL OF THE CINEMA IS THE "DELIGHT IN BODIES AND EXPRESSIVE MOVEMENT" THAT COMES FROM WATCHING ACTORS PERFORM. (P2)

THE RESULT WAS AN ERA OF WHAT GUNNING CALLS "EXHIBITIONIST CINEMA" (P39), IN WHICH PHYSICAL PERFORMANCE WAS EMPHASISED OVER NARRATIVE.

ONE OF THE MOST SKILLED SILENT STARS WAS **BUSTER KEATON**, A MAN WHO BUILT HIS CAREER ON THE APPEAL OF HIS SPECTACULAR PERFORMANCES.

FROM THE RUNAWAY TRAINS OF **THE GENERAL** (1927) TO THE COLLAPSING BUILDINGS OF **STEAMBOAT BILL JR.** (1928), KEATON EMBRACED THE EXAGGERATED PHYSICAL NATURE OF SILENT CINEMA WITH APLOMB, USING LONG SHOTS AND LONG TAKES TO EMPHASISE HIS BODY IN MOTION.

THE RESULTS ARE SOME OF CINEMA'S TRULY MAGICAL MOMENTS, WITH KEATON'S COMEDIC MASTERY OF HIS BODY AS FUNNY AND COMPELLING TODAY AS IT WAS IN THE SILENT ERA.

AS FILM-MAKING EVOLVED AND NARRATIVE CINEMA DEVELOPED, THE **NATURE** OF PERFORMANCE CHANGED.

LEGEND HAS IT THAT FILM-MAKING PIONEER **D.W. GRIFFITH** INVENTED THE CLOSE-UP TO BETTER REVEAL THE BEAUTY OF HIS LEADING LADY.

THE IMPLICATIONS OF THIS WERE ENORMOUS. NO LONGER SHOT ONLY AT A DISTANCE, THE SUBTLEST FACIAL MOVEMENTS WERE NOW AS IMPORTANT AS GRAND GESTURES, AND ACTORS WERE FORCED TO BECOME "MAESTROS OF THEIR FACIAL MUSCLES AND EYE MOVEMENTS". (BORDWELL, WEB)

IN TIME, THE DEMAND FOR ACTORS TO MORE FULLY INHABIT THEIR ROLES GAVE RISE TO **METHOD ACTING**, A TECHNIQUE IN WHICH AN ACTOR IMMERSES THEMSELVES IN THE ROLE, DRAWING ON THEIR OWN LIFE EXPERIENCES TO ENGAGE WITH THE CHARACTER THEY ARE PLAYING.

IN STRIVING FOR REALISM AND AUTHENTICITY OVER THEATRICALITY, AT TIMES METHOD ACTING HAS BEEN TAKEN TO ASTONISHING EXTREMES, WITH ACTORS SUCH AS **ROBERT DE NIRO**, **CHARLIZE THERON** AND **CHRISTIAN BALE** TRANSFORMING THEIR VERY BODIES TO MORE AUTHENTICALLY INHABIT THEIR CHARACTERS.

THE SPECTACLE AND APPEAL OF THE ACTOR'S BODY IS A THEME AT THE HEART OF SPIKE JONES' WITTY AND INVENTIVE **BEING JOHN MALKOVICH** (1999).

IN THE FILM, SAD-SACK PUPPETEER CRAIG DISCOVERS A PORTAL THAT LEADS HIM INTO THE MIND OF THE ACTOR JOHN MALKOVICH, ALLOWING HIM TO SEE WHAT MALKOVICH SEES FOR FIFTEEN MINUTES.

TURNING THE EXPERIENCE INTO A TWISTED FUNFAIR RIDE, CRAIG BEGINS CHARGING ENTRY TO MALKOVICH'S MIND, PROFITING FROM PEOPLE DESPERATE TO ESCAPE THEIR OWN MUNDANE BODIES AND BECOME SOMEONE ELSE.

CRAIG'S OWN ESCAPE COMES WHEN HE APPLIES HIS PUPPETRY SKILLS TO MALKOVICH, TAKING CONTROL OF HIM FROM WITHIN THE PORTAL.

NO LONGER BOUND BY HIS OWN BODY, CRAIG TAKES UP RESIDENCE IN MALKOVICH, USING THE ACTOR'S FAME TO START A NEW LIFE.

YET THIS TRANSFER TO ANOTHER BODY IS NOT THE SOLUTION TO HIS MISERY THAT CRAIG WISHES IT WAS.

AS CRITIC DAVID ULIN PUTS IT, "CRAIG SEEKS TO INHABIT MALKOVICH BECAUSE HE THINKS THIS WILL MAKE HIM MORE LIKE AN ACTOR - CONFIDENT, DESIRABLE, COOL. THE JOKE'S ON HIM, THOUGH, FOR THE OPPOSITE HAPPENS: MALKOVICH BECOMES LIKE CRAIG." (P57, QUOTED IN FALZON)

THE FILM IS A WONDERFUL ECHO OF MODERN CULTURE, WHERE DISSATISFACTION WITH OUR **OWN BODIES** HAS TRANSLATED INTO A CULTURAL OBSESSION WITH **THE BODIES OF CELEBRITIES**, WHO SERVE AS VESSELS FOR OUR IDENTIFICATION, BLANK SLATES ON WHICH WE **SUPERIMPOSE** OUR OWN HOPES AND ASPIRATIONS.

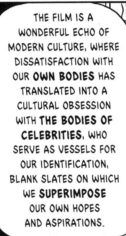

AS THE FILM STARKLY DEMONSTRATES, THIS CHANCE FOR ESCAPE IS AN ILLUSION, AND "THE MOVE TO ANOTHER BODY IS NOT REALLY A MODE OF ESCAPE AT ALL, BUT RATHER A CHANCE TO MERELY IMPRISON THE SELF IN SOMEONE ELSE'S BODY". (P47, FALZON)

THE FASHIONS FOR PERFORMANCE ARE ALWAYS EVOLVING, AND IN THE DIGITAL AGE IT HAS BECOME INCREASINGLY COMMON FOR AN ACTOR'S REAL BODILY PERFORMANCE TO BE MERGED WITH THE VIRTUAL.

PERFORMANCE CAPTURE ALLOWS FILM-MAKERS TO RECORD AN ACTOR'S PERFORMANCE AND MAP IT ONTO A DIGITAL CHARACTER, A TECHNIQUE SEEN IN FILMS LIKE **THE LORD OF THE RINGS: THE TWO TOWERS** (2002) AND **RISE OF THE PLANET OF THE APES** (2011).

THE 21ST CENTURY EQUIVALENT OF PUPPETEERING, THESE TECHNOLOGIES OFFER FILM-MAKERS UNPRECEDENTED CONTROL OVER THE CREATION OF UNIQUE, OFTEN NON-HUMAN, CHARACTERS AND ALLOW ACTORS A FANTASTIC OPPORTUNITY TO **EMBODY NEW FORMS.**

BUT THERE IS PERHAPS A DOWNSIDE TO THIS TECHNOLOGY, AS ACTORS LOSE THEIR AUTONOMY AND PRIMACY, "MERELY PROVIDING A SCREED OF DIGITAL INFORMATION" FOR ANIMATORS AND FILM-MAKERS TO WORK WITH AND HONE. (P208, FLEMING)

IN THE STERILE ENVIRONMENT OF THE COMPUTER, WE RISK LOSING THOSE LITTLE MOMENTS THAT MAKE THE MOVIES SUCH A JOY - THE MISTAKES, IMPROVISATIONS AND UNFORESEEN EVENTS THAT ADD TO THE RICHNESS OF THE FINISHED FILM AND CANNOT BE CONTROLLED ON A LIVING SET.

THE BODY'S ROLE IN CINEMA GOES BEYOND THE MERE SPECTACLE OF PERFORMANCE. WITH ITS PRIMACY IN CULTURE, CINEMA HAS A KEY ROLE IN REINFORCING AND CHALLENGING CULTURAL PERCEPTIONS OF BODILY 'NORMS'.

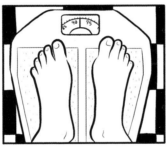

AS RICHARDSON PUTS IT: "IT IS CULTURE WHICH TELLS US THE 'IDEAL' WEIGHT FOR THE BODY, HOW THE BODY SHOULD BE GROOMED/STYLED AND HOW THE BODY SHOULD 'DO' ITS 'APPROPRIATE' GENDER." (p10)

CINEMA IS A SITE ON WHICH THESE **CULTURAL ANXIETIES** ABOUT THE BODY ARE EXPRESSED AND NEGOTIATED, AND WHERE THE **DIFFERENCES** BETWEEN BODIES ARE PUT ON SHOW AND EXAMINED.

THROUGHOUT FILM HISTORY, MAINSTREAM CINEMA HAS STRUGGLED WITH REPRESENTATIONS OF RACIAL DIVERSITY.

IN THE EARLY DECADES OF CINEMA, MOST BLACK CHARACTERS WERE DRAWN FROM "STEREOTYPES THAT HAD EXISTED SINCE THE DAYS OF SLAVERY" (p4, BOGLE) AND WERE COMMONLY PLAYED BY WHITE ACTORS IN 'BLACKFACE'.

MICKEY ROONEY IN **BREAKFAST AT TIFFANY'S** (1961)

THESE PRACTICES WOULD REMAIN COMMON INTO THE 1960s, AS WHITE ACTORS WERE BROUGHT IN TO PLAY NON-WHITE CHARACTERS, ALL WHILE REAL PEOPLE FROM ETHNIC MINORITIES WERE LARGELY ABSENT FROM THE SCREEN.

BURT LANCASTER IN **APACHE** (1954)

CRIMSON JIHAD WILL RAIN FIRE ON ONE MAJOR U.S. CITY EACH WEEK, UNTIL OUR DEMANDS ARE MET.

FROM **THE BIRTH OF A NATION** (1915) TO **TRUE LIES** (1994), RACIAL 'OTHERS' HAVE REGULARLY BEEN CAST AS VILLAINS, THEIR DIFFERENCE IN SKIN COLOUR AND APPEARANCE MARKING THEM IN OPPOSITION TO THE RIGHTEOUS WHITE HERO.

MEANWHILE, **UGLY RACIAL STEREOTYPES** WERE EVERYWHERE IN 20TH CENTURY CINEMA, SEEPING INTO EVEN THE MOST INNOCUOUS FAMILY FARE.

WHILE THE CIVIL RIGHTS MOVEMENT FOUGHT TO GAIN **EQUALITY**, MAINSTREAM CINEMA RESPONDED WITH INTERRACIAL BUDDY MOVIES, IN WHICH BLACK AND WHITE CHARACTERS WORKED TOGETHER ONSCREEN.

YET DESPITE THE EASY-GOING FUN THAT FILMS LIKE **48 HRS.** (1982) AND **LETHAL WEAPON** (1987) OFFER, AN UNDERCURRENT OF RACISM REMAINS.

WE'RE BACK, WE'RE BAD. YOU'RE BLACK, I'M MAD.

AS FILM HISTORIAN ED GUERRERO ARGUES, THESE FILMS "PUT THE BLACK FILMIC PRESENCE IN THE PROTECTIVE CUSTODY, SO TO SPEAK, OF A WHITE LEAD OR CO-STAR AND THEREFORE IN CONFORMITY WITH WHITE SENSIBILITIES AND THE EXPECTATIONS OF WHAT BLACKS, ESSENTIALLY, SHOULD BE." (p35, IN WILLIS)

BUT, AS MARY BELTRÁN ASSERTS, ALTHOUGH MODERN CINEMA HAS LARGELY ADOPTED A **MULTICULTURAL APPROACH** TO CASTING, "IDEOLOGIES OF WHITE SUPERIORITY AND NON-WHITE SUBORDINATION CONTINUE TO HAVE A POWERFUL INFLUENCE" (p63) AS WHITE MALE HEROES CONTINUE TO **DOMINATE** THE SCREEN.

MODERN CINEMA PERHAPS OFFERS HOPE AS STARS SUCH AS **WILL SMITH**, **LAURENCE FISHBURNE**, **SAMUEL L. JACKSON** AND **DENZEL WASHINGTON** TAKE ON ROLES WRITTEN WITHOUT RACE IN MIND - ROLES THAT AREN'T DEFINED BY THE BODY'S OUTWARD APPEARANCE.

THE BODIES OF WOMEN HAVE PERHAPS HAD THE MOST PRESCRIBED ROLE IN THE MOVIES, BROUGHT TO THE SCREEN TIME AND AGAIN AS A SOURCE OF **EROTIC SPECTACLE**.

INTRODUCED IN SLOW MOTION, FRACTURED CLOSE-UP OR SILHOUETTE, THESE CHARACTERS' "VISUAL PRESENCE TENDS TO WORK AGAINST THE DEVELOPMENT OF A STORYLINE, TO FREEZE THE FLOW OF ACTION IN MOMENTS OF EROTIC CONTEMPLATION". (P20, MULVEY)

A COMMON TREND SEEN THROUGHOUT FILM HISTORY, IT'S ALL PART OF CINEMA'S CONSTRUCTION OF WOMEN AS **OBJECTS**, PRESENT ONLY TO BE **LOOKED AT** AND CLAIMED AS THE HERO'S **PRIZE**.

THERE HAVE OF COURSE BEEN ALTERNATIVES. TOUGH, RESOURCEFUL AND COMPASSIONATE, RIPLEY IN **ALIENS** (1986) AND KATNISS IN **THE HUNGER GAMES** (2012) OFFER A REFRESHING TAKE ON THE ACTION HERO, DEFINED BY THEIR **WIT** AND **BRAVERY** RATHER THAN THEIR BODIES.

BUT SUCH EXAMPLES ARE FEW AND FAR BETWEEN. ALL TOO OFTEN, FEMALE BODIES ARE SHOWN TO BE OBJECTS, DESIGNED TO PLEASE MEN AND CONFORM TO MAINSTREAM IDEALS OF FEMININITY.

THE MALE BODY IS JUST AS PRONE TO **OBJECTIFICATION**, THOUGH OF A VERY DIFFERENT KIND. AS STEVE NEALE PUTS IT, "WHERE WOMEN ARE INVESTIGATED, MEN ARE TESTED." (p16)

RATHER THAN HALTING THE NARRATIVE FLOW, THE SPECTACULAR MALE BODY IS SHOWN IN ACTION, WITH AN EMPHASIS ON MUSCULATURE AND PHYSICAL PROWESS.

TESTED TO ITS LIMITS, THE MALE BODY IS SEEN AS "A MACHINE OF DESTRUCTION AND AS A CONSTANTLY ERODED AND MUTILATED FLESH." (p40, WILLIS)

FROM THE WESTERN TO THE SUPERHERO MOVIE, THE MALE BODY IS A SITE ON WHICH THE HERO'S CAUSE IS FOUGHT, HIS **BODY** TAKING THE PUNISHMENT SO THAT OTHERS DON'T HAVE TO.

YET, INCREASINGLY, MALE BODIES ARE UNDERGOING SIMILAR SCRUTINY TO FEMALE ONES IN MAINSTREAM CINEMA. **CASINO ROYALE** (2006) SEES JAMES BOND RISE EROTICALLY FROM THE SURF IN A MOMENT THAT KNOWINGLY ECHOES THE CLASSIC SCENE OF HONEY RYDER DOING THE SAME IN **DR. NO** (1962).

THIS IS A MALE BODY **ON SHOW** PURELY FOR THE SPECTACLE OF IT, SHOT IN THE SAME SLOW MOTION MANNER THAT WOMEN HAVE BEEN FOR YEARS.

THE OPPRESSIVENESS OF THE GENDERED BODY IS BEAUTIFULLY ILLUSTRATED IN DARREN ARONOFSKY'S **THE WRESTLER** (2008).

THE FILM FOLLOWS AGEING WRESTLER RANDY 'THE RAM' ROBINSON, A MAN WHOSE BODY HAS BEEN WRECKED BY YEARS OF ABUSE IN THE RING.

EVERY NIGHT, HE IS SMASHED WITH GLASS, SLAPPED, CUT, STAPLED AND BEATEN, ALL IN FRONT OF A SCREAMING CROWD.

AS HE STRIKES UP A RELATIONSHIP WITH 'CASSIDY', A STRIPPER NEARING THE END OF HER OWN CAREER, WE COME TO SEE THE VERY DIFFERENT WAYS IN WHICH THESE TWO CHARACTERS ARE AFFECTED BY THEIR **BODILY ROLES**.

WHILE CASSIDY EXPOSES HERSELF TO THE EROTIC GAZE OF MEN, HUSTLING FOR THEIR MONEY AND ATTENTION IN THE STRIP BAR, RANDY MUST SUBJECT HIS OWN BODY TO "EXTREME AND GROTESQUE ABUSE" (p110, GOLDENBERG) FOR HIS FANS' AMUSEMENT.

ECHOES OF EACH OTHER, THESE ARE PEOPLE UNABLE TO ESCAPE THE EXTREME GENDERED ROLES THAT HAVE COME TO DEFINE AND DELINEATE THEIR BODIES.

IN DIFFERENT WAYS, THEY ARE BOTH RUINED BY THE FILM'S GUT-WRENCHING END.

CINEMA HAS OFTEN REVEALED A **FASCINATION** WITH BODIES THAT CONFLICT WITH CULTURAL CONCEPTIONS OF 'NORMALITY', REGULARLY PORTRAYING CHARACTERS **DEFINED** BY BODIES THAT ARE ATYPICALLY SIZED, DISABLED OR AGEING, OR THAT DO NOT FIT INTO THE GENDER BINARY.

ALL TOO OFTEN, THE MOVIES USE MARGINALISED BODIES, AND ESPECIALLY DISABLED BODIES, AS "A KIND OF SHORTHAND TO SPICE CHARACTERS AND CONVEY INTERNAL QUALITIES OR PLOT FUNCTIONS VIVIDLY AND EFFICIENTLY". (P2, MOGK)

THIS IS SEEN CLEARLY IN THE CINEMATIC VILLAIN, WHOSE SCARS OR DEFORMITIES "MAKE HIS ALIENATION AND MORAL CORRUPTION VISIBLE" IN OPPOSITION TO THE ABLE-BODIED HERO. (P2, MOGK)

IT'S A CHILLING PATTERN OF REPRESENTATION AND THESE ARE DANGEROUS TRENDS WHICH DEFINE DISABLED PEOPLE BY THEIR BODIES AND EQUATE DISABILITY WITH **IMMORALITY** AND EVEN **EVIL**.

SOME FILMS HAVE ATTEMPTED TO REDRESS THE BALANCE, TRYING TO CONVEY THE LIVED REALITY OF DISABILITY WITH MORE SYMPATHETIC REPRESENTATIONS THAT SHOW PEOPLE WITH DISABILITIES ACHIEVING HAPPINESS AND ACCEPTANCE.

YET THESE **TRIUMPH OVER ADVERSITY** NARRATIVES ARE STILL LARGELY PROBLEMATIC, DEPICTING DISABILITY AS A 'PROBLEM' THAT NEEDS TO BE OVERCOME, WHILE IGNORING THE FAILINGS OF OUR INHERENTLY ABLEIST SOCIETY.

TOD BROWNING'S **FREAKS** (1932) IS A FILM THAT CONFRONTS IMAGES OF DISABILITY HEAD-ON, FEATURING A CAST OF PEOPLE WITH DISABILITIES WHO WORKED AS 'SIDESHOW FREAKS'.

CONSIDERED "A CATALOGUE OF HORRORS" ON RELEASE, THE FILM WAS PULLED FROM THEATRES DUE TO PUBLIC OUTCRY (p62, ADAMS). YET IT IS NOW CONSIDERED BY SOME TO BE ONE OF THE MOST COMPLEX DEPICTIONS OF DISABILITY EVER COMMITTED TO FILM.

SET AROUND A CIRCUS SIDESHOW, THE FILM TELLS THE STORY OF AN ABLE-BODIED TRAPEZE ARTIST NAMED CLEO WHO MARRIES HANS, A DWARF, TO SWINDLE HIM OUT OF HIS INHERITANCE.

WITH A SENSATIONALIST TITLE AND SETTING, ON THE SURFACE THE FILM SEEMS DESIGNED TO PLAY ON ITS AUDIENCE'S **ANXIETY** TOWARDS PHYSICAL DIFFERENCE.

YET, AS RACHEL ADAMS PUTS IT, "RATHER THAN USING THE CAMERA TO FURTHER DEGRADE THE DISABLED ACTOR, AS SOME NEGATIVE REVIEWS SUGGESTED, **FREAKS** PROVES THAT FILM MAY BE INSTRUMENTAL IN CREATING GREATER TOLERANCE TO VARIOUS KINDS OF DIFFERENCE." (p68)

FAR FROM **EXPLOITING** ITS CAST OF DISABLED PERFORMERS AS A TRUE 'FREAK SHOW' MIGHT, THE FILM SEEKS OUR IDENTIFICATION AND EMOTIONAL ENGAGEMENT WITH THEM, TURNING TYPICAL CINEMATIC VILLAINS INTO THE MOVIE'S HEROES.

BY SHOWING US THESE CHARACTERS LIVING THEIR EVERYDAY LIVES BEHIND THE SCENES AT THE CIRCUS, THE FILM NORMALISES THEIR SUPPOSED 'OTHERNESS' TO CREATE REALISTIC, RELATABLE CHARACTERS WHO AREN'T JUST DEFINED BY THEIR BODIES.

AND SO, WHILE CLEO CAN'T SEE HER COLLEAGUES AS "ANYTHING OTHER THAN THE FREAKISH PERSONAE THEY ENACT ONSTAGE" (p80, ADAMS), WE CAN.

WE ACCEPT HER. WE ACCEPT HER. ONE OF US. ONE OF US.

NO! DIRTY, SLIMY FREAKS, FREAKS, **FREAKS**! YOU **FILTH**, MAKE ME ONE OF YOU, WILL YOU?

THE FILM ENDS WITH THE SIDESHOW PERFORMERS ENACTING A GRISLY REVENGE ON CLEO FOR HER CRIMES.

YET, WHILE THIS SCENE IS FRAMED LIKE A HORROR FILM, IT DOESN'T FEEL LIKE ONE. THIS IS REVENGE, PURE AND SIMPLE; NOT THE ACT OF **MONSTERS** BUT OF **PEOPLE** PUSHED TOO FAR, FOR TOO LONG.

WHILE MUCH OF CINEMA FOCUSES ON CULTURE'S CONSTRUCTION OF THE BODY, SOME FILMS HAVE SOUGHT TO REVEAL THE MATERIAL REALITIES **INSIDE** IT.

FANTASTIC VOYAGE (1966) SEES A TEAM OF SCIENTISTS MINIATURISED AND INJECTED INTO A SOVIET DEFECTOR TO PERFORM LIFE-SAVING SURGERY ON HIM.

AS THEIR SHIP SAILS THROUGH THE VARIOUS ORGANS AND SYSTEMS OF THE BODY, WE COME TO SEE THE BODY AS SOMETHING OF A **LANDSCAPE** – A MAGNIFICENT BUT DANGEROUS ALIEN ENVIRONMENT THAT CAN BE MAPPED AND TRAVERSED.

CAPTIVATED BY THE UNKNOWABLE **INNER WORLD**, IT'S A FILM "FUELLED BY THE DESIRE TO KNOW WHAT IS HAPPENING INSIDE AND TO SEE THE INNER BODY AT WORK". (P20, SAWCHUK)

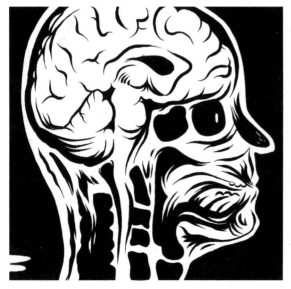

THIS WIDESPREAD FASCINATION HAS ONLY INCREASED IN RECENT YEARS DUE TO PROLIFERATING MEDICAL IMAGING TECHNOLOGY, WHICH HAS IN TURN SHAPED CINEMA'S PORTRAYAL OF THE INNER BODY IN FILMS LIKE **FIGHT CLUB** (1999) AND **ANATOMY** (2000).

THE COMPLEX RELATIONSHIP WE HAVE WITH OUR BODIES PARTLY STEMS FROM THE SPLIT WE PERCEIVE BETWEEN THE BODY AND THE 'SELF'.

AS RICHARDSON PUTS IT, "WHILE THE HEAD/MIND IS ASSOCIATED WITH THOUGHT, REASON, PHILOSOPHY, CONTROL AND TRANSCENDENCE, THE BODY DENOTES ONLY UNRULY PASSIONS, EXCESS AND IMMANENCE." (p13)

MANY FILM-MAKERS HAVE TURNED TO THE **GROTESQUE** SIDE OF OUR BODIES FOR INSPIRATION - STRIPPING AWAY THE SOFTENING FAÇADE OF CULTURE TO REVEAL THE DIRTY, SWEATY, GRIMY SIDE OF THE HUMAN FORM.

IN **LA GRANDE BOUFFE** (1973), FOUR MIDDLE-CLASS MEN RETREAT TO A MANSION FOR A GARGANTUAN FEAST.

AT FIRST A CULTURED, CIVILISED AFFAIR, THE HOLIDAY SOON GIVES WAY TO A DELICIOUSLY VULGAR ONSLAUGHT OF GORGING, COPULATION, VOMIT AND DIARRHOEA AS THE MEN ATTEMPT TO EAT THEMSELVES TO DEATH.

IF YOU DON'T EAT... YOU WON'T DIE!

A DARKLY HUMOROUS SATIRE OF CAPITALIST EXCESS, THE FILM PRESENTS THE HUMAN BODY AT ITS MOST BASE: A MASS OF FLESH, BURSTING AT THE SEAMS WITH VARIOUS BODILY FLUIDS.

FROM THE GRIMY CARNALITY OF **LA GRANDE BOUFFE** AND **TAXIDERMIA** (2006) TO THE INTENSE VIOLENCE OF **SPLATTER CINEMA**, FILM-MAKERS HAVE LONG DELIGHTED IN IMAGERY OF THE BODY AT ITS MOST CORPOREAL AND GROTESQUE. BUT WHY DO IMAGES OF VOMIT, EXCREMENT, BLOOD AND GUTS HAVE SUCH A POWER TO SHOCK AND REPEL US?

FOR JULIA KRISTEVA, THE ANSWER LIES IN THE FACT THAT THESE SUBSTANCES CROSS OR COLLAPSE THE BORDER BETWEEN OUR OUTSIDE AND INSIDE, REMINDING US OF OUR MORTAL, CORPOREAL NATURE. (P3)

AS SHE PUTS IT: "THESE BODY FLUIDS, THIS DEFILEMENT, THIS SHIT ARE WHAT LIFE WITHSTANDS, HARDLY AND WITH DIFFICULTY, ON THE PART OF DEATH. THERE, I AM AT THE BORDER OF MY CONDITION AS A LIVING BEING."

THESE SUBSTANCES ARE NORMALLY KEPT AT BAY, HIDDEN OR SOFTENED BY CULTURAL PROCESSES...

BUT WHEN THEY AREN'T, **ABJECTION** TAKES HOLD OF US: THE FEELING OF DISGUST OR HORROR THAT THESE IMPROPER OR UNCLEAN SUBSTANCES EVOKE.

THIS FEELING OF **BODILY REVULSION** IS AT THE HEART OF THE HORROR MOVIE, A GENRE DESIGNED TO PROVOKE VISCERAL REACTIONS FROM ITS AUDIENCE.

AS THE CULTURAL CRITIC BARBARA CREED ARGUES: "THE HORROR FILM ABOUNDS WITH IMAGES OF ABJECTION, FOREMOST OF WHICH IS THE CORPSE, WHOLE AND MUTILATED, FOLLOWED BY AN ARRAY OF BODILY WASTES SUCH AS BLOOD, VOMIT, SALIVA, SWEAT, TEARS AND PUTREFYING FLESH." (p40)

AS KNIVES TEAR THROUGH SKIN, ALIENS BURST FROM WITHIN AND BLOOD, GUTS AND BILE SPILL ACROSS THE SCREEN, THE BOUNDARY BETWEEN THE SELF AND THE OUTSIDE IS **FATALLY COLLAPSED**.

TURNING OUR OWN **BODIES** INTO A SITE OF HORROR, THESE FILMS DRAW ON THE VERY FUNDAMENTAL FEAR WE HAVE ABOUT THE BODY'S LIMITS, DELVING BELOW THE SKIN'S SURFACE TO EXPLORE THE BODY'S **FRAGILE** AND **MUTABLE NATURE**.

DIRECTOR DAVID CRONENBERG IS ONE OF CINEMA'S UNDOUBTED MASTERS OF BODY HORROR, HIS FILMS EXPLORING "THE BODY AND ITS INTERMINABLE TRANSFORMATIONS - ITS DECAY, ITS MUTATION, ITS POTENTIAL FOR POSSESSION AND INHABITATION BY OTHER LIFE FORMS". (p33, WILLIAMS)

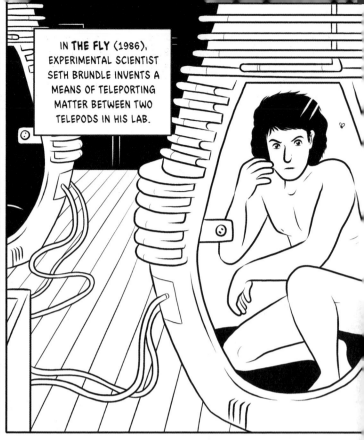

IN **THE FLY** (1986), EXPERIMENTAL SCIENTIST SETH BRUNDLE INVENTS A MEANS OF TELEPORTING MATTER BETWEEN TWO TELEPODS IN HIS LAB.

AFTER A TRIP THROUGH THE PODS, BRUNDLE DISCOVERS CHANGES IN HIS BODY. FILLED WITH STRENGTH AND ENERGY, HE BECOMES CONVINCED THAT HIS BODY HAS BEEN PURIFIED BY THE PROCESS AND TRIES TO CONVINCE HIS LOVER TO JOIN HIM.

YOU'RE AFRAID TO BE DESTROYED AND RECREATED, AREN'T YOU? I'LL BET YOU THINK THAT YOU WOKE ME UP ABOUT THE FLESH, DON'T YOU? BUT YOU ONLY KNOW SOCIETY'S **STRAIGHT LINE** ABOUT THE FLESH.

SLOWLY, HIS BODY AND MIND BEGIN TO CHANGE: HAIRS GROW IN STRANGE PLACES, HE BECOMES SPOTTY AND HIS AGGRESSION SOARS. IT'S A **MONSTROUS VISION OF MASCULINITY**, A PERVERSE SECOND PUBERTY.

TO HIS HORROR, BRUNDLE DISCOVERS THAT HE SHARED THE TELEPOD WITH A STRAY FLY AND WAS **COMBINED** WITH IT ON A GENETIC LEVEL DURING TELEPORTATION.

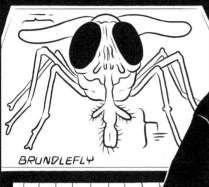

BRUNDLEFLY

AS BRUNDLE AND FLY COALESCE, THE BOUNDARIES OF HIS BODY **DISINTEGRATE**. HIS NAILS AND TEETH FALL OUT AND BODY PARTS SLUICE OFF AS HE SHEDS HIS HUMANITY PIECE BY PIECE.

THE FILM IS A HORRIFIC VISION OF THE BODY **UNBOUND**, A CHALLENGE TO THE VERY FUNDAMENTAL NOTION THAT OUR BODILY LIMITS ARE **STABLE**.

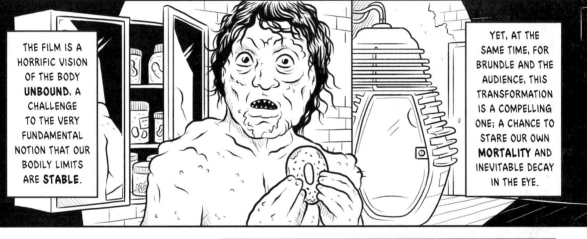

YET, AT THE SAME TIME, FOR BRUNDLE AND THE AUDIENCE, THIS TRANSFORMATION IS A COMPELLING ONE; A CHANCE TO STARE OUR OWN **MORTALITY** AND INEVITABLE DECAY IN THE EYE.

FOR CRONENBERG, DISEASE AND DECAY ARE NEITHER POSITIVE NOR NEGATIVE. AS LINDA WILLIAMS PUTS IT, "DISEASE HAS TO BE READ AS ONLY ANOTHER FORM OF NATURAL LIFE, DEGENERATION AND CHANGE BECOMING SIMPLY A MATTER OF PERSPECTIVE." (p33)

ALL THAT BRUNDLE CAN DO IS EMBRACE THE FLY INSIDE OF HIM AND COME TO TERMS NOT WITH HIS OWN DEATH, BUT WITH THE BIRTH OF THE FLY.

I'M SAYING... I'M SAYING I'M AN INSECT WHO DREAMT HE WAS A MAN AND LOVED IT. BUT NOW THE DREAM IS OVER... AND THE INSECT IS AWAKE.

ONSCREEN BODIES ARE ENDLESSLY FASCINATING, IN LARGE PART BECAUSE OF HOW THEY RELATE TO OUR OWN BODIES AS WE SIT BEFORE THE SCREEN.

WHILE FILM DOES INDEED SATISFY "A FASCINATION WITH LIKENESS AND RECOGNITION" (p18, MULVEY), OUR ENGAGEMENT WITH THE SCREEN IS ALSO A **PHYSICAL** ONE.

AS JENNIFER BARKER POSITS, "THE EMPATHY BETWEEN THE FILM'S AND VIEWER'S BODIES GOES SO DEEPLY THAT WE CAN FEEL THE FILM'S BODY, LIVE VICARIOUSLY THROUGH IT AND EXPERIENCE ITS MOVEMENTS TO SUCH AN EXTENT THAT WE OURSELVES BECOME MOMENTARILY AS GRACEFUL OR POWERFUL AS THE FILM'S BODY." (p83)

AS A RESULT, OUR HEARTS RACE DURING BUSTER KEATON'S DARING STUNTS, WE FLINCH IN FRIGHT DURING **THE FLY**, CRY WITH GRIEF DURING **THE WRESTLER** AND LEAVE THE CINEMA "FEELING INVIGORATED AND EXHAUSTED, THOUGH WE OURSELVES HAVE HARDLY MOVED A MUSCLE". (p83, BARKER)

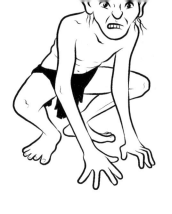
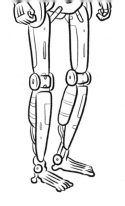

FILLED WITH BODILY SPECTACLE AND SUBVERSION, THE CINEMA HAS BECOME A PLACE WHERE THE CENTRAL NOTIONS OF THE BODY ARE CHALLENGED AND WHERE WE CAN STEP IN AND OUT OF SCREEN BODIES TO **RE-IMAGINE OUR OWN**.

SETS AND ARCHITECTURE

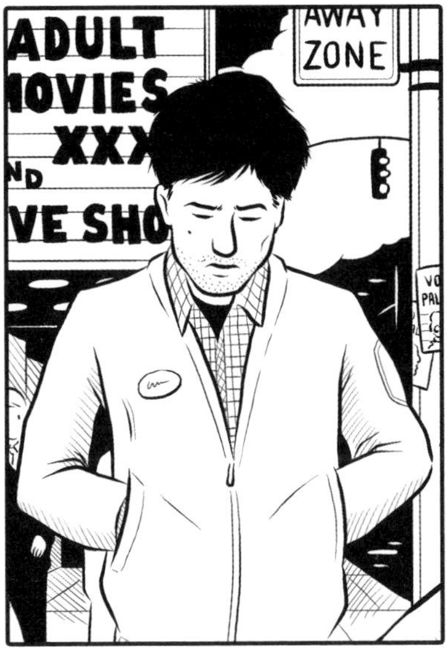

ADULT
IOVIES
XXX
ND
VE SHO
AWAY
ZONE

WHILE THE ONSCREEN BODY PROVIDES OUR POINT OF INVESTMENT IN THE MOVIES, THE **SPACES** AND **PLACES** THAT THESE CHARACTERS INHABIT ARE OF CRUCIAL IMPORTANCE.

THROUGHOUT ITS HISTORY, CINEMA HAS COMPELLED AUDIENCES WITH ITS CAPACITY TO SHOW US EXCITING WORLDS THAT ARE UNFAMILIAR TO US, TO REFLECT BACK NEW ASPECTS OF THE PLACES WE KNOW OR TO TAKE THE FAMILIAR WORLD WE LIVE IN AND TURN IT UPSIDE-DOWN.

WHETHER IT IS THE WAKING NIGHTMARE OF THE FILM-NOIR CITYSCAPE, THE DISTORTED BUT PRESCIENT FUTURESCAPES OF SCIENCE FICTION OR THE BANALITY OF SUBURBIA, THE MOVIES ALLOW US TO BETTER UNDERSTAND **OUR WORLD** AND OUR PLACE IN IT.

FOR THE FILM-MAKER, THE SPACES THAT CHARACTERS INHABIT ARE A COMPELLING SYMBOLIC TOOL, RICH WITH MEANING AND FULL OF CINEMATIC POTENTIAL.

AT ITS MOST BASIC, A FILM'S SETTING WORKS TO **SET THE TONE** OF THE STORY
AND MANY FILMS ARE MEMORABLE IN LARGE PART BECAUSE OF THEIR SETTING.

WHO CAN FORGET THE DARK DISTRUST OF NEW YORK IN **TAXI DRIVER** (1976), THE EDGY ROMANTICISM OF
PARIS IN **BREATHLESS** (1960) OR THE OPPRESSIVE POVERTY OF RIO DE JANEIRO IN **CITY OF GOD** (2002)?

LOCATIONS ARE INHERENTLY
LOADED WITH MEANING.
THE SHAPES OF BUILDINGS,
THE WAY PEOPLE LIVE, THE
ABSENCE OR PRESENCE
OF NATURE AND MORE,
ALL CONTRIBUTE TO
HOW WE PERCEIVE A SPACE.

STAR WARS (1977-2005), WITH
ITS GALAXY OF APPARENTLY
MONOCULTURAL PLANETS, IS A
PRIME EXAMPLE OF THIS.

FROM THE EARTHY INNOCENCE OF THE EWOK VILLAGE AND THE DANGER AND
ADVENTURE OF MOS EISLEY OR CLOUD CITY TO THE EVIL OF THE DEATH STAR,
THE SAGA'S **LOCATIONS** TELL US A GREAT DEAL ABOUT THEIR INHABITANTS.

IT IS NO ACCIDENT THAT THE SERIES' MOST HEROIC CHARACTERS HAIL FROM
RURAL, NATURAL ENVIRONMENTS; AS STARK AN OPPOSITION AS POSSIBLE TO
THE MONOCHROMATIC MACHINERY OF THE EVIL EMPIRE. (p233, LAMSTER)

FROM THE VERY BEGINNING, FILM HAS STRIVED TO SHOW US SOMEWHERE NEW. D.W. GRIFFITH'S EPIC **INTOLERANCE** (1916) CONFRONTS HUMANKIND'S CAPACITY FOR HATRED IN A MILLENNIA-SPANNING JOURNEY FROM ANCIENT BABYLON TO CONTEMPORARY NEW YORK.

MADE IN THE EARLY DAYS OF CINEMA, THE FILM REMAINS JAW-DROPPING TO THIS DAY FOR ITS ENORMOUSLY DETAILED RECREATION OF BABYLON, WHICH WAS POPULATED BY OVER 3,000 EXTRAS.

INTOLERANCE WAS NOT ALONE IN ITS AMBITION OR ITS FOLLY. FROM **CABIRIA** (1914) TO **TITANIC** (1997) AND BEYOND, FILM-MAKERS HAVE ALWAYS BEEN SEDUCED BY THE VERY EXPENSIVE DESIRE TO RECREATE HISTORICAL SETTINGS IN ALL THEIR SPLENDOUR.

KEEP OUT

UNSURPRISINGLY, THE PRODUCTION'S BUDGET SKYROCKETED, EVENTUALLY SINKING GRIFFITH'S STUDIO. THE CRUMBLING CINEMATIC CITY REMAINED STANDING UNTIL 1919, WHEN IT WAS TORN DOWN AS A FIRE HAZARD.

WHILE AN OBSESSION WITH SPECTACULAR SETS TOOK HOLD IN HOLLYWOOD, FILM-MAKERS WORKING WITH LOWER BUDGETS BEGAN TO SEE THE **EXPRESSIVE POTENTIAL** THAT EVEN A LICK OF PAINT AND MOODY LIGHTING COULD ACHIEVE.

UNABLE TO MATCH THE OPULENCE OF AMERICAN CINEMA, THE FLOURISHING **GERMAN EXPRESSIONIST** MOVEMENT OF THE 1920s HARNESSED THE METAPHORIC POTENTIAL OF BACKGROUNDS TO PERFECTLY EXPRESS THE THEMES OF **TORMENT**, **INSANITY** AND **BETRAYAL** THAT SATURATED GERMAN CINEMA.

IT WAS A REVOLUTIONARY DEVELOPMENT. AS CONTEMPORARY CRITIC HERMANN G. SCHEFFAUER WROTE:

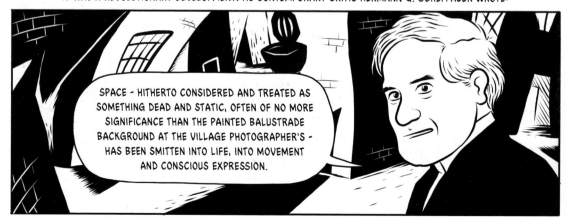

SPACE - HITHERTO CONSIDERED AND TREATED AS SOMETHING DEAD AND STATIC, OFTEN OF NO MORE SIGNIFICANCE THAN THE PAINTED BALUSTRADE BACKGROUND AT THE VILLAGE PHOTOGRAPHER'S - HAS BEEN SMITTEN INTO LIFE, INTO MOVEMENT AND CONSCIOUS EXPRESSION.

THE CABINET OF DR. CALIGARI (1920) IS AN ARCHETYPAL EXAMPLE OF THIS.

THE STORY OF AN UNHINGED INSANE ASYLUM DIRECTOR AND HIS SOMNAMBULISTIC SLAVE OVERCAME BUDGETARY CONSTRAINTS AND A LIMITED QUOTA OF ELECTRICITY BY PAINTING LIGHT AND SHADOW DIRECTLY ONTO THE SET'S FLOORS AND BACKDROPS.

THIS MOODY ATMOSPHERE, ALONG WITH THE WARPED, OFF-KILTER LOOK OF THE SCENERY, EVOKED A WORLD OVERWHELMED BY **MADNESS**.

IN AN ERA BEFORE SOUND, THESE EXPRESSIONIST ARTISTS HARNESSED EVERY INCH OF SCREEN SPACE TO EXPRESS THE UNSPOKEN AND GIVE VOICE TO THE WORLD THEY HAD CREATED.

IT IS AN AESTHETIC ALL THE MORE APT WHEN IT IS FINALLY REVEALED THAT THE WHOLE TALE IS THE DELUSION OF ONE OF CALIGARI'S INSANE INMATES.

AS VIDLER STATES, "NO LONGER AN INERT BACKGROUND, ARCHITECTURE NOW PARTICIPATES IN THE VERY EMOTIONS OF THE FILM. THE SURROUNDINGS NO LONGER SURROUNDED, BUT ENTERED THE EXPERIENCE AS PRESENCE." (p102)

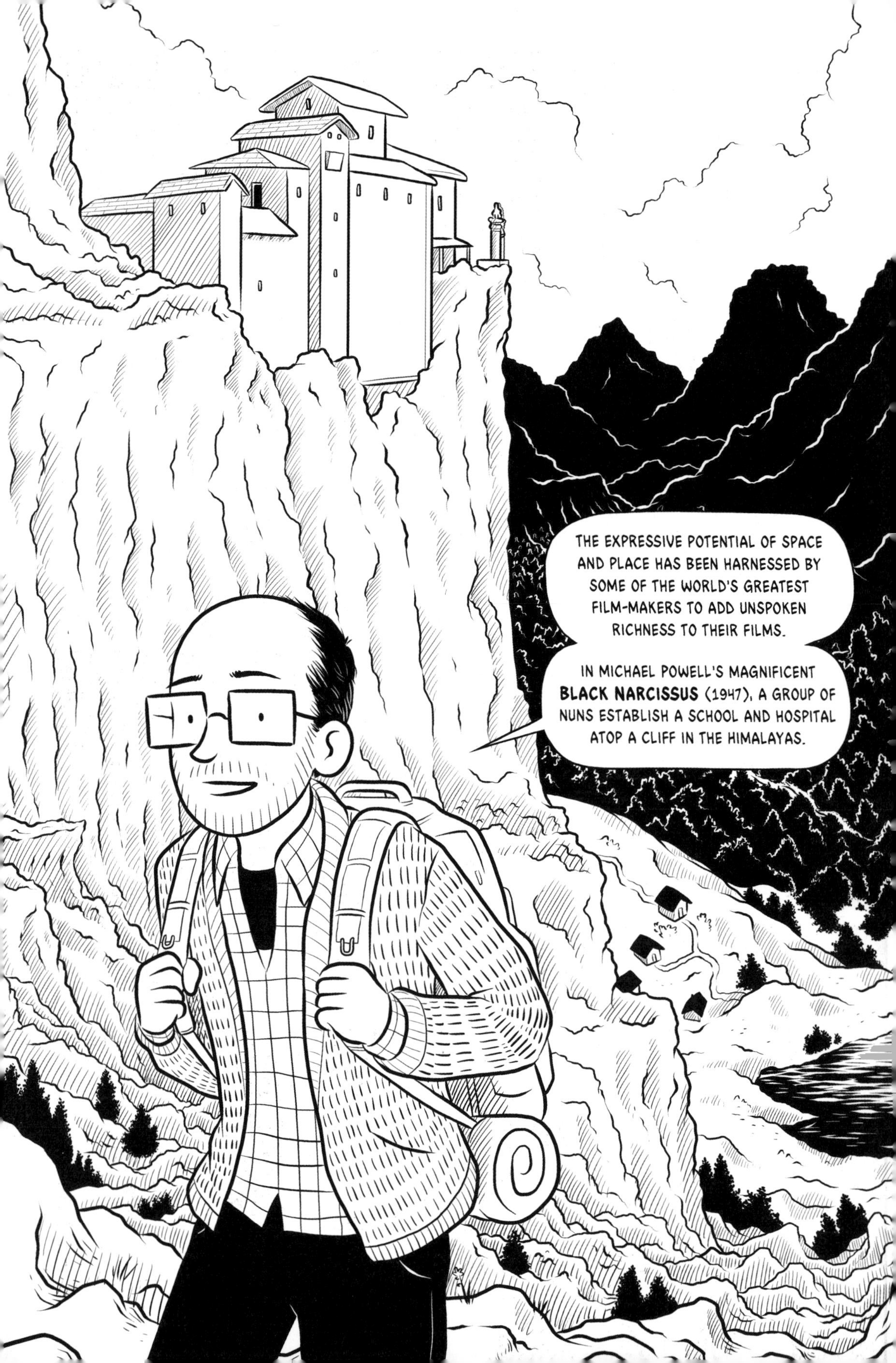
THE EXPRESSIVE POTENTIAL OF SPACE AND PLACE HAS BEEN HARNESSED BY SOME OF THE WORLD'S GREATEST FILM-MAKERS TO ADD UNSPOKEN RICHNESS TO THEIR FILMS.
IN MICHAEL POWELL'S MAGNIFICENT **BLACK NARCISSUS** (1947), A GROUP OF NUNS ESTABLISH A SCHOOL AND HOSPITAL ATOP A CLIFF IN THE HIMALAYAS.

IT'S A FORBIDDING, INHOSPITABLE ENVIRONMENT – AN EXPOSED YET CLAUSTROPHOBIC SPACE THAT ECHOES SISTER RUTH'S ISOLATION AND BECOMES THE PERFECT SETTING FOR HER TRAGIC **PSYCHOLOGICAL BREAKDOWN.**

AS THEORIST ANDREW MOOR ELOQUENTLY PUTS IT, THIS SETTING "IS NOT SO MUCH A GEOGRAPHICAL LOCATION AS A PLASTIC RENDERING OF THE PROTAGONIST'S INTERIORITY". (p181)

SET TO AN OVERPOWERING JAZZ SOUNDTRACK, THE INTERMINABLE IMAGES OF NEW YORK'S CLAUSTROPHOBIC STREETS, NEON SIGNS AND SHADY CHARACTERS SIGNAL THE **INESCAPABILITY** OF THE CITY AND THE FUTILITY OF BICKLE'S STRUGGLE AGAINST IT.

THE SAME COULD BE SAID FOR MARTIN SCORSESE'S **TAXI DRIVER** (1976), IN WHICH TRAVIS BICKLE SLOWLY DESCENDS INTO INSANITY AMONG NEW YORK'S OPPRESSIVE DIRT, SMOG AND CORRUPTION.

SOMEDAY A REAL RAIN WILL COME AND WASH ALL THIS SCUM OFF THE STREETS.

FROM THE BATES MOTEL IN **PSYCHO** (1960) TO THE MONROEVILLE MALL IN **DAWN OF THE DEAD** (1978), MANY OF THE GREATEST HORROR FILMS FEATURE UNFORGETTABLE SETTINGS THAT HELP BRING THE HORROR TO LIFE.

IN **SEVEN** (1995), THE BRUTAL SERIAL KILLER JOHN DOE'S DINGY APARTMENT IS A CLAUSTROPHOBIC, NEON-LIT SPACE, OVERFLOWING WITH **DISTURBING DETAIL.**

THIS IS A PSYCHOPATH'S INNER WORLD **MADE MANIFEST,** OFFERING THE VIEWER AN UNSETTLING INSIGHT INTO DOE'S TWISTED MIND.

HAUNTED HOUSE MOVIES GIVE ARCHITECTURE A LIFE OF ITS OWN, PRESENTING US WITH SPACES "PRONE TO METAMORPHOSIS AND AGITATION". (p10, CURTIS)

IN THE DERANGED JAPANESE MOVIE **HAUSU** (1977), A RURAL HOUSE BECOMES ENERGISED BY THE ANGRY SPIRIT OF ITS DECEASED OWNER.

AN EYE-POPPING MASSACRE ENSUES AS THE HOUSE USES POSSESSED PIANOS, MALICIOUS MATTRESSES AND BLOOD-SPRAYING CAT PAINTINGS TO CONSUME A GANG OF TEENAGE GIRLS ONE BY ONE.

FEATURING ONE OF THE MOST MEMORABLE HAUNTED HOUSES OF ALL, STANLEY KUBRICK'S **THE SHINING** (1980) SEES JACK, WENDY AND THEIR SON DANNY MOVING INTO THE ISOLATED **OVERLOOK HOTEL** AS WINTER CARETAKERS.

AS THE COLD SETS IN, A SERIES OF UNSETTLING GHOSTLY ENCOUNTERS IN THE HOTEL'S **LABYRINTHINE CORRIDORS** DRIVE THE FAMILY TOWARDS INSANITY.

COME AND PLAY WITH US, DANNY...

THE OVERLOOK HOTEL IS THE PERFECT SETTING FOR THIS CREEPING HORROR. RICH WITH UNFORGETTABLE ARCHITECTURAL DETAIL, IT'S A VAST AND CONFUSING BUILDING IN WHICH THE VIEWER IS NEVER GIVEN THE CHANCE TO ORIENT THEMSELVES.

AS THEORIST THOMAS NELSON PUTS IT, THIS IS A SPACE THAT "THE AUDIENCE FEELS BOTH AT HOME AND LOST WITHIN" (p211), A BUILDING AS WELCOMING AS IT IS ALIEN.

BUT THE OVERLOOK HOTEL IS MORE **DECEPTIVE** THAN FIRST MEETS THE EYE. A STRUCTURE THAT IS SUPERFICIALLY LOGICAL AT FIRST GLANCE, THIS IS A SET BUILT WITH **SPATIAL CONTRADICTIONS** AND **IMPOSSIBILITIES** IN MIND.

AS ROB AGER DOCUMENTS, THE OVERLOOK SET MAKES NO SPATIAL SENSE...

THE WINDOW IN THE HOTEL MANAGER'S OFFICE HAS A VIEW TO THE OUTSIDE BUT IS SITUATED ON AN **INTERIOR WALL**.

STUART ULLMAN

MEANWHILE, A NUMBER OF DOORS THROUGHOUT THE HOTEL CAN BE SEEN TO LEAD TO **IMPOSSIBLE LOCATIONS** WHICH WOULD EITHER HOVER IN MID-AIR OR OVERLAP WITH PRE-EXISTING FEATURES.

THIS "VAST LABYRINTH OF WINDING CORRIDORS, MYSTERIOUS OPEN DOORWAYS AND DISORIENTATING DESIGN" (AGER, WEB) PLAYS HAVOC WITH THE AUDIENCE'S **ORIENTATION**, INSTILLING AN UNCANNY FEELING THAT SOMETHING IS NOT QUITE RIGHT ABOUT THE BUILDING.

THE HOTEL IS A MAZE TO GET LOST IN, BOTH PHYSICALLY AND PSYCHOLOGICALLY. AS JACK SPIRALS TOWARDS A MURDEROUS, AXE-WIELDING FRENZY, EACH CHARACTER'S ABILITY TO NAVIGATE THIS **DECEPTIVE** AND **ILLOGICAL SPACE** DICTATES WHETHER THEY LIVE OR DIE.

IT'S NOT JUST UNIQUE OR OUTLANDISH SETTINGS THAT CAN HAVE AN EFFECT ON US. IN DAVID LYNCH'S **BLUE VELVET** (1986), A SLEEPY SMALL-TOWN SUBURBIA SHOWS ITS SEEDY, VIOLENT UNDERSIDE TO THE NAÏVE JEFFREY.

THE OPENING SEQUENCE JUXTAPOSES WHITE PICKET FENCES, SCHOOL KIDS AND RED ROSES WITH A WRITHING MASS OF INSECTS JUST BELOW THE SURFACE OF THE TOWN'S IMPECCABLE LAWNS; A STRIKING METAPHOR FOR THE TOWN'S **REPRESSED REALITY**.

THE TRUMAN SHOW (1998) FEATURES AN IMPOSSIBLY PERFECT SUBURBIA THAT IS REVEALED TO THE UNSUSPECTING TRUMAN TO BE A SET FOR THE TV SHOW OF HIS LIFE.

IN SEARCHING FOR THE IDEAL DEPICTION OF THIS ARTIFICIAL TOWN, IT TRANSPIRED THAT "HOLLYWOOD SET DESIGN SIMPLY LOOKED TOO REAL" FOR THE FILM-MAKERS...

"TO ACHIEVE THE LEVEL OF ARTIFICIALITY DEMANDED BY ANDREW NICCOL'S SCRIPT, THE FILM-MAKER TURNED TO SEASIDE, FLORIDA, A REAL PLACE THAT EXUDES PLASTIC PRETENSE." (p157, VALENTINE)

Greetings from SEASIDE FLORIDA

THE RESULT IS A PERFECT RENDERING OF SUBURBAN ARTIFICIALITY, MADE ALL THE MORE IRONIC BY THE FACT THAT THIS TOWN **REALLY EXISTS**.

IT IS IN THE 'CINEMATIC CITY' WHERE WE FIND SOME OF THE MOST POTENT ONSCREEN REFLECTIONS OF THE WORLD WE LIVE IN.

CURRENTLY AROUND HALF OF THE WORLD'S POPULATION LIVE IN CITIES, AND IN THE LAST FEW CENTURIES THE CITY HAS BECOME AN **INTEGRAL PART** OF HUMAN EXISTENCE.

MORE THAN JUST A HOME TO HUMANITY, CITIES ARE A **PROBLEMATIC SPACE** - A BATTLEGROUND FOR OUR HOPES AND FEARS ABOUT CRIME, FREEDOM, IDENTITY AND ANONYMITY.

IT IS THESE QUALITIES THAT MAKE THE CITY A SOURCE OF UNENDING **INSPIRATION** FOR FILM-MAKERS AND THE IDEAL BACKDROP FOR SOME OF CINEMA'S GREATEST STORIES.

PERHAPS THE MOST FAMOUS EARLY CINEMATIC CITY IS FRITZ LANG'S TRIUMPHANT VISION OF THE FUTURE, **METROPOLIS** (1927).

SET IN A FUTURISTIC CITY OF TIGHTLY PACKED **ART DECO** ARCHITECTURE, THE FILM DEALS WITH A WORKERS' UPRISING WHICH HAS BEEN INCITED BY A BEAUTIFUL HUMANOID ROBOT.

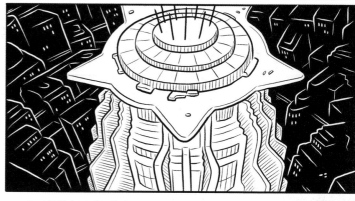

IN THIS **VERTICALLY STRATIFIED SOCIETY**, THE POOR ARE BURIED IN THE DARKNESS OF CATACOMBS AND UNDERGROUND FACTORIES, WHILE THE RICH LIVE IN TOWERING, BIBLICAL STRUCTURES OVERLOOKING THE VAST METROPOLIS.

IT IS A COMPELLING VISION, YET ONE THAT SCIENCE FICTION MASTER **H.G. WELLS** THOUGHT WAS "STALE OLD STUFF."

SO FAR FROM BEING A HUNDRED YEARS HENCE, **METROPOLIS**, IN ITS FORMS AND SHAPES, IS ALREADY AS A POSSIBILITY A THIRD OF A CENTURY **OUT OF DATE**.

BUT AS DIETRICH NEUMANN NOTES, "LANG HAD NOT INTENDED TO PRODUCE A REALISTIC PROJECTION OF URBAN DEVELOPMENT OR EVEN AN IDEAL CITY." (p35)

INSTEAD, LANG AND WRITER THEA VON HARBOU SET OUT TO PORTRAY A CITY "WHOSE INDIVIDUAL BUT INTERDEPENDENT SPACES - THE SKYSCRAPERS, MACHINE HALLS AND CATACOMBS - FULFILLED A BODY'S FUNCTION AS ITS HEART, HANDS AND MIND." (p34, NEUMANN)

THIS IS THE CITY AS A **LIVING BEING**, WITH ITS WORKING INHABITANTS MERELY EXPENDABLE, ENSLAVED **CELLS**, LABOURING AND DYING TO FEED THE INSATIABLE FIRES OF INDUSTRY, THE HEART OF THE CITY.

A PRODUCT OF GROWING DISCONTENT IN WEIMAR GERMANY, THE CAPITALIST CITY OF **METROPOLIS** IS A MONSTER: DARK, CRUEL AND **ALL-CONSUMING**.

MORE THAN JUST A BACKDROP, THIS CITY IS A METAPHOR, A LIVING, BREATHING PRESENCE, A **CHARACTER** IN ITSELF.

FOR HIS CINEMATIC FUTURESCAPES IN **BLADE RUNNER** (1982), DIRECTOR RIDLEY SCOTT CONJURED IMAGES OF A DYSTOPIC METROPOLIS THAT FRITZ LANG COULD ONLY HAVE DREAMT OF.

THE FILM FOLLOWS RICK DECKARD AS HE SEARCHES LOS ANGELES FOR FOUR RENEGADE REPLICANTS, ANDROIDS THAT ARE VIRTUALLY INDISTINGUISHABLE FROM HUMANS.

AS RIDLEY SCOTT STATES:

I'M TRYING TO MAKE THE CITY AS REAL AS POSSIBLE... RICH, COLOURFUL, NOISY, GRITTY, FULL OF TEXTURES AND TEEMING WITH LIFE... THIS IS A **TANGIBLE** FUTURE, NOT SO EXOTIC AS TO BE UNBELIEVABLE... LIKE TODAY, **ONLY MORE SO.**

TO ACHIEVE THIS, SCOTT FUSED SETS, REAL LOCATIONS AND AMAZING SPECIAL EFFECTS, CREATING A RICH TAPESTRY OF VISUALS.

THE RESULT IS AN ENDLESS, SMOG-WRAPPED CITY, "A RETROFITTED FUTURE BUILT ON THE DEBRIS OF THE PAST" (p263, BUKATMAN) WHERE OLD ARCHITECTURE MESHES WITH NEW, CULTURES MELT TOGETHER AND **BOUNDARIES COLLAPSE.**

THIS **BREAKDOWN OF BOUNDARIES** IS REFLECTED IN THE RELATIONSHIP THE REPLICANTS HAVE WITH THE CITY.

WHILE ITS CITIZENS LIVE IN (BUT APART FROM) THE CITY, OCCUPYING THE CONVENTIONAL SPACES OF ITS STREETS, BARS AND APARTMENTS, THE REPLICANTS BLEND IN AND BECOME AT ONE WITH THEIR ENVIRONMENT.

TO THE REPLICANTS, THE BOUNDARIES OF THE CITY MEAN LITTLE. AS HE HUNTS DECKARD DOWN, REPLICANT LEADER ROY BATTY TRAVERSES ROOFTOPS AND BURSTS THROUGH WALLS AND WINDOWS, **UNIMPEDED** BY THE CITY'S CRUMBLING GEOGRAPHY.

IN HIS FRANTIC ESCAPE, DECKARD QUICKLY LEARNS TO THINK LIKE BATTY, CLIMBING THROUGH A HOLE IN THE APARTMENT ROOF AND CLAMBERING AROUND THE OUTSIDE OF THE BUILDING AS BATTY HUNTS HIM.

FORESHADOWING THE REVELATION THAT DECKARD HIMSELF MAY BE A REPLICANT, THE FILM SHOWS HIM TO BE AN EMERGING **EXPLORER OF SPACE**, A SUBVERTER OF URBAN CONVENTIONS, AN ECHO OF BATTY.

THIS EXPLORATION OF URBAN SPACE CONTINUES IN JOHN MCTIERNAN'S GENRE-DEFINING ACTION CLASSIC **DIE HARD** (1988).

SET IN A MUNDANE CORPORATE HIGH-RISE, THE FILM SEES BARE-FOOTED COP JOHN MCCLANE ACT AS THE LONE RESISTANCE AGAINST A GANG OF EUROPEAN TERRORISTS WHO TAKE CONTROL OF THE BUILDING AND HOLD ITS EMPLOYEES HOSTAGE.

WITH ITS NORMAL SPACES OCCUPIED AND DISABLED, THIS "ORDINARY OFFICE BUILDING BECOMES A **TERRIFYING PRISON**, SINCE IT IS VIRTUALLY UNMANAGEABLE FOR THE SCALE OF THE HUMAN BODY". (P48, WILLIS)

IN HIS FIGHT BACK, MCCLANE IS FORCED INTO THE **HIDDEN SPACES** OF THE BUILDING, MOVING THROUGH THE NAKATOMI PLAZA'S STRUCTURE "IN BASICALLY EVERY CONCEIVABLE WAY BUT PASSING THROUGH ITS DOORS AND HALLWAYS". (MANAUGH, WEB)

NOW I KNOW WHAT A TV DINNER FEELS LIKE.

IT'S A FASCINATING REINTERPRETATION OF THE RULES OF SPATIAL NAVIGATION: "IF THERE IS NOT A CORRIDOR, HE MAKES ONE; IF THERE IS NOT AN OPENING, THERE WILL BE SOON." (MANAUGH, WEB)

IN A THRILLING **SUBVERSION** OF THE INTENTIONS OF THIS DULL CORPORATE SPACE, MCCLANE ULTIMATELY OVERCOMES THE OCCUPYING HUMAN FORCE BY TURNING THE BUILDING INTO A **WEAPON** AND A **SHIELD**.

MCCLANE CRAWLS THROUGH AIR VENTS AND MAINTENANCE PASSAGES, RIDES ON TOP OF ELEVATORS AND USES A FIRE HOSE TO ABSEIL DOWN THE SIDE OF THE BUILDING AND RE-ENTER IT THROUGH A PLATE-GLASS WINDOW.

AS WRITER GEOFF MANAUGH STATES, THESE ARE "ACTS OF VIRTUOSO NAVIGATION THAT WERE NEITHER IMAGINED NOR PHYSICALLY PLANNED FOR BY THE ARCHITECTS." (WEB)

HE IS ACTION CINEMA'S GREAT URBAN EXPLORER, PLAYFULLY **REINTERPRETING** HIS RELATIONSHIP WITH THE **BUILT WORLD**.

WELCOME TO THE PARTY, PAL!

CHRISTOPHER NOLAN'S LABYRINTHINE THRILLER **INCEPTION** (2010) PROVIDES US WITH A VISION OF THE BUILT WORLD AS EVEN MORE MUTABLE THAN IN **DIE HARD**.

IN THE FILM, DOMINICK COBB IS A CORPORATE SPY WHO USES A TECHNOLOGY THAT ALLOWS HIM TO **ENTER THE DREAMS** OF OTHERS AND STEAL SECRETS FROM THEIR SUBCONSCIOUS.

IN A SEQUENCE SHOT ON THE STREETS OF PARIS, COBB COACHES ARCHITECTURE STUDENT ARIADNE ON HOW TO **CONSTRUCT** THE DREAMSCAPES IN WHICH THEY WILL PULL OFF THEIR LATEST HEIST.

HUNGRY TO EXPERIMENT WITH THIS LIVING, TANGIBLE DREAM CITY, ARIADNE BEGINS CREATING AND DESTROYING STRUCTURES AT WILL, LITERALLY **FOLDING** THE CITY ON TOP OF ITSELF.

MORE THAN JUST AN URBAN EXPLORER, IN THE DREAMSCAPES OF **INCEPTION** ARIADNE IS AN ARCHITECTURAL GOD, ABLE TO CONJURE SPACES OUT OF PURE IMAGINATION.

YET, AS COBB WARNS, THESE SPACES MUST REMAIN **BELIEVABLE** TO THE DREAMING SUBJECT, LEST THEY CATCH WIND OF ARIADNE'S INTERFERENCE AND BRING THE DREAM **TUMBLING DOWN**.

IT'S A PERFECT ANALOGY FOR THE FRAGILE ILLUSION OF THE CINEMA AND THE SIGNIFICANCE AND IMPORTANCE OF SETTING IN FILM.

JUST AS THE DREAMWORLDS OF **INCEPTION** ARE FRAGILE AND PRONE TO COLLAPSE WHEN BENT TOO MUCH OUT OF LINE WITH REALITY, SO TOO MUST CINEMA WORK TO CONVINCE US THAT ITS OWN DREAMWORLDS ARE REAL.

IN THE WORLD OF FILM, SETS ARE SURFACE - PLYWOOD AND POLYSTYRENE POSING AS REALITY - BUT THEY HAVE **CRUCIAL** SYMBOLIC AND ILLUSORY IMPORTANCE.

WHEN WE LOSE FAITH IN THE ILLUSION, WHEN THE FILM WORLD LOOKS FAKE, THE SPELL OF THE **CINEMATIC DREAM** IS BROKEN AND FOR A MOMENT WE RETURN TO REALITY.

FOR POLITICAL THEORIST IVAN CHTCHEGLOV, "ARCHITECTURE IS THE SIMPLEST MEANS OF ARTICULATING TIME AND SPACE, OF MODULATING REALITY, OF **ENGENDERING DREAMS**." (P3, QUOTED IN PINDER)

HE MAY BE REFERRING TO BUILDINGS, BUT I HAVE NEVER HEARD SUCH A LOVELY DESCRIPTION OF **FILM**.

DURING THE COURSE OF THEIR COMMON HISTORY, FILM AND ARCHITECTURE HAVE INFLUENCED EACH OTHER TO AN ENORMOUS DEGREE.

WHILE ARCHITECTURE HAS HELPED TO LITERALLY CONSTRUCT THE WORLDS WE SEE ONSCREEN, FILM HAS **SHAPED** OUR TOWNS, CITIES AND SUBURBS IN A MORE SUBTLE MANNER BY GIVING US A WAY TO CONTEMPLATE OUR PLACE WITHIN THE BUILT WORLD.

AS THE PHILOSOPHER JEAN BAUDRILLARD SUGGESTS, THE MOVIES HAVE LED TO OUR CITIES BECOMING INVESTED "WITH A MYTHICAL ATMOSPHERE" (P56), LINKED IN OUR MEMORIES WITH THE FILMS THAT PORTRAYED THEM AND SLOWLY MAKING THE **REAL WORLD** THAT LITTLE BIT MORE **CINEMATIC**.

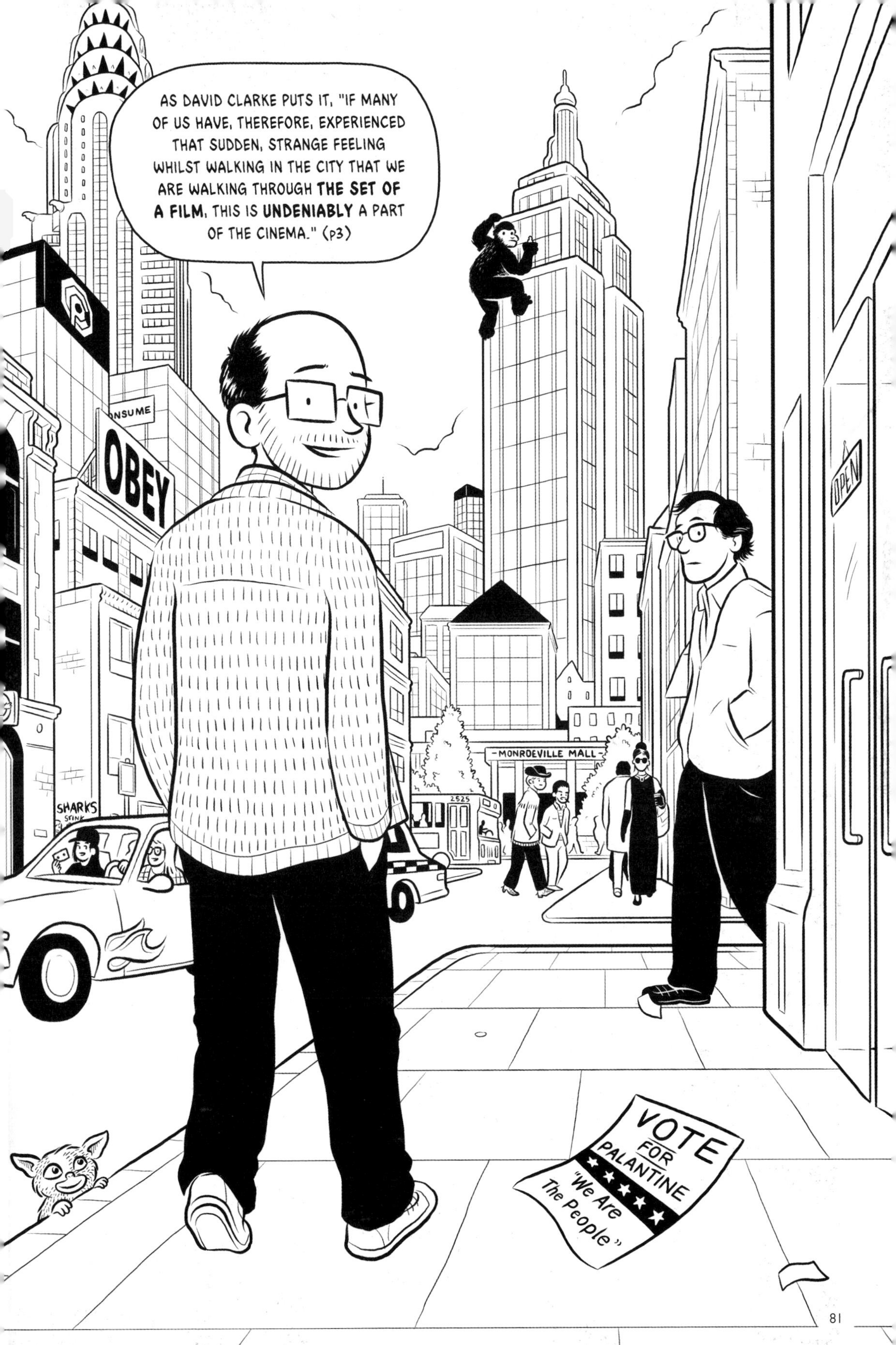
AS DAVID CLARKE PUTS IT, "IF MANY OF US HAVE, THEREFORE, EXPERIENCED THAT SUDDEN, STRANGE FEELING WHILST WALKING IN THE CITY THAT WE ARE WALKING THROUGH **THE SET OF A FILM**, THIS IS **UNDENIABLY** A PART OF THE CINEMA." (p3)
ONSUME
OBEY
SHARKS
2525
MONROEVILLE MALL
OPEN
VOTE FOR PALANTINE
"We Are The People"

TIME

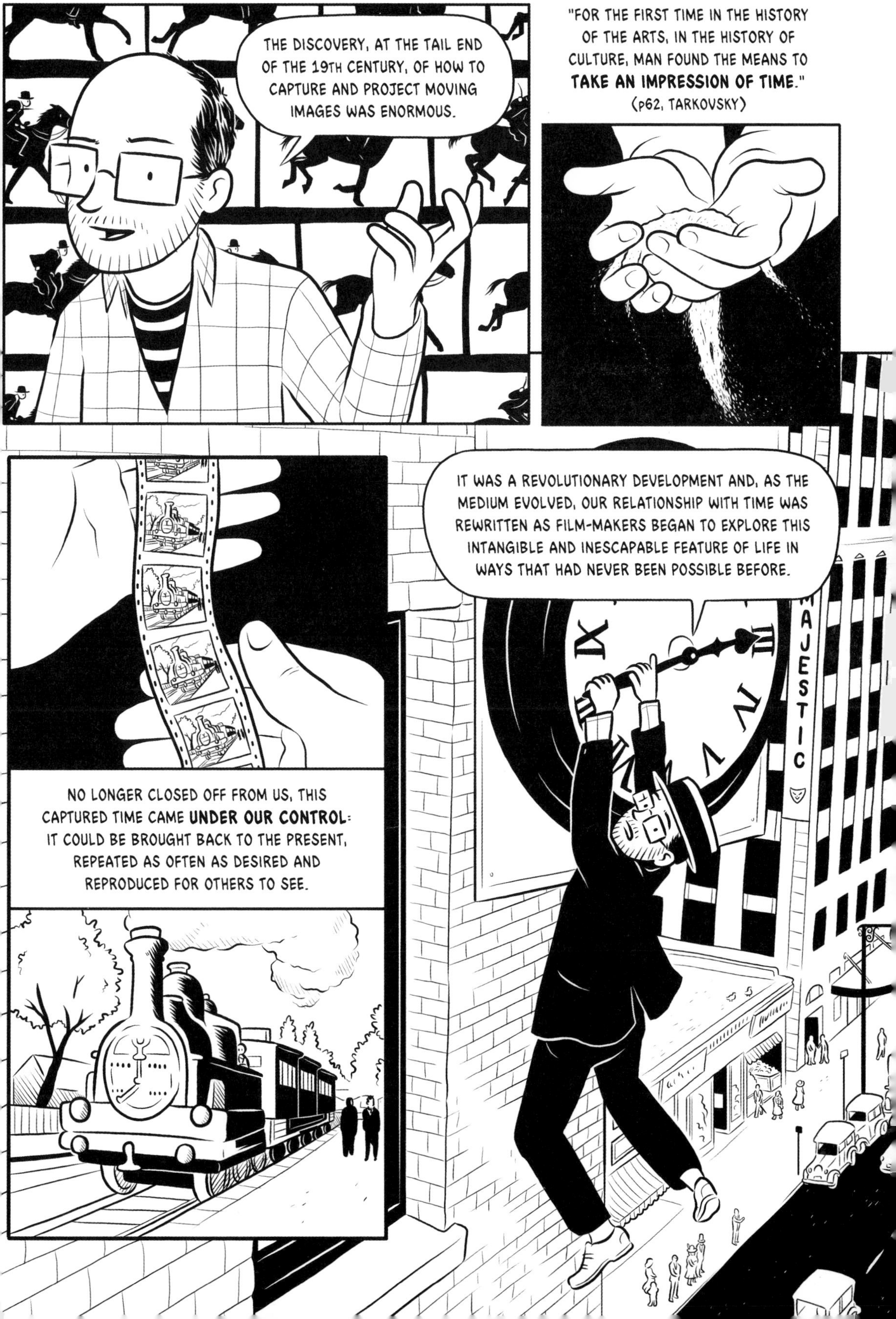
THE DISCOVERY, AT THE TAIL END OF THE 19TH CENTURY, OF HOW TO CAPTURE AND PROJECT MOVING IMAGES WAS ENORMOUS.
"FOR THE FIRST TIME IN THE HISTORY OF THE ARTS, IN THE HISTORY OF CULTURE, MAN FOUND THE MEANS TO **TAKE AN IMPRESSION OF TIME**."
(P62, TARKOVSKY)
IT WAS A REVOLUTIONARY DEVELOPMENT AND, AS THE MEDIUM EVOLVED, OUR RELATIONSHIP WITH TIME WAS REWRITTEN AS FILM-MAKERS BEGAN TO EXPLORE THIS INTANGIBLE AND INESCAPABLE FEATURE OF LIFE IN WAYS THAT HAD NEVER BEEN POSSIBLE BEFORE.
MAJESTIC
NO LONGER CLOSED OFF FROM US, THIS CAPTURED TIME CAME **UNDER OUR CONTROL**: IT COULD BE BROUGHT BACK TO THE PRESENT, REPEATED AS OFTEN AS DESIRED AND REPRODUCED FOR OTHERS TO SEE.

FOR FILM-MAKERS, THE THEME OF TIME HAS BEEN ONE OF CONSTANT FASCINATION. FROM THE MEDITATIVE TURNING OF THE SEASONS IN **SPRING, SUMMER, FALL, WINTER... AND SPRING** (2003) TO THE TICKING-CLOCK TENSION OF **RUN LOLA RUN** (1998) AND THE INTRICATE FLASHBACK STRUCTURE OF **FIGHT CLUB** (1999), THE MOVIES ALLOW US TO EXAMINE AND EXPLORE TIME, UNCOUPLED FROM OUR OWN CHRONOLOGIES.

THIS IS YOUR LIFE, AND IT'S ENDING ONE MOMENT AT A TIME...

FOR DIRECTOR ANDREI TARKOVSKY, TIME IS THE MOST FUNDAMENTAL AND DEFINING ELEMENT OF CINEMA; THE 'BASE MATERIAL' THAT A FILM-MAKER WORKS WITH...

JUST AS A SCULPTOR TAKES A LUMP OF MARBLE, AND, INWARDLY CONSCIOUS OF THE FEATURES OF HIS FINISHED PIECE, REMOVES EVERYTHING THAT IS NOT A PART OF IT...

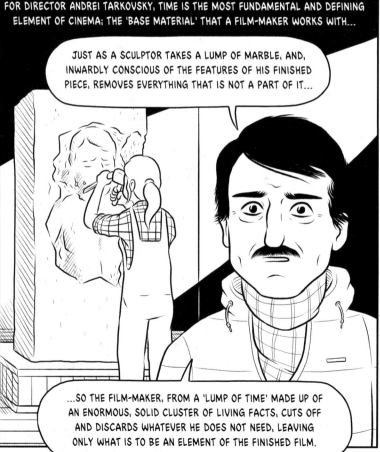

...SO THE FILM-MAKER, FROM A 'LUMP OF TIME' MADE UP OF AN ENORMOUS, SOLID CLUSTER OF LIVING FACTS, CUTS OFF AND DISCARDS WHATEVER HE DOES NOT NEED, LEAVING ONLY WHAT IS TO BE AN ELEMENT OF THE FINISHED FILM.

THIS EDITING PROCESS, WHICH TARKOVSKY CALLS 'SCULPTING IN TIME', IS ONE OF THE KEY TOOLS OF THE FILM-MAKER, ALLOWING THEM TO EXPLORE THE VERY IDEA OF TIME IN A MANNER IMPOSSIBLE IN ANY OTHER MEDIUM.

IN MAINSTREAM CINEMA, EDITING OFTEN HAS A PURELY PRACTICAL ROLE, ALLOWING FILM-MAKERS TO CUT BETWEEN IMAGES OF INTEREST AND OMIT UNIMPORTANT PERIODS OF TIME.

BUT EDITING CAN BE A POWERFUL TOOL, A FACT ABLY DEMONSTRATED IN SERGEI EISENSTEIN'S **BATTLESHIP POTEMKIN** (1925).

FOR THE ODESSA STEPS SEQUENCE, DURING WHICH TSARIST TROOPS MASSACRE CIVILIANS, EISENSTEIN IGNORED TRADITIONS OF CHRONOLOGY AND TEMPORALITY TO PRODUCE A SCENE OF FEROCIOUS EMOTIONAL AND IDEOLOGICAL POWER.

AS THE MASSACRE UNFOLDS, THE EDITING TEMPO INCREASES RHYTHMICALLY, SCENES OF CHAOS INTERCUTTING WITH INCREASINGLY FRENETIC CLOSE-UPS OF ANGUISHED FACES AND TERRIFIED SCREAMS.

MEANWHILE, TIME IS DRAWN OUT PAINFULLY AS A CHILD IS SHOT AND TRAMPLED UNDERFOOT - AND AGAIN AS A PRAM TEETERS ON THE EDGE OF THE STEPS.

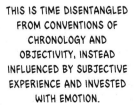

IT'S A REVOLUTIONARY SEQUENCE IN MORE WAYS THAN ONE, IN WHICH "STRICT TEMPORALITY IS DISCARDED" IN FAVOUR OF **RHYTHM** AND VISUAL ASSOCIATION. (p154, SKLAR)

THIS IS TIME DISENTANGLED FROM CONVENTIONS OF CHRONOLOGY AND OBJECTIVITY, INSTEAD INFLUENCED BY SUBJECTIVE EXPERIENCE AND INVESTED WITH EMOTION.

THE EXPRESSIVE POTENTIAL OF EDITING IS FURTHER EXPLORED IN JEAN-LUC GODARD'S **BREATHLESS** (1960), AN UNAPOLOGETICALLY COOL DECONSTRUCTION OF HOLLYWOOD CRIME CINEMA.

FILMED HANDHELD AND WITHOUT PERMISSION ON THE STREETS OF PARIS, THE HIGHLY IMPROVISED FILM WAS SHOT AND EDITED IN A **VERITÉ STYLE** - MAKING IT LOOK MORE LIKE A DOCUMENTARY THAN A FICTION FILM.

BUT EVEN MORE STRIKING FOR THE TIME WAS GODARD'S USE OF **JUMP CUTS** - EDITS WHERE A SEGMENT OF TIME IS REMOVED FROM THE MIDDLE OF A SINGLE SHOT, CREATING A JARRING 'JUMP' THROUGH TIME.

IT WAS A DISTANCING EFFECT, DESIGNED TO SHATTER THE IMMERSION ENCOURAGED BY THE **INVISIBLE STYLE** OF MAINSTREAM CINEMA.

A STATEMENT OF INTENT FOR A GENERATION OF AUDACIOUS FILM-MAKERS DETERMINED TO RIP UP THE HOLLYWOOD RULEBOOK, THE JUMP CUT WAS AN IMPORTANT STEP FORWARD FOR CINEMA, KICKSTARTING CINEMA'S GRADUAL "EMANCIPATION OF TIME". (P39, DELEUZE)

NO LONGER A BACKGROUND ELEMENT, TIME COULD NOW BECOME A PLAYFUL PART OF FILM STYLE, AND FILM-MAKERS WERE FREED FROM THE CONSTRAINTS OF PRESENTING TIME REALISTICALLY.

STANLEY KUBRICK'S **2001: A SPACE ODYSSEY** (1968) FEATURES PERHAPS THE MOST FAMOUS LEAP THROUGH TIME IN CINEMA HISTORY. THE OPENING SEQUENCE BEARS WITNESS TO THE DAWN OF MAN, AS HUMANOID APES DISCOVER TOOLS.

A SHOT OF A BONE TOOL, FLUNG INTO THE AIR, CUTS TO AN IMAGE OF A SPACESHIP, ORBITING EARTH MILLIONS OF YEARS LATER.

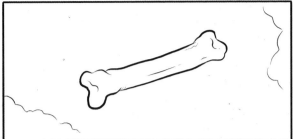

IT'S A CUT THAT SPANS THE COURSE OF HUMAN EVOLUTION AND TECHNOLOGICAL DEVELOPMENT IN THE **BLINK OF AN EYE.**

SIMILARLY AUDACIOUS, TERRENCE MALICK'S SPRAWLING AND GLORIOUS **THE TREE OF LIFE** (2011) SETS ITS STORY OF A TROUBLED FATHER-SON RELATIONSHIP IN THE CONTEXT OF GEOLOGICAL TIME.

IN A SPELLBINDING SEQUENCE AT THE CENTRE OF THE MOVIE, THE THIRTEEN-BILLION-YEAR HISTORY OF THE UNIVERSE AND THE EVOLUTION OF LIFE ON EARTH IS CONDENSED INTO FIFTEEN MINUTES.

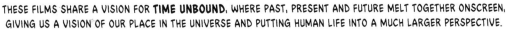

THESE FILMS SHARE A VISION FOR **TIME UNBOUND**, WHERE PAST, PRESENT AND FUTURE MELT TOGETHER ONSCREEN, GIVING US A VISION OF OUR PLACE IN THE UNIVERSE AND PUTTING HUMAN LIFE INTO A MUCH LARGER PERSPECTIVE.

WHILE EDITING ALLOWS FILM-MAKERS TO OMIT ANYTHING FROM A MILLISECOND TO A MILLENNIUM, SOME HAVE TRIED TO GROUND THEIR FILMS IN A TEMPORALITY MORE **IN SYNCH** WITH THAT OF THE VIEWERS WATCHING THE FILM.

IN **CLEO FROM 5 TO 7** (1962), WE FOLLOW CLEO FOR A TENSE TWO HOURS AS SHE WANDERS THE STREETS OF PARIS AWAITING A CANCER DIAGNOSIS.

IN REFUSING TO JUMP AHEAD AND REVEAL HER DESTINY, THE FILM COMPELS US TO SHARE IN CLEO'S ANXIOUS WAIT, BUILDING DREAD WITH ITS AGONISING, DELIBERATE PACE.

THE WESTERN CLASSIC **HIGH NOON** (1952) ALSO PLAYS OUT IN REAL TIME AS A RETIRED SHERIFF TRIES TO RECRUIT A POSSE TO DEFEND HIM FROM A GANG DUE ON THE NOON TRAIN.

WHEN THE TOWNSPEOPLE REFUSE TO HELP, ALL THAT REMAINS IS TO WAIT, AS TIME TICKS DOWN ON CLOCKS ACROSS TOWN AND THE SHERIFF'S DESTINY APPROACHES.

AWARE OF EVERY MOMENT LEFT ON THE CLOCK, THESE FILMS DWELL ON THE SLOW PASSING OF TIME TO HEIGHTEN TENSION AND REMIND US OF THE INEVITABILITY THAT OUR OWN TIME WILL EVENTUALLY RUN OUT.

LONG, UNINTERRUPTED TAKES CAN MAKE US ESPECIALLY AWARE OF THE PASSING OF TIME.

ORSON WELLES' **TOUCH OF EVIL** (1958) FEATURES AN ELABORATE THREE-AND-A-HALF-MINUTE SHOT THAT FOLLOWS A CAR CARRYING A TICKING TIMEBOMB TOWARDS THE MEXICAN-AMERICAN BORDER.

AS THE CAR SLOWLY WINDS ITS WAY THROUGH BUSY STREETS, THE TENSION RATCHETS UP AND ANTICIPATION OF THE EXPLOSION GROWS UNBEARABLE.

TIC TIC TIC TIC TIC TIC TIC TIC

PARK CHAN-WOOK'S **OLDBOY** (2003) FEATURES AN EXTENDED CORRIDOR FIGHT SHOWN ENTIRELY IN ONE LONG TAKE WHICH SUBTLY ECHOES THE LOOK OF A SIDE-SCROLLING ARCADE BEAT 'EM UP.

THE INITIALLY FAST AND FIERCELY VIOLENT FIGHT DESCENDS INTO A WEARY BRAWL AS THE MINUTES TICK BY AND OH DAE-SU PROGRESSES DOWN THE CORRIDOR.

IT'S A FAR CRY FROM THE EFFORTLESS VIOLENCE OF MOST ACTION HEROES, THE LONG TAKE EMPHASISING THE PUNISHING PHYSICALITY OF DAE-SU'S FIGHT.

WHILE IN THE PAST THE LENGTH OF A SINGLE SHOT WAS LIMITED TO THE LENGTH OF A REEL OF FILM, MODERN DIGITAL TECHNOLOGY MEANS A CAMERA CAN KEEP ROLLING INDEFINITELY.

RUSSIAN ARK (2002) IS A SPELLBINDING JOURNEY THROUGH 300 YEARS OF RUSSIAN HISTORY, ALL CAPTURED IN ONE UNINTERRUPTED NINETY-MINUTE SHOT.

THE FILM FOLLOWS A MAN WANDERING THROUGH THE WINTER PALACE IN ST. PETERSBURG AS CHARACTERS FROM THROUGHOUT RUSSIAN HISTORY INTERACT AROUND HIM.

YET THIS IS NO MERE CHRONOLOGICAL HISTORY. DESPITE THE UNINTERRUPTED CHRONOLOGY OF THE FILM'S SINGLE SHOT, THE HISTORY IT TAKES IN IS PRESENTED AS **FLUID** AND **NON-CHRONOLOGICAL**.

FROM THE DAYS OF EMPIRE THROUGH TO COMMUNISM, THE FILM OBSERVES RUSSIAN HISTORY AS A TOTALITY, USING THE SINGLE UNINTERRUPTED SHOT TO CREATE "THE SENSATION OF FLOATING THROUGH HISTORY". (BEUMERS, p251)

HERE, TIME IS BOTH INTEGRAL TO THE VIEWING EXPERIENCE AND **OBSOLETE**, AS RUSSIAN HISTORY COLLAPSES IN ON ITSELF INSIDE THIS RUSSIAN ARK.

NUMEROUS FILMS HAVE SOUGHT TO BREAK FREE FROM THE BASIC **CHRONOLOGY** AND CAUSE-AND-EFFECT NARRATIVES THAT DOMINATE MAINSTREAM CINEMA.

GOING BEYOND "THE PURELY EMPIRICAL SUCCESSION OF TIME - PAST-PRESENT-FUTURE" (DELEUZE, pXII) WITH THEIR USE OF FLASHBACKS, FRACTURED TIMELINES AND TEMPORAL LEAPS, THESE FILMS USE THE FULL POTENTIAL OF THE MEDIUM TO BETTER EXPLORE OUR RELATIONSHIP WITH TIME.

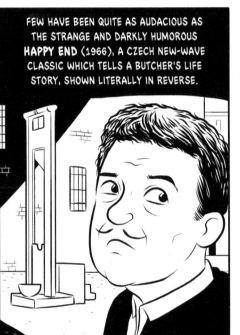

FEW HAVE BEEN QUITE AS AUDACIOUS AS THE STRANGE AND DARKLY HUMOROUS **HAPPY END** (1966), A CZECH NEW-WAVE CLASSIC WHICH TELLS A BUTCHER'S LIFE STORY, SHOWN LITERALLY IN REVERSE.

STARTING WITH HIS BIRTH BY EXECUTION, THE FILM **REWINDS** THROUGH HIS LIFE AS HE GRADUATES FROM PRISON, CONSTRUCTS A WIFE OUT OF BODY PARTS, GROWS YOUNGER AND EVENTUALLY MEETS HIS HAPPY END: HIS DEATH BY BIRTH.

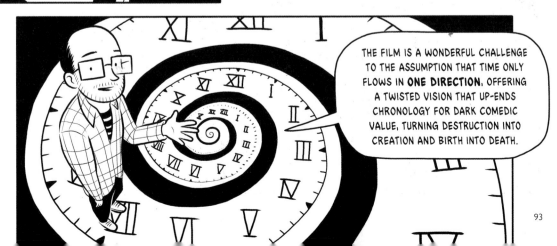

THE FILM IS A WONDERFUL CHALLENGE TO THE ASSUMPTION THAT TIME ONLY FLOWS IN **ONE DIRECTION**, OFFERING A TWISTED VISION THAT UP-ENDS CHRONOLOGY FOR DARK COMEDIC VALUE, TURNING DESTRUCTION INTO CREATION AND BIRTH INTO DEATH.

TIME'S ARROW IS REVERSED AGAIN IN CHRISTOPHER NOLAN'S **MEMENTO** (2000), WHICH FOLLOWS AMNESIAC LEONARD SHELBY'S HUNT FOR HIS WIFE'S KILLER.

FACT 1: MALE

FACT 2: WHITE

UNABLE TO FORM NEW MEMORIES, LEONARD'S ONLY CLUES TO HIS PURPOSE AND THE IDENTITY OF HIS WIFE'S KILLER ARE THE TATTOOS THAT COVER HIS BODY AND THE NOTES AND PHOTOS THAT FILL HIS POCKETS.

IN A THRILLING INVERSION OF NARRATIVE STORYTELLING, **MEMENTO** PRESENTS ITS SCENES IN **REVERSE CHRONOLOGICAL ORDER**, AN INGENIOUS AND DISORIENTATING MOVE WHICH THRUSTS US INTO LEONARD'S VIEWPOINT BY MIMICKING HIS ANTEROGRADE AMNESIA.

> SO WHERE ARE YOU? YOU'RE IN SOME MOTEL ROOM. YOU JUST... YOU JUST WAKE UP AND YOU'RE IN... IN A MOTEL ROOM.

AS THEORIST ALLAN CAMERON PUTS IT, "RATHER THAN SHOWING US WHAT THE CHARACTER REMEMBERS, THEY PROGRESSIVELY REVEAL WHAT HE IS UNABLE TO REMEMBER" (p65), ALLOWING THE AUDIENCE TO PIECE TOGETHER THE MYSTERY THAT DRIVES LEONARD'S ACTIONS.

IT'S A MESMERISING TECHNIQUE WHICH OFFERS US A CHANCE TO LIVE LIFE **AGAINST TIME'S FLOW**.

> YET THERE'S A UNIQUE TRAGEDY TO LEONARD'S POSITION. STRIPPED OF MEMORY, HE IS A MAN FOR WHOM IT IS NOT JUST THE FUTURE THAT IS UNKNOWABLE, BUT THE PAST, TOO.

TEDDY
-555 1154

TRAPPED FOREVER IN THE PRESENT, HIS PERSONAL TRAUMAS WILL NEVER LEAVE HIM, BECAUSE MAKING NEW MEMORIES AND MOVING ON IS IMPOSSIBLE...

> HOW AM I SUPPOSED TO HEAL IF I CAN'T FEEL TIME?

THIS PROBLEMATIC FANTASY OF ESCAPING THE CONFINES OF THE PRESENT IS DEPLOYED MORE LITERALLY IN THE ETERNALLY POPULAR **TIME-TRAVEL** GENRE.

TIMECRIMES (2007) SEES ORDINARY, MIDDLE-AGED HÉCTOR DRAWN INTO A TIME-TRAVEL LOOP AS HE TRIES TO CATCH A MYSTERIOUS ATTACKER AT HIS ISOLATED COUNTRY HOME.

TRICKED BY A LOCAL SCIENTIST INTO AN EXPERIMENTAL TIME MACHINE, HÉCTOR EMERGES ONE HOUR IN THE PAST AND SOON BECOMES THE VERY ATTACKER HE WAS ORIGINALLY OUT TO CATCH.

IT QUICKLY BECOMES APPARENT THAT HÉCTOR'S ATTEMPTS TO UNDO THE MISTAKES OF HIS PAST AND FUTURE ARE MERELY **REINFORCING EVENTS**, AND THE FILM SPIRALS TOWARDS ITS INEXORABLE CONCLUSION.

A GRITTY COUNTERPOINT TO THE TIME-HOPPING ADVENTURE OF FILMS LIKE **BACK TO THE FUTURE** (1985), **TIMECRIMES** PROVIDES A FATALISTIC VISION OF TIME-TRAVEL THAT SEEMS TO CONSCIOUSLY CONTRADICT **THE TERMINATOR** FRANCHISE'S ASSERTION THAT THERE IS "NO FATE BUT WHAT WE MAKE".

THE QUESTION OF INEVITABILITY ALSO COMES UP IN **LA JETÉE** (1962), WIDELY CONSIDERED TO BE ONE OF THE GREATEST TIME-TRAVEL MOVIES EVER MADE.

COMPRISED ALMOST ENTIRELY OF **STILL PHOTOGRAPHS**, THE FILM SEES A SURVIVOR IN POST-APOCALYPTIC PARIS ENLISTED TO TRAVEL THROUGH TIME TO "SUMMON PAST AND FUTURE TO RESCUE THE PRESENT".

UNDERGOING A TORTUROUS AND PSYCHOLOGICALLY PUNISHING TIME-TRAVEL PROCESS, THE SURVIVOR RETURNS TO BEFORE THE APOCALYPSE TO DISCOVER THERE IS NOTHING HE CAN DO TO ALTER THE COURSE OF HISTORY.

A PESSIMISTIC VISION, **LA JETÉE** SUGGESTS THAT OUR FATES ARE PREDETERMINED AND THAT FREE WILL IS AN ILLUSION.

A PRECURSOR TO TERRY GILLIAM'S EQUALLY WONDERFUL **TWELVE MONKEYS** (1995), THE FILM ENDS AS THE PROTAGONIST BECOMES THE VERY MAN HE SAW SHOT DEAD AS A CHILD, COMPLETING A **LOOP OF FATE** DESTINED NEVER TO BE BROKEN.

WHILE FILMS LIKE **THE TIME MACHINE** (1960) AND **THE TERMINATOR** (1984) TAKE CENTRE STAGE IN OUR UNDERSTANDING OF CINEMATIC TIME-TRAVEL, "WITH ITS CAPACITY TO MANIPULATE THE ILLUSION OF TIME" FILM ITSELF CAN BE SEEN AS A FORM OF TIME-TRAVEL. (P307, COATES)

ONE ONLY NEED THINK OF THE IMMERSIVE, TANGIBLE PASTS OF **CABIRIA** (1914) AND **SAVING PRIVATE RYAN** (1998) OR THE FUTURISTIC VISIONS OF **METROPOLIS** (1927) AND **ELYSIUM** (2013) TO SEE THAT THE MOVIES FACILITATE JOURNEYS THROUGH TIME ON A REGULAR BASIS.

ON A MORE FUNDAMENTAL LEVEL, FILM ALLOWS US TO CAPTURE IMAGES THAT WOULD OTHERWISE BE LOST TO HISTORY, OFFERING US AN UNPRECEDENTED ABILITY TO RECONSTRUCT IMAGES OF THE PAST AND EVOKE OUR MEMORIES LONG INTO THE FUTURE.

WHETHER IT IS THE SPECTACLE OF THE HISTORICAL DRAMA OR THE SIMPLE PLEASURES OF THE FAMILY HOME VIDEO, THE MOVING IMAGE TAPS INTO OUR DESIRE TO **RELIVE THE PAST** AND ACCESS PERSONAL AS WELL AS CULTURAL MEMORY.

HIROSHIMA MON AMOUR (1959) IS A POETIC, ENTRANCING FILM THAT CENTRES AROUND A FLEETING LOVE AFFAIR BETWEEN A JAPANESE MAN AND A FRENCH WOMAN IN POST-WAR HIROSHIMA.

OVER A SERIES OF CONVERSATIONS, THEY DEBATE THE NATURE OF MEMORY AND RECALL THROUGH DREAMLIKE FLASHBACKS THE HISTORICAL TRAUMAS THAT HAVE SHAPED THEIR LIVES.

IN THE FILM'S POWERFUL OPENING SEQUENCE, WE SEE DOCUMENTARY FOOTAGE OF BOMBED-OUT HIROSHIMA, AS THE WOMAN NARRATES AN EVENT SHE NEVER WITNESSED.

YOU SAW NOTHING IN HIROSHIMA. NOTHING.

I SAW EVERYTHING. EVERYTHING.

THE SEQUENCE PLAYS ALMOST LIKE A **FLASHBACK** - HAVING SEEN THE NEWSREELS AND MUSEUMS THAT DOCUMENT THE ATROCITY, THE WOMAN IS ADAMANT THAT SHE REMEMBERS THIS EVENT LIKE SHE WAS THERE.

YOU ARE NOT ENDOWED WITH MEMORY.

WHILE WE MAY AT TIMES CONFLATE MEMORY WITH HISTORY, AS THIS FILM POINTS OUT, THE TWO ARE ENTIRELY DIFFERENT THINGS.

IT'S A DISTURBING SEQUENCE, WHICH JUXTAPOSES HER NAÏVE TESTIMONY WITH IMAGES OF UNSPEAKABLE HORROR TO EXPOSE JUST HOW UNRELIABLE AND MISLEADING MEMORY CAN BE.

MEMORIES OF THE PAST ALSO HAUNT DIRECTOR ARI FOLMAN IN HIS DOCUMENTARY **WALTZ WITH BASHIR** (2008).

TROUBLED BY VIVID DREAMS, THE FILM CHARTS FOLMAN'S STRUGGLE TO REMEMBER HIS INVOLVEMENT IN THE 1982 **LEBANON WAR**, WHICH APPEARS LOST FROM HIS MEMORY.

INTERVIEWING OTHERS WHO WERE THERE, HE BEGINS TO REMEMBER A MASSACRE OF PALESTINIAN REFUGEES BY A LEBANESE MILITIA, WHICH THE ISRAELIS ASSISTED BY BLOCKADING AND FIRING FLARES INTO THE CAMP.

AMIDST ITS HALLUCINATORY ANIMATED VISUALS, THE FILM REFLECTS ON THE ABILITY OF A CULTURE TO COLLECTIVELY **MISREMEMBER** OR BLOCK OUT ELEMENTS OF ITS HISTORY, LEAVING CLEANER, EASIER-TO-HANDLE MEMORIES IN THEIR PLACE.

IN MANY WAYS IT'S THE OPPOSITE OF THE MEMORIES BROUGHT TO LIGHT IN **HIROSHIMA MON AMOUR**.

HIROSHIMA IS AN EVENT SEARED INTO THE MEMORIES OF ALL, EVEN THOSE WHO WEREN'T THERE. THIS MASSACRE IS ONE THAT RISKS BEING **FORGOTTEN**, EVEN BY ITS PERPETRATORS, AND LOST FROM THE TIMELINE COMPLETELY.

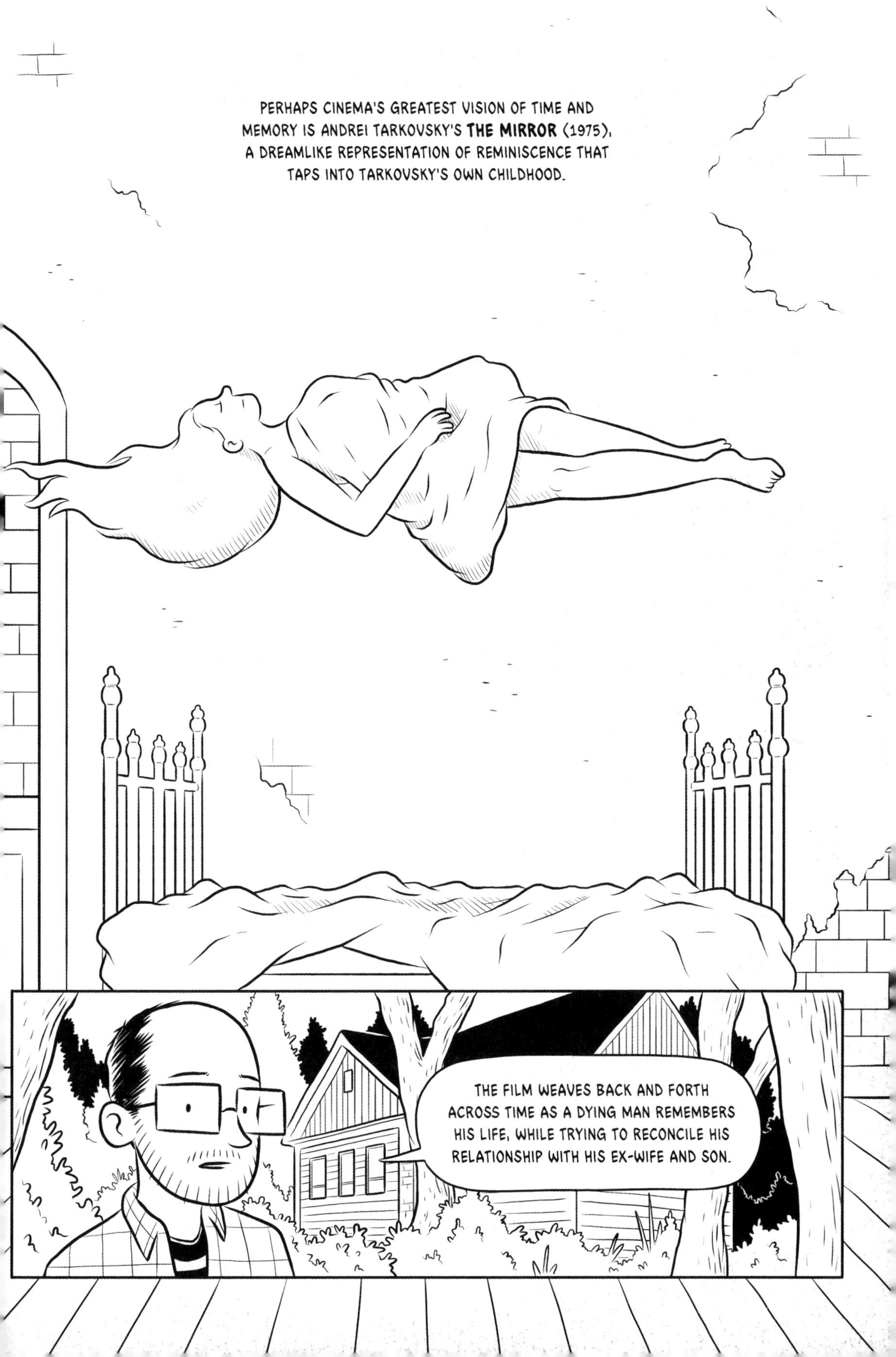
PERHAPS CINEMA'S GREATEST VISION OF TIME AND MEMORY IS ANDREI TARKOVSKY'S **THE MIRROR** (1975), A DREAMLIKE REPRESENTATION OF REMINISCENCE THAT TAPS INTO TARKOVSKY'S OWN CHILDHOOD.
THE FILM WEAVES BACK AND FORTH ACROSS TIME AS A DYING MAN REMEMBERS HIS LIFE, WHILE TRYING TO RECONCILE HIS RELATIONSHIP WITH HIS EX-WIFE AND SON.

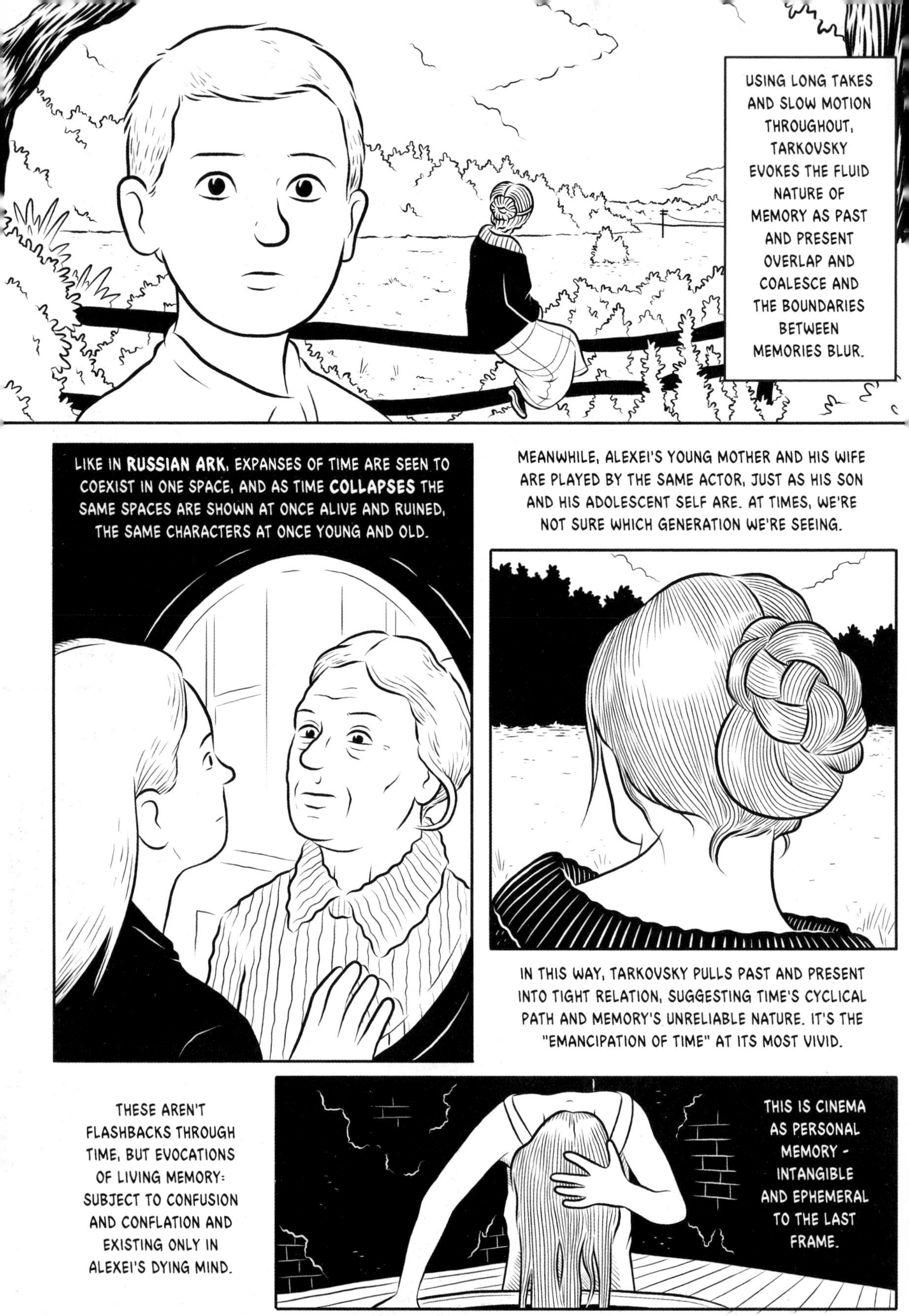
USING LONG TAKES AND SLOW MOTION THROUGHOUT, TARKOVSKY EVOKES THE FLUID NATURE OF MEMORY AS PAST AND PRESENT OVERLAP AND COALESCE AND THE BOUNDARIES BETWEEN MEMORIES BLUR.
LIKE IN **RUSSIAN ARK**, EXPANSES OF TIME ARE SEEN TO COEXIST IN ONE SPACE, AND AS TIME **COLLAPSES** THE SAME SPACES ARE SHOWN AT ONCE ALIVE AND RUINED, THE SAME CHARACTERS AT ONCE YOUNG AND OLD.
MEANWHILE, ALEXEI'S YOUNG MOTHER AND HIS WIFE ARE PLAYED BY THE SAME ACTOR, JUST AS HIS SON AND HIS ADOLESCENT SELF ARE. AT TIMES, WE'RE NOT SURE WHICH GENERATION WE'RE SEEING.
IN THIS WAY, TARKOVSKY PULLS PAST AND PRESENT INTO TIGHT RELATION, SUGGESTING TIME'S CYCLICAL PATH AND MEMORY'S UNRELIABLE NATURE. IT'S THE "EMANCIPATION OF TIME" AT ITS MOST VIVID.
THESE AREN'T FLASHBACKS THROUGH TIME, BUT EVOCATIONS OF LIVING MEMORY: SUBJECT TO CONFUSION AND CONFLATION AND EXISTING ONLY IN ALEXEI'S DYING MIND.
THIS IS CINEMA AS PERSONAL MEMORY - INTANGIBLE AND EPHEMERAL TO THE LAST FRAME.

TIME IS AT THE HEART OF HOW WE PERCEIVE THE MOVIES, "THE VERY FOUNDATION OF CINEMA". (p119, TARKOVSKY)

FROM THE TICKING-CLOCK TENSION OF **TOUCH OF EVIL** AND **HIGH NOON** TO THE LEAPS AND REVERSALS THROUGH TIME OF **2001: A SPACE ODYSSEY** AND **MEMENTO**, THE MOVIES HAVE HARNESSED TIME IN UNCOUNTABLE WAYS.

IN WAYS **UNIQUE** TO THE MEDIUM, FILM ALLOWS US TO PLAY WITH TIME, TO JUMP BACK AND FORTH THROUGH TIME AND TO SEE OUR WORLD 'OUTSIDE OF TIME' AND BEYOND THE CHRONOLOGY THAT DICTATES OUR DAY-TO-DAY LIVES.

TARKOVSKY PUTS IT BEST WHEN HE SAYS WE GO TO THE CINEMA "FOR TIME LOST OR SPENT OR NOT YET HAD..."

"FOR CINEMA, LIKE NO OTHER ART, WIDENS, ENHANCES AND CONCENTRATES A PERSON'S EXPERIENCE - AND NOT ONLY ENHANCES IT BUT MAKES IT LONGER, SIGNIFICANTLY LONGER." (p63)

BACK TO THE FUTURE

VOICE AND
LANGUAGE

EVER SINCE SOUND FIRST GRACED THE CINEMA, THE MOVIES HAVE BEEN FASCINATED BY THE POWER OF THE HUMAN VOICE.

INTEGRAL TO HUMAN EXISTENCE, OUR SOPHISTICATED ABILITY TO COMMUNICATE HAS DEFINED US AS A SPECIES.

AS FILM THEORIST MICHEL CHION STATES, "SINCE THE VERY DAWN OF TIME, **VOICES HAVE PRESENTED IMAGES**, MADE ORDER OF THINGS IN THE WORLD, BROUGHT THINGS TO LIFE AND NAMED THEM." (p49)

LANGUAGE IS THE FORCE THAT BINDS US TOGETHER AS SOCIAL BEINGS, HELPS US MAKE SENSE OF THE WORLD AROUND US AND PROVIDES THE FOUNDATIONS OF EVERYTHING WE HAVE ACHIEVED THROUGHOUT HUMAN HISTORY.

YET, FOR ALL THEIR POWER, LANGUAGE AND THE VOICE ARE FRAGILE FORCES. WORDS CAN BE USED TO MANIPULATE AND DECEIVE, AND LANGUAGE CONTROLS OUR PERCEPTIONS OF THE WORLD AS MUCH AS IT LIBERATES US.

FOR THE MOVIES, THE CRUCIAL AND COMPLEX ROLE THAT THE VOICE PLAYS IN OUR LIVES HAS BEEN A SOURCE OF ENDLESS INSPIRATION, LEADING TO A PROFOUND PREOCCUPATION WITH LANGUAGE AND THE HUMAN VOICE ONSCREEN...

FROM THE PIERCING SCREAMS THROUGHOUT **KING KONG** (1933) TO THE SONG AND DANCE EXCITEMENT OF **SINGIN' IN THE RAIN** (1952) AND THE WHISPERS OF LOSS AND LONGING IN **THE THIN RED LINE** (1998), THE HUMAN VOICE HAS TAKEN ON EVERY TONE AND VOLUME IMAGINABLE DURING CINEMA'S HISTORY.

THE MOVIES DEMAND THAT ACTORS BRING BOTH A BODILY AND VOCAL PERFORMANCE, OFTEN REQUIRING NOT JUST THE MASTERY OF ACCENT, BUT OF TIMBRE, PITCH AND SPEECH PATTERNS AS WELL. (p173, CHION)

HEATH LEDGER'S HYPNOTISING TURN AS THE JOKER IN **THE DARK KNIGHT** (2008) IS A PRIME EXAMPLE OF THIS.

LEDGER "CALLS FORTH AN INTERRUPTED RHYTHM FROM WITHIN HIMSELF" (p104, STERNAGEL), DELIVERING A BROKEN, WAVERING VOCAL PERFORMANCE THAT SOUNDS LIKE A CHILD'S TOY RUNNING OUT OF BATTERIES.

I BELIEVE WHATEVER DOESN'T KILL YOU, SIMPLY MAKES YOU...

...STRANGER.

WITH A CHARACTER SO CAKED IN CLOWN MAKE-UP THAT WE CAN'T SEE THE MAN UNDERNEATH, IT'S HIS VOICE THAT TELLS THE STORY, SUGGESTING AN INDIVIDUAL DAMAGED BOTH VOCALLY AND PSYCHOLOGICALLY.

GROUNDED AND UNSETTLING, **THE EXORCIST** (1973) USES REAGAN'S CHANGING VOICE TO HELP PORTRAY HER GRADUAL POSSESSION BY THE DEMON PAZUZU.

ONCE SOFT AND SWEET, HER VOICE IS DEFORMED AS THE POSSESSION TAKES HOLD, BECOMING GUTTURAL AND ANIMALISTIC, USHERING FROM DEEP WITHIN HER.

KEEP AWAY... THE SOW IS MINE.

MUCH OF THE FILM'S TERROR COMES FROM THE INCONGRUITY OF THE VICIOUS DEMONIC VOICE OF PAZUZU COMING OUT OF THIS INNOCENT CHILD'S MOUTH.

CONVERSELY, IN **SEVEN** (1995), THE SERIAL KILLER JOHN DOE IS MADE ALL THE MORE UNSETTLING DUE TO KEVIN SPACEY'S MEASURED VOCAL PERFORMANCE.

WE SEE A DEADLY SIN ON EVERY STREET CORNER, IN EVERY HOME, AND WE TOLERATE IT.

FOREGOING CONVENTIONAL SERIAL KILLER THEATRICS, DOE SPEAKS ELOQUENTLY, HIS VOICE STEADY AND CALM AS HE RATIONALISES HIS CRIMES.

WELL, NOT ANY MORE. I'M SETTING THE EXAMPLE...

IT'S A CHILLING TECHNIQUE THAT EMPHASISES DOE'S PSYCHOPATHIC LACK OF HUMAN EMPATHY.

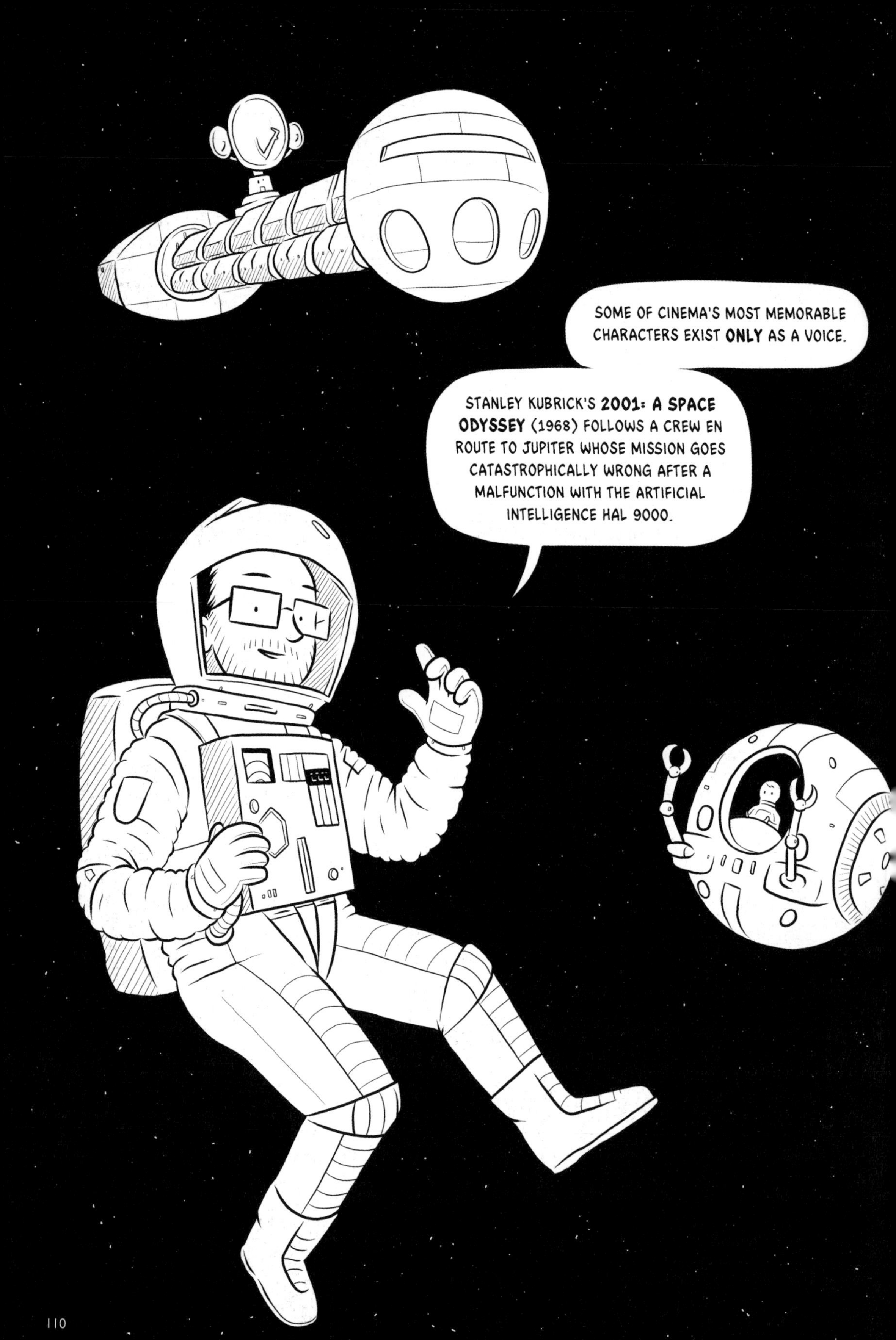
SOME OF CINEMA'S MOST MEMORABLE CHARACTERS EXIST **ONLY** AS A VOICE.
STANLEY KUBRICK'S **2001: A SPACE ODYSSEY** (1968) FOLLOWS A CREW EN ROUTE TO JUPITER WHOSE MISSION GOES CATASTROPHICALLY WRONG AFTER A MALFUNCTION WITH THE ARTIFICIAL INTELLIGENCE HAL 9000.

A DISEMBODIED VOCAL PRESENCE HEARD THROUGHOUT THE SHIP, HAL'S VOICE IS AT ONCE LIFELIKE AND YET ODDLY FLAT AND ARTIFICIAL, DISCONCERTINGLY STRADDLING THE BOUNDARY BETWEEN HUMAN AND MACHINE.

WHEN HAL TURNS VIOLENT, KILLING OFF MOST OF THE CREW, DAVE MUST DISCONNECT THE MALEVOLENT AI TO SAVE HIMSELF.

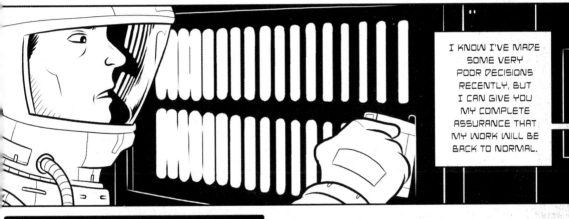

AS HE IS TURNED OFF, HAL REGRESSES TOWARDS A SORT OF INFANCY, HIS VOICE MODULATING AND SLOWING AS HIS MIND IS SHUT DOWN. SINGING HIMSELF TO SLEEP, WE CAN'T HELP BUT FEEL SORRY FOR HIM.

EXISTING ONLY AS A VOICE, "IT'S BY HIS VOICE, IN HIS VOICE, THAT HE DIES" (P45, CHION). ONCE HE FINALLY FALLS SILENT, HE CEASES TO EXIST.

AS KUBRICK SHOWS, THERE IS A CERTAIN UNCANNY POWER TO THE DISEMBODIED VOICE. WITH "THE ABILITY TO BE EVERYWHERE, TO SEE ALL, TO KNOW ALL AND TO HAVE COMPLETE POWER... ITS WORD IS LIKE THE WORD OF GOD." (P24, CHION)

THIS IS EXPERTLY DEMONSTRATED IN FRITZ LANG'S **THE TESTAMENT OF DR. MABUSE** (1933). IN THE FILM, THE INSANE MASTERMIND MABUSE IS ONLY HEARD FROM BEHIND A CURTAIN, INSTRUCTING HIS CRIMINAL GANG TO BUILD AN EMPIRE OF CRIME.

THE FAILURE TO OBEY IS TANTAMOUNT TO TREASON!

MADE DURING THE RISE OF FASCISM, LANG'S FILM CAN BE SEEN AS A COMMENT ON THE ALLURING, TERRIFYING POWER OF THE AUTHORITATIVE VOICE, WHICH ATTRACTS THE DESPERATE UNEMPLOYED WITH ITS PROMISES FOR THE FUTURE.

AS WITH **THE WIZARD OF OZ** (1939), ONCE THE SOURCE OF THE DISEMBODIED VOICE IS REVEALED, ITS POWER COMES TUMBLING DOWN, ITS SPELL BROKEN.

YET MABUSE'S DISEMBODIED VOICE IS NOT INVULNERABLE. WHEN THE CURTAIN IS FINALLY PULLED AWAY, MABUSE'S VOICE IS REVEALED TO BE A RECORDING AND HIS PLANS BEGIN TO UNWIND.

YOU WILL NEVER LEAVE THIS ROOM ALIVE!

THE CORRUPTING POWER OF THE VOICE IS AT THE HEART OF CHARLIE CHAPLIN'S MASTERPIECE **THE GREAT DICTATOR** (1940), WHICH OFFERS A MORE DIRECT TAKE ON FASCISM.

THE FILM FOLLOWS THE INTERSECTING STORIES OF ADENOID HYNKEL, THE FASCIST LEADER OF THE INVENTED LAND OF TOMAINIA, AND AN INNOCENT JEWISH BARBER.

BOTH PLAYED BY CHAPLIN, THESE CHARACTERS COULDN'T BE MORE DIFFERENT. HYNKEL IS LOUD, BRASH AND EGOMANIACAL, WHILE THE BARBER IS A GENTLE, QUIET MAN.

AGAIN OFTEN SEPARATED FROM HIS BODY, HYNKEL'S VOICE IS HEARD THROUGHOUT THE FILM, SCREAMING NONSENSE FAUX-GERMAN OUT OF RADIOS AND LOUDSPEAKERS AND AT POLITICAL RALLIES. IT'S AN OPPRESSIVE, INVASIVE PRESENCE IN THE BARBER'S LIFE.

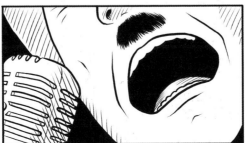

CHAPLIN WAS ESPECIALLY WARY OF THE POWERS OF THE HUMAN VOICE, HAVING STRUGGLED AS A STAR SINCE THE ADVENT OF CINEMA SOUND, MORE THAN A DECADE EARLIER.

AS CULTURAL THEORIST SLAVOJ ŽIŽEK PUTS IT, WITH THE COMING OF SOUND, "THE INNOCENT VULGAR VITALITY OF THE SILENT MOVIE IS LOST", MAKING WAY FOR THE MORE AMBIGUOUS ERA OF SOUND CINEMA. (P2)

THE GREAT DICTATOR IS A REFLECTION OF THIS LOSS, PRESENTING A CONFLICT BETWEEN THE INNOCENCE OF SILENCE AND THE CORRUPTING FORCE OF LANGUAGE.

AT THE FILM'S END, THE BARBER IS MISTAKEN FOR HYNKEL AND IS FORCED TO THE STAGE AT A MASSIVE RALLY.

SPEAKING AT LENGTH FOR THE FIRST TIME, THE BARBER UNLEASHES THE POWER OF HIS OWN VOICE TO CHALLENGE HYNKEL'S FASCIST POLICIES.

I'M SORRY, BUT I DON'T WANT TO BE AN EMPEROR. THAT'S NOT MY BUSINESS. I DON'T WANT TO RULE OR CONQUER ANYONE.

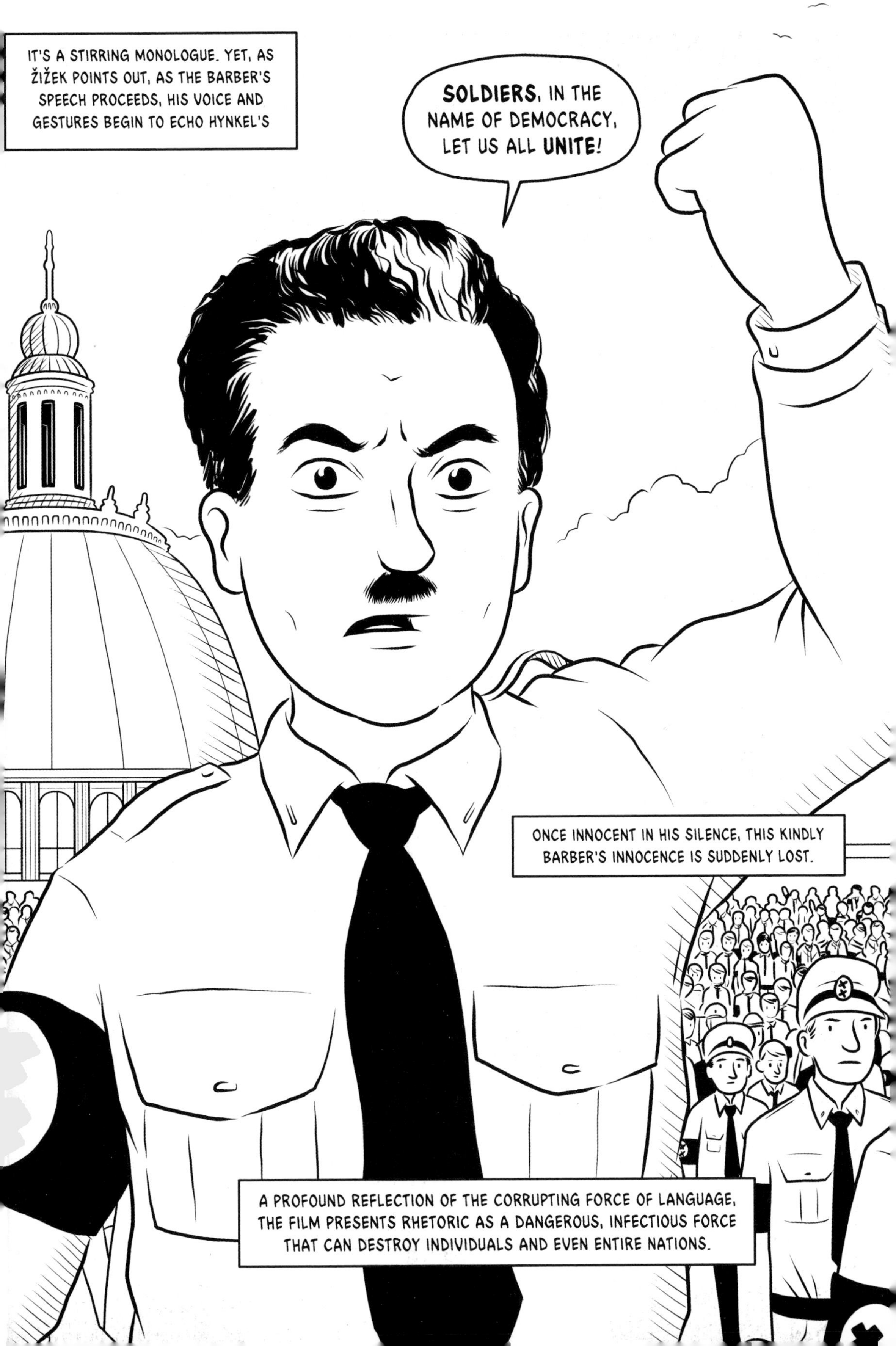
IT'S A STIRRING MONOLOGUE. YET, AS ŽIŽEK POINTS OUT, AS THE BARBER'S SPEECH PROCEEDS, HIS VOICE AND GESTURES BEGIN TO ECHO HYNKEL'S
SOLDIERS, IN THE NAME OF DEMOCRACY, LET US ALL **UNITE**!
ONCE INNOCENT IN HIS SILENCE, THIS KINDLY BARBER'S INNOCENCE IS SUDDENLY LOST.
A PROFOUND REFLECTION OF THE CORRUPTING FORCE OF LANGUAGE, THE FILM PRESENTS RHETORIC AS A DANGEROUS, INFECTIOUS FORCE THAT CAN DESTROY INDIVIDUALS AND EVEN ENTIRE NATIONS.

THE TAUT AND INVENTIVE **PONTYPOOL** (2009) SEES WORDS AND THEIR MEANINGS AS THE DANGER.

THE FILM FOLLOWS RADIO PRESENTER GRANT MAZZY, HOLED UP AT HIS STATION AS A ZOMBIE-LIKE VIRUS SPREADS ACROSS TOWN.

ON AIR

FROM THIS ENCLOSED PERSPECTIVE, THE APOCALYPSE IS DESCRIBED TO MAZZY AND THE VIEWER, RATHER THAN SEEN, "ALLOWING SPECTATORS TO VISUALIZE THE HORRORS OUTSIDE THE RADIO STUDIO IN THEIR OWN MINDS". (P6, CHRISTIANSEN)

THEY'RE BITING, THEY'RE JUST BITING. THEY LOOK LIKE A SCHOOL OF FISH, LIKE A FRENZY OF PIRANHA. IT'S ALMOST LIKE, UH, IT LOOKS LIKE THESE PEOPLE ARE TRYING TO CLIMB OR EAT THEIR WAY INSIDE...

THIS TECHNIQUE OF PRIVILEGING VOICE OVER VISUALS IS AS EFFECTIVE AS IT IS FITTING. AS THE FILM UNFOLDS, IT IS DISCOVERED THAT THE VIRUS IS TRANSMITTED VIA LANGUAGE, WITH SPECIFIC WORDS CARRYING THE VIRUS FROM PERSON TO PERSON.

ON AIR

IT'S A CLEVER TWIST ON RICHARD DAWKINS' NOTION OF THE **'MEME'** - AN IDEA OR CULTURAL CONCEPT THAT SPREADS AND PROLIFERATES BETWEEN HUMAN HOSTS VIA LANGUAGE.

THE MALIGNANT MEMES OF **PONTYPOOL** ARE WORDS WITH SPECIAL MEANING FOR THE HEARER, WHICH LATCH ONTO THE VICTIM'S MIND, CAUSING THEM TO BABBLE AND ECHO OTHER VOICES TO FURTHER SPREAD THE DISEASE.

AS THE OUTBREAK WORSENS, THE RADIO STATION IS OVERRUN AND MAZZY'S ASSISTANT SYDNEY DISCOVERS SHE IS INFECTED.

REALISING THE SOLUTION LIES IN DIVORCING WORDS FROM THEIR MEANING, MAZZY FRANTICALLY ATTEMPTS TO UNDO THE CONVENTIONAL CONNOTATIONS OF 'KILL'.

AS MAZZY AND SYDNEY 'KILL' EACH OTHER, HER INFECTION IS VANQUISHED. ONLY BY BREAKING THE WORD FROM ITS MEANING, THE SIGNIFIER FROM ITS SIGNIFIED, CAN THE DISEASE BE COMBATTED.

AS CRITIC MICHAEL ATKINSON ARGUES, "IN PONTYPOOL, RHETORIC ITSELF IS THE POISONING AGENT, LITERALLY AND IRRATIONALLY TRANSFORMING AN ORDERLY SOCIETY INTO RAVING MADNESS." (WEB)

THE FILM IS A NEAT PIECE OF SATIRE IN AN AGE OF DOUBLESPEAK AND MISINFORMATION, OF 'COLLATERAL DAMAGE' AND 'ENHANCED INTERROGATION', WHERE WORDS AND THEIR MEANINGS ARE INCREASINGLY PROBLEMATIC.

THIS STRUGGLE FOR MEANING IS A RECURRING THEME IN THE MOVIES. AS THE CULTURAL THEORIST MLADEN DOLAR PROPOSES, "THE VOICE IS THE INSTRUMENT, THE VEHICLE, THE MEDIUM, AND THE MEANING IS THE GOAL." (p15)

FRANCIS FORD COPPOLA'S **THE CONVERSATION** (1974) SEES SURVEILLANCE EXPERT HARRY CAUL TASKED WITH RECORDING A COUPLE'S CONVERSATION FOR A WEALTHY CLIENT.

AS HARRY USES HIS EQUIPMENT TO CLEAN UP THE VOICES, HE BECOMES OBSESSED WITH THIS CONVERSATION, UNABLE TO WORK OUT WHAT IT ALL MEANS.

HE'D **KILL** US IF HE HAD THE CHANCE...

THE ENTIRE FILM HINGES ON THIS SINGLE PIECE OF DIALOGUE. FEARING FOR THESE PEOPLE'S LIVES, HARRY TRIES TO PREVENT THE EVIDENCE GETTING INTO HIS CLIENT'S HANDS.

ONLY TOO LATE DOES HE REALISE THE TRUE MEANING OF THEIR CONVERSATION.

HE'D KILL **US** IF HE HAD THE CHANCE...

THE FILM TWISTS ON THIS SINGLE EMPHASIS, A NUANCE OF DELIVERY THAT REVEALS THE MURDEROUS INTENT OF THE COUPLE ONLY AFTER HARRY'S CLIENT WINDS UP DEAD.

EQUALLY FASCINATED BY THE BREAKDOWN OF LANGUAGE, **SYNECDOCHE, NEW YORK** (2008) FOLLOWS CADEN COTARD, A DEPRESSED PLAYWRIGHT ATTEMPTING TO DEVELOP AN AMBITIOUS NEW PLAY THAT WILL BE A BRUTALLY HONEST REPRESENTATION OF LIFE.

THROUGHOUT THE FILM, LANGUAGE FLOUNDERS AS CHARACTERS REPEATEDLY MISUNDERSTAND EACH OTHER, THEIR WORDS FAILING TO PROVIDE THE MEANING THEY WISH TO EXPRESS.

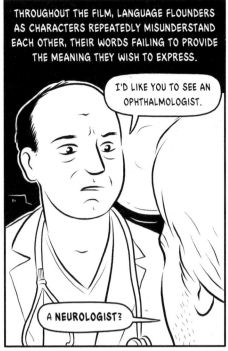

I'D LIKE YOU TO SEE AN OPHTHALMOLOGIST.

A **NEUROLOGIST?**

THIS INABILITY TO COMMUNICATE SPILLS OVER INTO COTARD'S PLAY...

STAGED IN AN IMPOSSIBLY MASSIVE AMPHITHEATRE, THE PLAY'S SCOPE EXPANDS STEADILY AS COTARD STRUGGLES TO COMMUNICATE HIS IDEAS.

A WHOLE CITY IS GRADUALLY CONSTRUCTED WITHIN THE THEATRE AND EACH EXTRA IS GIVEN A RICH INNER LIFE THAT FORMS A PART OF THE PLAY'S INFINITE TAPESTRY.

CADE   NG ROOM

ACTORS ARE BROUGHT IN TO PLAY COTARD AND HIS ASSISTANT AND, AS THEIR LIVES INTERTWINE WITH COTARD'S, THEY TOO REQUIRE ACTORS TO REPRESENT THEM.

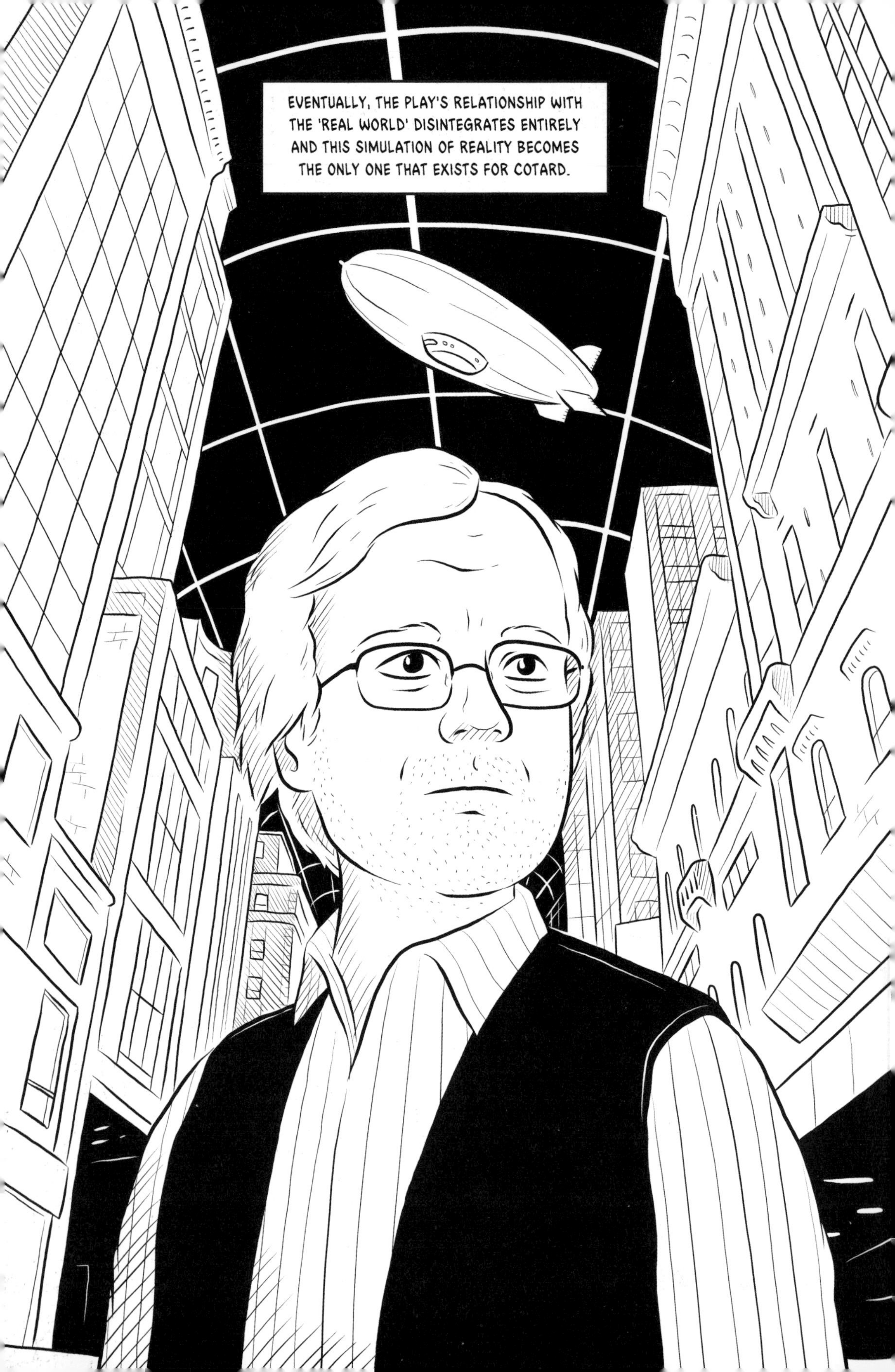
EVENTUALLY, THE PLAY'S RELATIONSHIP WITH THE 'REAL WORLD' DISINTEGRATES ENTIRELY AND THIS SIMULATION OF REALITY BECOMES THE ONLY ONE THAT EXISTS FOR COTARD.

IT'S A WONDERFUL EXAMPLE OF JEAN BAUDRILLARD'S THEORY OF SIMULACRA AND SIMULATION, WHICH THE CULTURAL PHILOSOPHER SET FORWARD TO CRITIQUE THE EVER-WIDENING GAP IN MODERN CULTURE BETWEEN REPRESENTATION AND REALITY.

AS HE POSITS, THE MODERN WORLD IS AWASH WITH REPRESENTATIONS OF THINGS THAT NO LONGER EXIST, OR NEVER EXISTED TO BEGIN WITH - SO MUCH SO, THAT WE ARE SLOWLY LOSING OUR GRIP ON WHAT IS REAL.

JUST LIKE COTARD, WE TOO ARE BECOMING LOST IN OUR OWN FICTIONS, LET DOWN BY LANGUAGE, AND EVER MORE DISCONNECTED FROM REALITY.

THE FILM ENDS IN APPROPRIATE STYLE, AS COTARD'S WORLD COLLAPSES INTO ANARCHY. DYING, HE WANDERS DEEPER INTO HIS CREATION, THROUGH A SUCCESSION OF AMPHITHEATRES, EACH CONTAINED WITHIN THE LAST.

BY THE END, NOT ONLY HAS LANGUAGE BROKEN DOWN, BUT SO TOO HAS THE RELATIONSHIP BETWEEN REPRESENTATION AND REALITY ITSELF, WITH COTARD'S WORLD NOW A SERIES OF INFINITELY REGRESSING COPIES WITH NO ORIGINAL.

IN THE 1960S, FILM THEORIST CHRISTIAN METZ SUGGESTED THAT CINEMA ITSELF SHOULD BE SEEN AS A KIND OF LANGUAGE, WITH ITS OWN GRAMMAR, SYNTAX AND VOCABULARY.

IN THIS FIGURATION, SINGLE SHOTS CAN BE SEEN AS SOMETHING LIKE THE "EQUIVALENT TO AN ORAL SENTENCE", WHICH CAN BE STRUNG TOGETHER WITH OTHER SHOTS TO GENERATE MEANING. (p66, METZ)

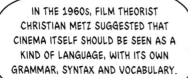

THIS CONCEPT WAS ABLY DEMONSTRATED BY RUSSIAN FILM-MAKER LEV KULESHOV, WHO SPLICED TOGETHER THE SAME SHOT OF AN EXPRESSIONLESS FACE WITH A SERIES OF DIFFERENT IMAGES.

A SIMPLE EXPERIMENT, IT EXPOSED THE FOUNDATIONS OF HOW CINEMA WORKS. AS HE DISCOVERED, EACH JUXTAPOSITION CREATED A NEW 'READING' OF THAT FACE FOR THE AUDIENCE.

LIKE WORDS, IMAGES ALONE MEAN ONLY SO MUCH...

BUT AS IMAGES AND SYMBOLS PILE UP, RICH NEW TAPESTRIES OF MEANING CAN BE CREATED.

AS METZ PUTS IT, "GOING FROM ONE IMAGE TO TWO IMAGES IS TO GO FROM IMAGE TO LANGUAGE." (p46)

THIS NOTION OF FILM AS LANGUAGE IS REFLECTED IN THE IDEA, POPULAR SINCE THE 1950s, OF THE FILM DIRECTOR AS AN 'AUTEUR'.

AUTEUR THEORY PROPOSES THAT THE FILM-MAKER IS THE SOLE VISIONARY AUTHOR OF A FILM, SKILFULLY DEPLOYING FILM LANGUAGE TO COMMUNICATE THEIR MESSAGE TO THE AUDIENCE.

IN THIS EQUATION, THE DIRECTOR IS THE SPEAKER, THE FILM THEIR VOICE, ITS MEANING THEIRS TO DICTATE.

NOT ONLY DOES THIS IDEA COMPLETELY IGNORE THE CAST AND CREW WHOSE CREATIVE INPUT SHAPES FILM PRODUCTION, BUT IT ALSO SUGGESTS THAT THE DIRECTOR'S INTERPRETATION OF THEIR WORK IS THE ONLY VALID ONE.

PSYCHO 9401
DIR. MR. HITCHCOCK
SLATE | SCENE
TAKE

AS LITERARY THEORIST ROLAND BARTHES PUTS IT, "TO GIVE A TEXT AN AUTHOR IS TO IMPOSE A LIMIT ON THAT TEXT, TO FURNISH IT WITH A FINAL SIGNIFIED, TO CLOSE THE WRITING." (p147)

FIN

IN AN ARTFORM HISTORICALLY DOMINATED BY WHITE, MALE, HETEROSEXUAL VOICES, THIS IS A TROUBLING NOTION.

YET DISSENTING VOICES DO EXIST. FOR NATIVE AMERICAN AUDIENCES, HOLLYWOOD CINEMA RARELY OFFERED A RESPITE FROM THE NEGATIVE IMAGES PROVIDED BY THE 'COWBOYS AND INDIANS' FORMULA, WHERE WHITE AMERICAN VOICES DOMINATED.

JOHN FORD'S **CHEYENNE AUTUMN** (1964) OSTENSIBLY OFFERED AN APOLOGY FOR THIS, TELLING THE STORY OF CHEYENNE NATIVE AMERICANS JOURNEYING TO THEIR HOMELAND, GUIDED BY AMERICAN TROOPS.

YET, FOR ALL HIS EFFORTS, THE LEGENDARY DIRECTOR'S FILM WAS GREETED WITH MOCKERY FROM NATIVE AMERICAN AUDIENCES.

WHILE ON THE SURFACE THE FILM IS A STOIC, SINCERE APOLOGY TO SUBJUGATED NATIVE AMERICANS, THE NAVAJO CAST BROUGHT IN TO PLAY THE CHEYENNE PEOPLE FILLED THE FILM WITH LEWD, MOCKING NAVAJO DIALOGUE. (p271, REAL)

THIS MAN HAS NO PENIS.

THE RESULT WAS TWO FILMS IN ONE, WITH NAVAJO SCREENINGS ACCOMPANIED BY LAUGHTER AND CELEBRATION, A STARK CONTRAST TO FORD'S WORTHY INTENT.

RECLAIMING THEIR VOICE AFTER DECADES OF SCREEN MISREPRESENTATION, IT WAS A WONDERFUL ACT OF RESISTANCE TO HOLLYWOOD'S ENGLISH LANGUAGE DOMINATION.

FOR GAY, LESBIAN, BISEXUAL AND TRANSGENDER AUDIENCES, THE SITUATION WAS PERHAPS EVEN WORSE, WITH STRICT CENSORSHIP DEPRIVING THEM OF ANY KIND OF POSITIVE OR COMPLEX REPRESENTATION ONSCREEN FOR MUCH OF THE 20TH CENTURY.

AS LGBT ACTIVIST AND FILM HISTORIAN VITO RUSSO PUTS IT: "AMERICA WAS A DREAM THAT HAD NO ROOM FOR THE EXISTENCE OF HOMOSEXUALS. LAWS WERE MADE AGAINST DEPICTING SUCH THINGS ONSCREEN. AND WHEN THE FACT OF OUR EXISTENCE BECAME UNAVOIDABLE, WE WERE REFLECTED ONSCREEN AND OFF AS DIRTY SECRETS." (pXII)

TO COMBAT THIS ATTEMPTED EFFACEMENT, LGBT CHARACTERS HAD TO HIDE IN PLAIN SIGHT, RETREATING TO A FILM'S SUBTEXT AND HINTED AT THROUGH LONGING LOOKS, SUGGESTIVE DIALOGUE OR COSTUME AND PERFORMANCE.

IN A HOSTILE CULTURE, THESE HIDDEN SUBTEXTS OFFERED LGBT AUDIENCES THE CHANCE TO RESIST MAINSTREAM CULTURE, MAKING THE INVISIBLE VISIBLE AND ALLOWING THEIR MARGINALISED VOICES TO BE HEARD.

THE COMPLEX ROLE THAT THE VOICE AND LANGUAGE PLAY IN OUR LIVES HAS RESULTED IN A MEDIUM FASCINATED BY THE WONDERFUL, AND AT TIMES TERRIFYING, POTENTIAL OF THE HUMAN VOICE.

A POWERFUL FORM OF COMMUNICATION IN ITSELF, FILM HAS BEEN USED THROUGHOUT ITS HISTORY TO SPREAD MESSAGES AND IDEAS ACROSS THE WORLD, COMMUNICATING WITH AUDIENCES THROUGH SOUND AND IMAGE.

BUT AS WE HAVE SEEN, THESE MESSAGES ARE FAR FROM SET. AS FILM-MAKER ANDREI TARKOVSKY PUTS IT, ONCE A FILM IS RELEASED INTO THE WORLD, "IT SEPARATES FROM ITS AUTHOR, STARTS TO LIVE ITS OWN LIFE, UNDERGOES CHANGES IN FORM AND MEANING". (p118)

IT IS WHEN **BEYOND** THE GRASP OF THEIR CREATORS THAT THE MOVIES ARE AT THEIR MOST EXCITING, OFFERING AUDIENCES THE CHANCE TO REJECT A FILM'S SUPERFICIAL, SANCTIONED MESSAGE, AND UNCOVER STORIES OF THEIR OWN.

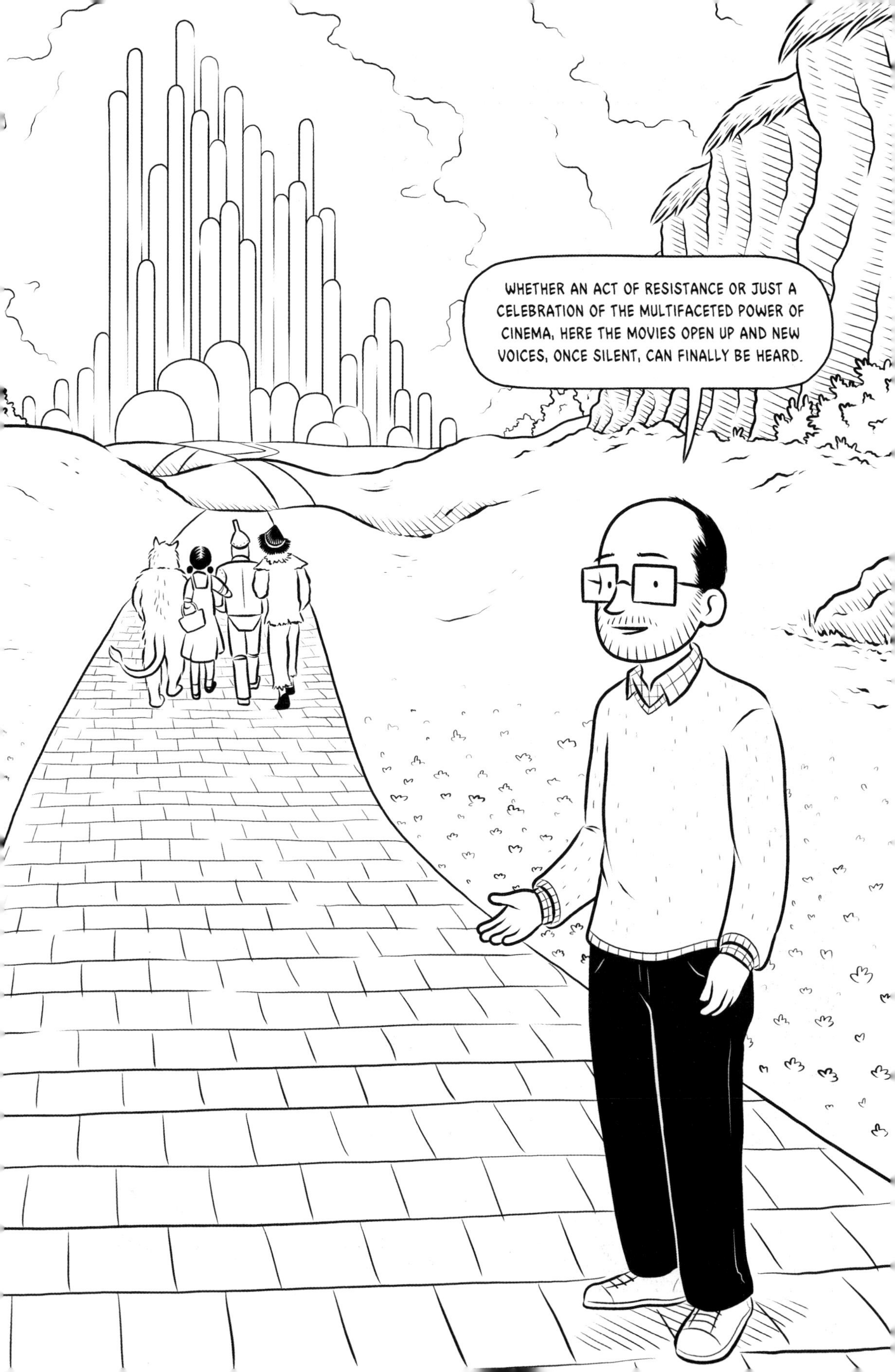
WHETHER AN ACT OF RESISTANCE OR JUST A CELEBRATION OF THE MULTIFACETED POWER OF CINEMA, HERE THE MOVIES OPEN UP AND NEW VOICES, ONCE SILENT, CAN FINALLY BE HEARD.

POWER AND IDEOLOGY

A RICH AND COMPLICATED KIND OF LANGUAGE, THE MOVING IMAGE IS AN IMMENSELY POWERFUL VEHICLE FOR THE COMMUNICATION OF IDEAS.

MUCH MORE THAN MERE ENTERTAINMENT, UNDER CINEMA'S SURFACE LIE **IDEOLOGIES** THAT PLAY A HUGE ROLE IN **SHAPING** OUR PERSPECTIVE ON THE WORLD.

IN THEIR PORTRAYAL OF EVERYTHING FROM SOCIETY, FAMILY AND THE GOVERNMENT TO GENDER, RACE AND SEXUALITY, THE MOVIES PLAY A VITAL ROLE IN INSCRIBING OUR **MORAL VALUES** AND RE-ENFORCING SOCIAL NORMS AND EXPECTATIONS.

THIS POWER THAT THE CINEMA HAS OVER US HAS NOT GONE UNNOTICED.

IF I COULD CONTROL THE MEDIUM OF THE AMERICAN MOTION PICTURE, I WOULD NEED **NOTHING ELSE** TO CONVERT THE ENTIRE WORLD TO COMMUNISM.

AS A RESULT, THE MOVIES HAVE LONG BEEN A BATTLEGROUND ON WHICH IDEOLOGIES HAVE FOUGHT, CONSCIOUSLY OR UNCONSCIOUSLY, FOR THE HEARTS AND MINDS OF VIEWERS ACROSS THE GLOBE.

THE NOTION THAT IDEOLOGY HIDES WITHIN CULTURE IS AT THE HEART OF JOHN CARPENTER'S CULT CLASSIC **THEY LIVE** (1988).

IN THE FILM, DOWN-AND-OUT DRIFTER JOHN NADA CHANCES UPON A PAIR OF SUNGLASSES THAT ALLOW HIM TO SEE PAST THE **SURFACE** OF SOCIETY TO THE IDEOLOGY **HIDDEN BELOW**, REVEALING AN ALIEN CONSPIRACY TO SUBJUGATE HUMANITY.

ON BILLBOARDS, MAGAZINES, PACKAGING AND MONEY, NADA SEES THE TRUTH BEHIND THE CONSUMER SYMBOLISM: INSTRUCTIONS TO "OBEY", "CONSUME" AND "CONFORM".

I HAVE COME HERE TO CHEW BUBBLEGUM AND KICK ASS... AND I'M ALL OUT OF BUBBLEGUM.

AS ŽIŽEK PUTS IT: "WHEN YOU PUT THE GLASSES ON, YOU SEE DICTATORSHIP IN DEMOCRACY. IT'S THE INVISIBLE ORDER WHICH SUSTAINS YOUR APPARENT FREEDOM."

THE SAME GOES FOR MAINSTREAM CINEMA. WHILE THE MAJORITY OF IT MAY SEEM APOLITICAL, BELOW THE SURFACE LIE INJUNCTIONS TO LIVE LIFE A CERTAIN WAY.

WHETHER IT IS THE NUCLEAR FAMILY, HETEROSEXUALITY, DEMOCRACY OR PATRIARCHY, MAINSTREAM CINEMA PRESENTS THE **DOMINANT IDEOLOGY** AS IF IT WERE "A TRUTHFUL AND NATURAL REPRESENTATION OF LIFE" RATHER THAN A **SYSTEM** SUPERIMPOSED UPON SOCIETY. (PVII, PARENTI IN ALFORD)

IT IS THIS IDEA THAT THE MOVIES SHOW US THE **TRUTH** THAT MAKES THEM SUCH A POWERFUL FORM OF IDEOLOGICAL CONTROL.

WHEN DEPICTING THE PAST, MANY FILMS PORTRAY A MYTHIC VISION OF THEIR NATION'S HISTORY, INJECTING CONTEMPORARY POLITICS INTO HISTORICAL EVENTS TO MAKE CURRENT STRUGGLES SEEM HISTORICALLY JUSTIFIED.

THIS WAS THE CASE FOR MUCH OF SOVIET CINEMA, WHERE THE IMAGES OF PRE-REVOLUTIONARY CLASS STRUGGLE SEEN IN **STRIKE** (1925) AND **BATTLESHIP POTEMKIN** (1925) PAINTED A MYTHIC PICTURE OF RUSSIA'S COMMUNIST DESTINY.

IT DIDN'T MATTER THAT **BATTLESHIP POTEMKIN**'S ODESSA STEPS MASSACRE WAS A FICTION ADDED FOR DRAMATIC AND IDEOLOGICAL EFFECT - THESE WERE INCENDIARY IMAGES THAT UPHELD THE COMMUNIST CAUSE.

THE MARTIAL ARTS EPIC **HERO** (2002) PAINTS A MYTHIC PICTURE OF ANCIENT CHINA THAT CONCEALS CONTEMPORARY NATIONALISM AMONG ITS COLOURFUL CHOREOGRAPHED FIGHT SCENES AND SPLENDID PERIOD DETAIL.

THE FILM SEES ITS HERO SACRIFICE HIMSELF SO THAT CHINA MAY BE UNITED UNDER ONE LEADER, **MYTHOLOGISING** THE MODERN CHINESE STRUGGLE TO RECLAIM HISTORIC TERRITORIES AND UNIFY THE NATION ONCE AGAIN. (P32, XU)

THIS KIND OF HISTORICAL MYTHOLOGY IS PARTICULARLY EVIDENT IN HOLLYWOOD CINEMA.

DURING THE 1950s AND '60s, THE **WESTERN** WAS HOLLYWOOD'S PRE-EMINENT GENRE, ENTHRALLING AUDIENCES WITH ITS IMAGES OF WHITE MALE FRONTIERSMEN DEFENDING THEIR LAND AND KIN AGAINST THE SAVAGERY OF INDIANS, OUTLAWS AND NATURE.

AS POLITICAL THEORIST STEPHEN MEXAL ARGUES, THE WESTERN OFFERED CONTEMPORARY AUDIENCES A MYTHIC TAKE ON AMERICAN HISTORY THAT ALLOWED THEM TO BETTER UNDERSTAND THE ROLE OF AMERICA IN THE COLD WAR ERA. (p80)

BY SHOWING AMERICAN HISTORY AS A **RIGHTEOUS STRUGGLE** ON BEHALF OF CIVILISATION AND FREEDOM, THE WESTERN PROVIDED SUPPORT TO THE COLD WAR, TRANSFORMING AN IDEOLOGICAL BATTLE INTO A **MORAL** ONE.

AT THE SAME TIME, WITH THE CIVIL RIGHTS MOVEMENT AND FEMINISM ON THE RISE, THE WESTERN OFFERED A REASSURING **PATRIARCHAL VISION** OF SOCIETY IN AN ERA OF "DECAYING MASCULINE POTENCY". (p39, CAWELTI)

THE WOMEN OF VIETNAM ARE OUR SISTERS

WOMEN'S LIBERATION

WOMAN POWER

WITH ITS RIGHTEOUS MASCULINE HEROES, THE HOLLYWOOD WESTERN PROVIDED A REACTIONARY IMAGE OF AMERICA AS A LAND BUILT BY WHITE MEN FOR WHITE MEN, A MYTH THAT HELPED JUSTIFY ONGOING INEQUALITY AND DISCRIMINATION.

SUCH REACTIONARY VISIONS ARE NOT UNCOMMON AND FILM REGULARLY PLAYS A ROLE IN BOLSTERING THE STATUS QUO WHEN IT IS MOST AT THREAT.

THROUGHOUT THE REAGAN ERA, HOLLYWOOD CINEMA WAS RIFE WITH NARRATIVES THAT REFLECTED A POLITICAL LANDSCAPE WHICH WAS "CENTRED AROUND ISSUES OF ANTI-FEMINISM, COVERT RACISM, CLASS PRIVILEGE, CONSERVATIVE RELIGION AND TRADITIONAL VALUES AND LIFESTYLES". (p145, PRATT)

MOVIES OF THE 1980s AND EARLY '90s WERE DOMINATED BY MUSCULAR MEN VIOLENTLY TAKING THE LAW INTO THEIR OWN HANDS TO PROTECT AMERICAN INTERESTS AND REINFORCE **CONSERVATIVE FAMILY VALUES**.

MEANWHILE, FILMS LIKE **FATAL ATTRACTION** (1987) AND **BASIC INSTINCT** (1992), WITH THEIR SEXUALLY LIBERATED, MURDEROUS CAREER WOMEN, EQUATED FEMALE INDEPENDENCE WITH IRRESPONSIBILITY AND EVEN **PSYCHOSIS**.

AS JOURNALIST SUSAN FALUDI PUTS IT, FOR '80s CINEMA, "THE GOOD WOMEN ARE ALL SUBSERVIENT AND BLAND HOUSEWIVES", WHILE "THE FEMALE VILLAINS ARE ALL WOMEN WHO FAIL TO GIVE UP THEIR INDEPENDENCE". (p145)

AFTER YEARS OF PROGRESS TOWARDS EQUALITY, THESE CONSERVATIVE VISIONS WORKED TO RE-INSCRIBE GENDER ROLES AND PROMOTE TRADITIONAL FAMILY VALUES, TURNING MAINSTREAM ENTERTAINMENT INTO AN **IDEOLOGICAL BLUEPRINT**.

EVEN THE MOST INNOCUOUS FAMILY FILMS HAVE AN IMPORTANT IDEOLOGICAL ROLE. BELOVED BY CHILDREN AND ADULTS ACROSS THE GLOBE, THE ANIMATED FILMS OF **DISNEY** ARE A MAJOR SHAPING INFLUENCE ON HOW YOUNG PEOPLE SEE THE WORLD.

FROM **SNOW WHITE AND THE SEVEN DWARFS** (1937) TO **BEAUTY AND THE BEAST** (1991) AND BEYOND, DISNEY HAS LONG CHARACTERISED ITS FEMALE CHARACTERS AS DAMSELS IN NEED OF RESCUE, FOR WHOM MARRIAGE IS THE ULTIMATE GOAL.

AS SUSAN WHITE PUTS IT, **THE LITTLE MERMAID** (1989) PRESENTS ARIEL AS "LITTLE MORE THAN A HAPPY HOUSEWIFE IN THE MAKING" (p188), WHOSE QUEST FOR THE LOVE OF PRINCE ERIC COMES AT AN UNSPOKEN PRICE.

TO MARRY PRINCE ERIC, ARIEL MUST GIVE UP HER HOME, HER FRIENDS, HER FAMILY AND, PERHAPS MOST IMPORTANTLY, HER NATURAL MERMAID FORM.

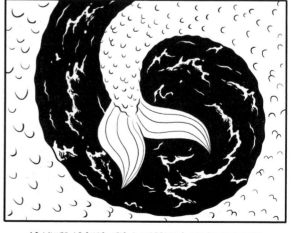

AS WHITE ARGUES, IT'S A WORRYING IMAGE IN A TIME "WHEN ACCEDING TO WOMANHOOD MEANS MORE THAN EVER TO CARVE ONE'S FLESH INTO THE APPROPRIATE SHAPE". (p188)

RACE ALSO PLAYS A MAJOR ROLE IN DISNEY MOVIES. FROM THE AFRICAN-AMERICAN-STYLED CROWS IN **DUMBO** (1941) TO THE PREDOMINANTLY VICIOUS ARABS IN **ALADDIN** (1992), DISNEY FILMS HAVE REGULARLY RELIED ON BROADLY DRAWN AND OFTEN NEGATIVE RACIAL STEREOTYPES IN THEIR CONSTRUCTION OF CHARACTER.

BROTHER, NOW I'VE SEEN EVERYTHING!

IN **THE JUNGLE BOOK** (1967), RACIST DEHUMANISATION MANIFESTS LITERALLY IN THE ORANG-UTAN KING LOUIE, WHOSE AFRICAN-AMERICAN-SOUNDING VOICE SINGS ABOUT WANTING TO BE "HUMAN, TOO".

RELEASED AT THE HEIGHT OF THE CIVIL RIGHTS MOVEMENT, THIS APPARENT EQUATION OF AFRICAN-AMERICANS WITH APES WAS A CALLOUS SLAP IN THE FACE TO MANY AUDIENCE MEMBERS.

ACCORDING TO ALEX WAINER, THE FILM "IS AT WORST A DISPLAY OF RETROGRADE RACIST RHETORIC CODED AS A CHILDREN'S TALE, OR AT BEST AN INSENSITIVE THROWBACK TO EARLIER CARTOON STEREOTYPES." (p91, QUOTED IN PINSKY)

DELIBERATELY OR NOT, IN THESE RACIAL STEREOTYPES AND CONSERVATIVE GENDER ROLES, DISNEY HELPS TO SET **EXPECTATIONS** FOR YOUNG PEOPLE, INSCRIBING IDEOLOGICAL VALUES ABOUT RACE, SEXUALITY AND GENDER BEFORE MANY CHILDREN ARE EVEN IN SCHOOL.

WHILE MOVIE HEROES REPRESENT AND CONFORM TO DOMINANT IDEOLOGY, CINEMA'S VILLAINS OFTEN REFLECT THE ANXIETIES THAT THE MAINSTREAM HAS TOWARDS OUTSIDERS.

FROM MURDEROUS HOMOSEXUALS AND LASCIVIOUS BLACKS TO CRAZED CAREER WOMEN AND SAVAGE NATIVE AMERICANS, MAINSTREAM CINEMA HAS REPEATEDLY PORTRAYED OUTSIDER GROUPS AS A DANGEROUS THREAT TO SOCIETY AND THE STATUS QUO.

IT RUBS THE LOTION ON ITS SKIN...

THIS IS THE SIMPLEST KIND OF **SOCIAL CONTROL**, A FORM OF REPRESENTATIONAL VIOLENCE THAT TEACHES OUTSIDERS THAT THEY DESERVE PUNISHMENT FOR NON-CONFORMANCE AND TELLS INSIDERS JUST WHO TO HATE.

FOR CULTURAL CRITIC JACK SHAHEEN, FEW GROUPS HAVE BEEN QUITE AS AGGRESSIVELY VILIFIED AS ARABS, WHO ARE REGULARLY PORTRAYED AS "BRUTAL, HEARTLESS, UNCIVILIZED RELIGIOUS FANATICS AND MONEY-MAD CULTURAL 'OTHERS' BENT ON TERRORIZING CIVILIZED WESTERNERS". (p7)

FROM ACTION BLOCKBUSTERS LIKE **INDIANA JONES AND THE RAIDERS OF THE LOST ARK** (1981) TO BELOVED ANIMATIONS LIKE **ALADDIN**, ARABS HAVE LONG BEEN A CONVENIENT STEREOTYPICAL VILLAIN FOR MAINSTREAM CINEMA, A SUPPOSEDLY ALIEN CULTURE WHOSE VISIBLE DIFFERENCE MAKES THEM AN EASY TARGET FOR DEFAMATION.

JAMES CAMERON'S ACTION-PACKED **TRUE LIES** (1994) SETS ARNOLD SCHWARZENEGGER'S MUSCULAR, WHITE, FAMILY-FOCUSED SPY AGAINST A GANG OF ARAB TERRORISTS INTENT ON DETONATING NUCLEAR BOMBS ON AMERICAN SOIL.

IT'S AN AGE-OLD SET-UP: "IF SCHWARZENEGGER'S CHARACTER WORE JEANS INSTEAD OF A TUX, CARRIED A SIX-GUN INSTEAD OF A BERETTA, RODE A PALOMINO INSTEAD OF A HARRIER JET, AND KILLED REDSKINS WEARING FEATHERS INSTEAD OF BROWNSKINS WEARING BEARDS, WE'D HAVE A CLASSIC (AND RACIST) COWBOY AND INDIAN MOVIE." (AL-MARAYATI AND BUSTANY, WEB)

FOR SHAHEEN, SUCH "DAMAGING PORTRAITS HAVE BECOME SO PREVALENT THAT VIEWERS OF FILM AND TV SHOWS DEMONSTRATING THESE STEREOTYPES MAY COME TO PERCEIVE REEL ARABS AS REAL ONES." (P1)

WITH FILMS LIKE **TRUE LIES**, HOLLYWOOD HAS VASTLY SKEWED AMERICA'S (AND THE WORLD'S) PERCEPTION OF ARAB AND MUSLIM PEOPLES - PERHAPS IN THE PROCESS HELPING TO JUSTIFY MILITARY INVOLVEMENT THROUGHOUT THE MIDDLE EAST.

AS AL-MARAYATI AND BUSTANY ARGUE, "IT'S AN ECHO OF THE NAZI PROPAGANDA - LESS LETHAL, WE HOPE - THAT DEHUMANIZED JEWS IN THE 1930s AND MADE THE HOLOCAUST POSSIBLE." (WEB)

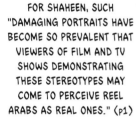

INDEED, THE MOVIES WERE A KEY COMPONENT IN HITLER'S IDEOLOGICAL REGIME, PLAYING A VITAL ROLE IN THE SCAPEGOATING AND DEHUMANISATION OF THE JEWS.

THE ETERNAL JEW (1940) WAS PERHAPS PROPAGANDA MINISTER JOSEPH GOEBBELS' MOST BLATANT AND DESPICABLE PIECE OF CINEMATIC VILIFICATION.

OSTENSIBLY A DOCUMENTARY, THE FILM JUXTAPOSED SHOTS OF JEWISH PEOPLE WITH IMAGES OF RATS, AS VOICEOVER NARRATION WORKED TO PORTRAY JEWS AS SUB-HUMAN VERMIN.

YET DESPITE GOEBBELS' FIRM GRIP ON THE INDUSTRY, "VERY FEW NAZI FEATURES SIMPLY RANT AND RAGE; MOST OF THEM APPEAR TO HAVE NOTHING TO DO WITH POLITICS". (p140, RENTSCHLER)

INSTEAD, LIKE HOLLYWOOD CINEMA, MUCH OF GERMANY'S OUTPUT AT THE TIME FOCUSED ON ENTERTAINMENT AND SPECTACLE, OFFERING FAR MORE INSIDIOUS PROPAGANDA IN THE PROCESS.

LENI RIEFENSTAHL'S TRIUMPH OF THE WILL (1935) DOCUMENTS THE NUREMBERG RALLIES IN A WAY THAT MYTHOLOGISES THE NAZI STATE.

DELIBERATELY EPIC, THE FILM SEES HITLER DESCENDING FROM THE CLOUDS IN A PLANE TO GREET THRONGS OF SUPPORTERS.

THESE ARE ICONIC IMAGES, ENGINEERED TO UNITE THE NATION BEHIND "A MYTHIC, GODLIKE FIGURE". (p219, CHAPMAN)

THE BRITISH AND AMERICANS TURNED TO FILM AS WELL, TO HELP BOOST MORALE AND INSPIRE THE FIGHT AGAINST FASCISM.

FRANK CAPRA'S HUGELY SUCCESSFUL **WHY WE FIGHT** DOCUMENTARIES (1942-1945) WERE COMMISSIONED BY THE US GOVERNMENT TO CONVINCE THE ISOLATIONIST AMERICAN PEOPLE TO INTERVENE IN EUROPE.

CAPRA WANTED HIS FILMS TO BE AN ANTIDOTE TO RIEFENSTAHL'S NAZI EPIC, WHICH HE VIEWED AS "THE OMINOUS PRELUDE TO HITLER'S HOLOCAUST OF HATE". (p22, QUOTED IN DOHERTY)

TO DO THIS, HE CLEVERLY TURNED NAZI PROPAGANDA AGAINST THE NAZIS, USING THE PARTY'S OWN MOVIES TO CONDEMN THEM IN AMERICA'S EYES.

YET ALLIED PROPAGANDA WAS NO MORE FREE OF RACISM THAN THAT CREATED BY GERMANY AND JAPAN, AND ALLIED IMAGES OF THE JAPANESE ARE ESPECIALLY DISCOMFITING TODAY.

HATE IS A POWERFUL WEAPON. AS WILLIAM GREIDER ARGUES, "THE POWER TO DEPICT CERTAIN 'OTHERS' AS INNATELY STRANGE AND DANGEROUS - AS FOUL CREATURES NOT LIKE THE REST OF US - IS SURELY AS DEVASTATING AS THE PHYSICAL FORCE OF WEAPONRY." (pVIII, IN SHAHEEN)

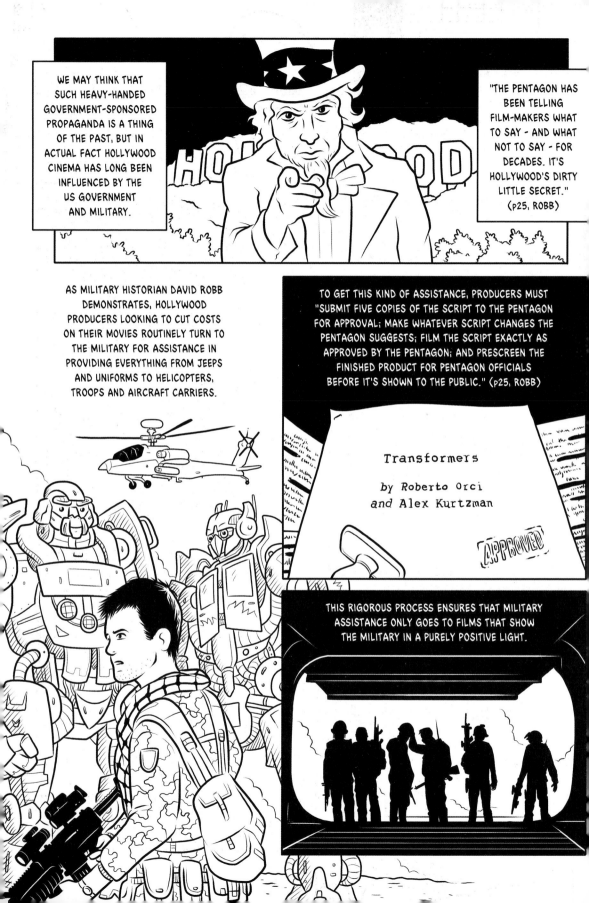

WE MAY THINK THAT SUCH HEAVY-HANDED GOVERNMENT-SPONSORED PROPAGANDA IS A THING OF THE PAST, BUT IN ACTUAL FACT HOLLYWOOD CINEMA HAS LONG BEEN INFLUENCED BY THE US GOVERNMENT AND MILITARY.

"THE PENTAGON HAS BEEN TELLING FILM-MAKERS WHAT TO SAY - AND WHAT NOT TO SAY - FOR DECADES. IT'S HOLLYWOOD'S DIRTY LITTLE SECRET." (p25, ROBB)

AS MILITARY HISTORIAN DAVID ROBB DEMONSTRATES, HOLLYWOOD PRODUCERS LOOKING TO CUT COSTS ON THEIR MOVIES ROUTINELY TURN TO THE MILITARY FOR ASSISTANCE IN PROVIDING EVERYTHING FROM JEEPS AND UNIFORMS TO HELICOPTERS, TROOPS AND AIRCRAFT CARRIERS.

TO GET THIS KIND OF ASSISTANCE, PRODUCERS MUST "SUBMIT FIVE COPIES OF THE SCRIPT TO THE PENTAGON FOR APPROVAL; MAKE WHATEVER SCRIPT CHANGES THE PENTAGON SUGGESTS; FILM THE SCRIPT EXACTLY AS APPROVED BY THE PENTAGON; AND PRESCREEN THE FINISHED PRODUCT FOR PENTAGON OFFICIALS BEFORE IT'S SHOWN TO THE PUBLIC." (p25, ROBB)

Transformers

by Roberto Orci and Alex Kurtzman

APPROVED

THIS RIGOROUS PROCESS ENSURES THAT MILITARY ASSISTANCE ONLY GOES TO FILMS THAT SHOW THE MILITARY IN A PURELY POSITIVE LIGHT.

FROM WAR FILMS LIKE **THE GREEN BERETS** (1968) AND **ZERO DARK THIRTY** (2012) TO FAMILY ENTERTAINMENT LIKE **THE MICKEY MOUSE CLUB** TV SHOW (1950s) AND **TRANSFORMERS** (2007), HUNDREDS OF HOLLYWOOD PRODUCTIONS HAVE TAILORED THEIR CONTENT TO PLEASE THE PENTAGON.

IN AN INSANE PIECE OF ORWELLIAN IRONY, EVEN THE 1956 ADAPTATION OF **NINETEEN EIGHTY-FOUR**, THE CLASSIC PARABLE ABOUT GOVERNMENT OPPRESSION, WAS ALTERED BY THE CIA'S **AMERICAN COMMITTEE FOR CULTURAL FREEDOM** TO MAKE BIG BROTHER MORE ASSOCIATED WITH COMMUNISM. (p12, ALFORD)

MEANWHILE, FILMS LIKE **FAIL-SAFE** (1964), **PLATOON** (1989) AND **THIRTEEN DAYS** (2000), WHICH SHOW THE NEGATIVE IMPACT OF WAR AND REFUSE TO MYTHOLOGISE AMERICA'S MILITARY HISTORY, ARE DENIED ANY KIND OF ASSISTANCE.

THE PENTAGON'S TECHNIQUE HAS CERTAINLY WORKED. **TOP GUN** (1986) LED TO A 500% SPIKE IN AIRFORCE RECRUITMENT AFTER THE FILM WAS RELEASED (p182, ROBB), WHILE FILMS CRITICAL OF THE US MILITARY ARE INCREASINGLY ABSENT FROM CINEMAS.

BY OFFERING SIMPLE ECONOMIC INCENTIVES, THE PENTAGON HAS ENSURED THAT "MAINSTREAM PRODUCTIONS REPEATEDLY ENDORSE US FORCE AND DO NOT CRITICISE THE FUNDAMENTAL ASSUMPTIONS OF US BENEVOLENCE ON THE WORLD STAGE". (p169, ALFORD)

WHEN ECONOMIC INCENTIVES DON'T WORK, THOSE IN POWER CAN ALWAYS ACTIVELY CONTROL WHAT THE PUBLIC DOES AND DOESN'T SEE, USING **CENSORSHIP** TO KEEP DISSENTING VOICES SILENT.

IN IRAN, FILM IS HEAVILY CONTROLLED BY THE MINISTRY OF CULTURE AND ISLAMIC GUIDANCE, WHICH FORCES MOVIES TO CONFORM TO THE CONSERVATIVE IDEALS OF THE REIGNING GOVERNMENT.

YET IRAN PRODUCES SOME OF THE MOST EXCITING FILMS IN THE WORLD TODAY, FEATURING COMPLEX DISCOURSES ABOUT THE ROLES OF WOMEN, CHILDREN AND ETHNIC MINORITIES IN MODERN IRAN.

AS RICHARD TAPPER POSITS, MUCH OF IRANIAN CINEMA IS COVERTLY POLITICAL, USING SYMBOLISM TO EXPRESS FORBIDDEN POINTS OF VIEW.

FOR FILM HISTORIAN NORA GILBERT, THERE'S SOMETHING POSITIVE IN THIS: "BY FORCING CERTAIN NARRATIVE IMPULSES UNDERGROUND, CENSORSHIP CREATES AN OPEN SPACE, BETWEEN TEXT AND SUBTEXT, WHERE THE AGILE INTERPRETER WITHIN EACH ONE OF US CAN COME OUT TO PLAY." (p14)

NONETHELESS, FILM-MAKERS HAVE BEEN IMPRISONED AS A RESULT OF THEIR WORK - THEIR FILMS BANNED OR SMUGGLED OUT OF THE COUNTRY TO TOUR FESTIVALS ELSEWHERE.

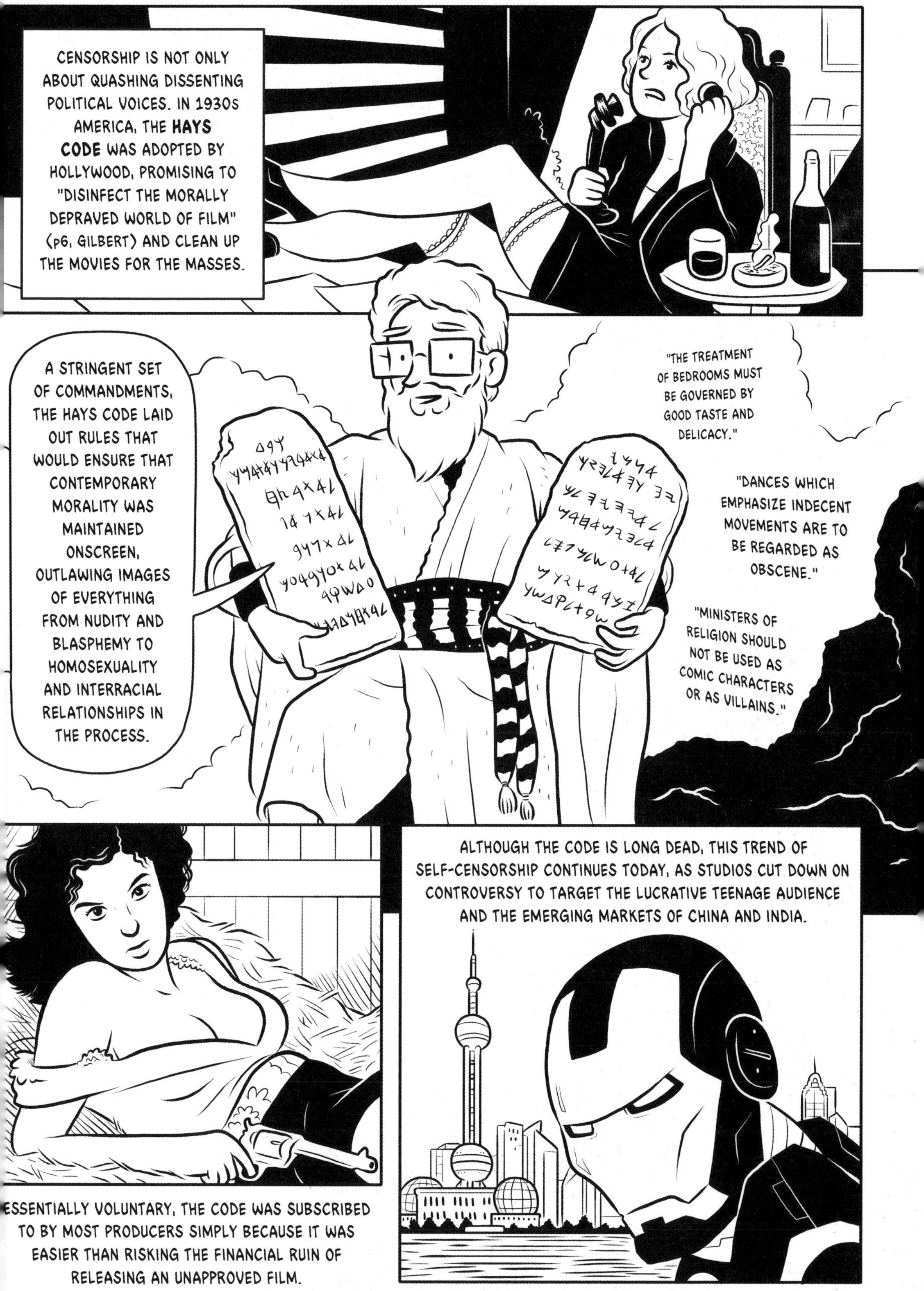
CENSORSHIP IS NOT ONLY ABOUT QUASHING DISSENTING POLITICAL VOICES. IN 1930S AMERICA, THE **HAYS CODE** WAS ADOPTED BY HOLLYWOOD, PROMISING TO "DISINFECT THE MORALLY DEPRAVED WORLD OF FILM" (P6, GILBERT) AND CLEAN UP THE MOVIES FOR THE MASSES.
A STRINGENT SET OF COMMANDMENTS, THE HAYS CODE LAID OUT RULES THAT WOULD ENSURE THAT CONTEMPORARY MORALITY WAS MAINTAINED ONSCREEN, OUTLAWING IMAGES OF EVERYTHING FROM NUDITY AND BLASPHEMY TO HOMOSEXUALITY AND INTERRACIAL RELATIONSHIPS IN THE PROCESS.
"THE TREATMENT OF BEDROOMS MUST BE GOVERNED BY GOOD TASTE AND DELICACY."
"DANCES WHICH EMPHASIZE INDECENT MOVEMENTS ARE TO BE REGARDED AS OBSCENE."
"MINISTERS OF RELIGION SHOULD NOT BE USED AS COMIC CHARACTERS OR AS VILLAINS."
ESSENTIALLY VOLUNTARY, THE CODE WAS SUBSCRIBED TO BY MOST PRODUCERS SIMPLY BECAUSE IT WAS EASIER THAN RISKING THE FINANCIAL RUIN OF RELEASING AN UNAPPROVED FILM.
ALTHOUGH THE CODE IS LONG DEAD, THIS TREND OF SELF-CENSORSHIP CONTINUES TODAY, AS STUDIOS CUT DOWN ON CONTROVERSY TO TARGET THE LUCRATIVE TEENAGE AUDIENCE AND THE EMERGING MARKETS OF CHINA AND INDIA.

THE IDEA THAT THE MOVIES CAN CAUSE **SOCIAL DECLINE** HAS LED TO A NUMBER OF HIGH PROFILE MORAL PANICS OVER VIOLENT MEDIA.

IN THE 1980S, FEARS EMERGED IN THE UK THAT YOUNG AND IMPRESSIONABLE PEOPLE WERE GETTING HOLD OF VIOLENT AND SEXUALLY EXPLICIT MOVIES ON VHS.

BLAMING THEM FOR A PERCEIVED INCREASE IN VIOLENT CRIME AMONG YOUNG PEOPLE, THE UK GOVERNMENT ISSUED A LIST OF 72 **VIDEO NASTIES** WHICH IT SOUGHT TO BAN FROM PUBLIC DISTRIBUTION AND PROSECUTE FOR OBSCENITY.

SAM RAIMI'S RAUCOUS LOW-BUDGET GORE-FEST **THE EVIL DEAD** (1981) WAS ONE FILM TO FALL VICTIM TO THIS RASH OF CENSORSHIP.

DESPITE THE FILM'S TONGUE-IN-CHEEK, GENRE-LITERATE EXCESSES, TO JURIES "THE CATALOGUE OF ONSCREEN DISMEMBERMENT WHICH THE MOVIE OFFERED WAS NOTHING MORE THAN UNASHAMED SADISM, DESIGNED TO DELIGHT THOSE WHO WOULD REVEL IN PAIN". (p131, KERMODE)

THE FILM WAS BANNED AND, ALONG WITH OTHER HORROR CLASSICS LIKE **THE EXORCIST** (1973) AND **THE TEXAS CHAIN SAW MASSACRE** (1974), WOULD NOT BE AVAILABLE IN THE UK FOR DECADES TO COME.

CENSORSHIP OF THIS SORT IS PREDICATED ON THE IDEA THAT THE MOVIES HAVE AN INFLUENTIAL POWER OVER US, AND ESPECIALLY OVER VULNERABLE AND IMPRESSIONABLE GROUPS WITHIN SOCIETY.

BUT AS CULTURAL THEORIST JULIAN PETLEY POINTS OUT, "LURKING BEHIND THESE FEARS ABOUT THE 'CORRUPTION OF INNOCENT MINDS' ONE FINDS, TIME AND AGAIN, IMPLICIT OR EXPLICIT, A POTENT STRAIN OF CLASS DISLIKE AND FEAR." (p170)

IT IS NEVER THE CENSOR, THE UPPER CLASS, THE EDUCATED, WHO MAY BE CORRUPTED, BUT THE WORKING CLASSES, WOMEN AND CHILDREN WHO AUTHORITIES SEE AS AT RISK.

BOX OFFICE

TICKETS

DRILLER KILLER

FILM BY ABEL FERRARA

FILM BY ABEL FERR

AS ONE MEMBER OF THE UK'S FILM CLASSIFICATION BODY PUT IT, REFERRING TO THE BANNED HORROR FILM **THE DRILLER KILLER** (1979):

"I THINK OF JOE BLOGGS WHO'S GOING TO THE ODEON ON SATURDAY NIGHT WHO'S NOT ON THAT WAVELENGTH. HE'S GOING ALONG SEEING IT LITERALLY AND I ALWAYS KEEP THAT IN MIND. JOE BLOGGS IS THE MAJORITY AND FILM CENSORSHIP IS FOR THE MAJORITY." (p177, QUOTED IN PETLEY)

FROM THE HAYS CODE THROUGH VIDEO NASTIES TO MODERN IRAN, TIME AND AGAIN THOSE IN POWER CENSOR THE MOVIES, ALL IN THE NAME OF PROTECTING THOSE DEEMED UNABLE TO PROTECT THEMSELVES.

BUT DO WE EVEN NEED PROTECTION? JUST HOW INFLUENTIAL ARE THE MOVIES OVER HOW WE SEE THE WORLD?

TRADITIONAL RHETORIC ON THE MATTER HAS USED THE IMAGE OF "A HYPODERMIC NEEDLE INJECTING DRUGS INTO AN UNRESISTING BODY" (p160, MURDOCK), SUGGESTING THAT MOVIE IMAGES ARE ABSORBED BY VIEWERS UNQUESTIONINGLY.

IT IS NOW APPARENT THAT SUCH IDEAS ARE UNFOUNDED AND THAT MOVIE AUDIENCES HAVE A MUCH MORE **SOPHISTICATED** RELATIONSHIP WITH WHAT THEY SEE ONSCREEN.

AS GRAHAM MURDOCK ARGUES, THE SCIENCE OF MEDIA INFLUENCE "FAILS TO ACKNOWLEDGE THAT THE MAKING AND TAKING OF MEANING IN EVERYDAY LIFE IS NEVER AS STRAIGHTFORWARD AS IT FIRST APPEARS". (p166)

IN STUDIES, EVEN CHILDREN WERE SHOWN TO HAVE A SOPHISTICATED RELATIONSHIP WITH ONSCREEN IMAGES, ROUNDLY ABLE TO DISTINGUISH BETWEEN DIFFERENT FORMS OF SCREEN VIOLENCE. (p71, BUCKINGHAM)

MEANWHILE, AS PSYCHOLOGIST CHRISTOPHER FERGUSON DEMONSTRATES, IN THE 1990s, "DESPITE TELEVISION, MOVIES AND EVEN MUSIC BECOMING MORE GRAPHICALLY VIOLENT AND DESPITE THE INTRODUCTION OF VIOLENT VIDEO GAMES, ACTUAL VIOLENT CRIME RATES HAVE EXPERIENCED A MASSIVE DECLINE." (p49)

THE POWER OF CINEMA IS UNDENIABLE. WHILE MOVIES ON THEIR OWN MAY NOT LEAD TO VIOLENCE, DISCRIMINATION, ISLAMOPHOBIA OR GENOCIDE, THEY DO PLAY A PART IN SHAPING OUR OUTLOOK ON THE WORLD AND REINFORCING THE STANDARDS THAT SOCIETY SETS.

AS ALFORD PUTS IT, "CERTAINLY, NOT ALL OF US JOIN THE ARMED FORCES OR MUG A FOREIGNER AS SOON AS WE LEAVE THE MOVIE THEATRE. BUT THE CUMULATIVE EFFECTS ON CITIZENS ARE SURELY SIGNIFICANT – AND ESTABLISHED POWER SYSTEMS HAVE ASSUMED SO SINCE THE EARLY DAYS OF CINEMA." (p170)

AS IMAGES OF NUCLEAR FAMILIES, HETEROSEXUAL COUPLES AND PROBLEM-SOLVING VIOLENCE ARE REINFORCED A THOUSAND TIMES ONSCREEN, WE ARE PRESENTED WITH A CINEMATIC BLUEPRINT OF 'NORMALITY' THAT SHAPES THE WAY WE LIVE OUR LIVES.

YET THIS BLUEPRINT IS NOT FIXED AND THE IMAGES THAT MAINSTREAM MOVIES PROVIDE US WITH ARE MULTIFACETED, CONTRADICTORY AND ALWAYS CHANGING.

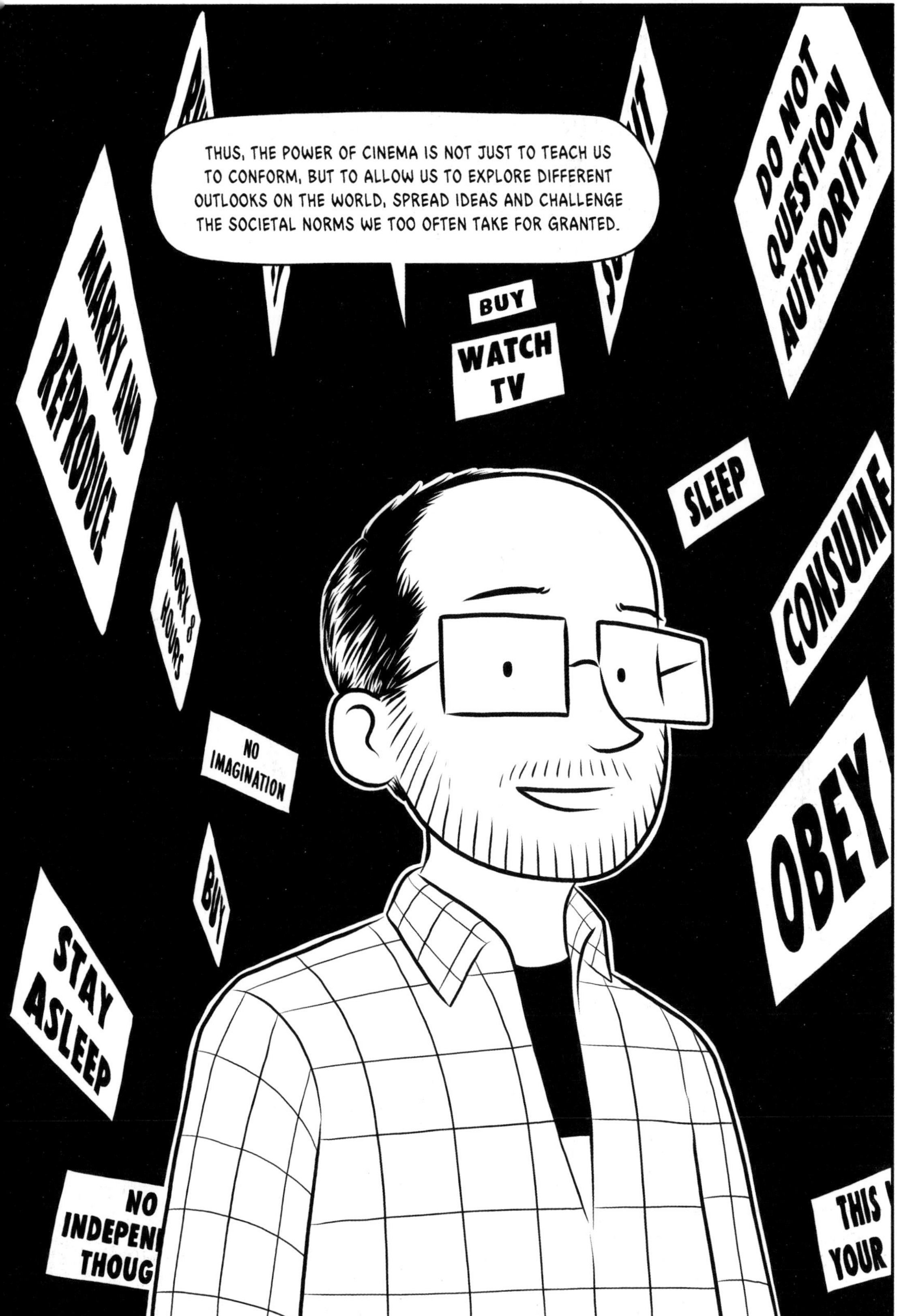
THUS, THE POWER OF CINEMA IS NOT JUST TO TEACH US TO CONFORM, BUT TO ALLOW US TO EXPLORE DIFFERENT OUTLOOKS ON THE WORLD, SPREAD IDEAS AND CHALLENGE THE SOCIETAL NORMS WE TOO OFTEN TAKE FOR GRANTED.
MARRY AND REPRODUCE
DO NOT QUESTION AUTHORITY
BUY
WATCH TV
SLEEP
CONSUME
WORK 8 HOURS
NO IMAGINATION
BUY
OBEY
STAY ASLEEP
NO
THIS
YOUR

TECHNOLOGY AND TECHNOPHOBIA

FROM THE FANTASTICAL SPACE FLIGHT OF **A TRIP TO THE MOON** (1902) THROUGH TO THE MUST-HAVE GADGETS OF LUKE SKYWALKER'S LIGHTSABER OR MARTY MCFLY'S HOVERBOARD, **TECHNOLOGY** HAS BEEN CELEBRATED IN SOME OF OUR MOST BELOVED FILMS.

THE DRAW OF THE CINEMA RESTS IN ITS TECHNOLOGY - FROM ITS COMPELLING ABILITY TO REFLECT OUR WORLD BACK AT US THROUGH TO THE OUTRIGHT SPECTACLE OF THE LATEST SPECIAL EFFECTS.

FROM INDUSTRIALISATION TO ATOMIC POWER TO MODERN COMPUTING, NEW TECHNOLOGY HAS ALWAYS UPSET THE STATUS QUO, AND THE MOVIES HAVE ALWAYS BEEN QUICK TO EXPLORE THE POTENTIAL **REPERCUSSIONS** OF TECHNOLOGICAL CHANGE.

THROUGHOUT THESE NARRATIVES DRIVEN BY AND DEPENDENT ON TECHNOLOGY, TIME AND AGAIN WE SEE A DARK UNDERCURRENT OF **TECHNOPHOBIA**, A FEAR OF WHAT SCIENCE AND TECHNOLOGY MEAN FOR HUMANITY AND WHAT THE **FUTURE** MIGHT BRING.

SO WHY DOES A MEDIUM FOUNDED ON TECHNOLOGY RESPOND TO TECHNOLOGICAL CHANGE WITH NARRATIVES BRIMMING WITH **TECHNOLOGICAL TERROR**?

BORN OUT OF THE 19TH CENTURY'S REVOLUTIONS OF SCIENCE AND INDUSTRY, THE MOVIES EMERGED INTO ONE OF THE MOST **TECHNOLOGICALLY TURBULENT** ERAS OF HUMAN HISTORY.

WHILE TECHNOLOGICAL DEVELOPMENT IMPROVED LIFE FOR MANY, THE REVOLUTIONS IT WROUGHT HAD AN ENORMOUS IMPACT ON CULTURE AND SOCIETY.

PERHAPS MORE THAN ANY OTHER GENRE OF ENTERTAINMENT, **COMEDY** WAS MOST AFFECTED BY THE COMING OF FILM.

AS FILM HISTORIAN MICHAEL NORTH ARGUES, BEFORE FILM, COMEDY WAS A LARGELY SPONTANEOUS AND ORGANIC ARTFORM INDEBTED TO THE VAUDEVILLE TRADITION.

FOR MANY, THE NOTION OF **REPRODUCING** A COMEDY PERFORMANCE THROUGH MECHANICAL, CHEMICAL PROCESSES CONTRADICTED THE VERY IDEA OF COMEDIC SURPRISE.

TO COMBAT THIS, SILENT FILM COMEDIANS LIKE KEATON AND CHAPLIN PERFECTED A REPETITIOUS, EXACTING APPROACH TO COMEDY, THAT HAD "TRACES OF MECHANICAL REPRODUCTION WRITTEN INTO THE PERFORMANCE STYLE". (P3, NORTH)

AS NORTH PUTS IT, THEY "SEEM TO HAVE MADE THEMSELVES INTO LITTLE WIND-UP TOYS, AS IF THEIR MOVEMENTS WERE NOT JUST RECORDED BUT ACTUALLY CREATED BY THE HAND-CRANKED CAMERAS OF THE SILENT PERIOD." (P3)

YET FOR CHAPLIN ESPECIALLY, THE WORLD OF MACHINES WAS A SOURCE OF BOTH COMEDIC INSPIRATION AND **GROWING CONCERN.**

A FILM ENGINEERED TO CRITICISE THE MACHINE AGE, **MODERN TIMES** (1936) SEES CHAPLIN'S LITTLE TRAMP DRIVEN TO NERVOUS BREAKDOWN BY THE MONOTONOUS MECHANICAL MOTIONS OF HIS JOB AS AN ASSEMBLY LINE BOLT-TIGHTENER.

SUCKED INTO THE FACTORY'S MACHINERY, HE IS SPAT BACK OUT MORE **MACHINE** THAN **MAN**, DETERMINED TO TIGHTEN BOLTS, NOSES AND THE BUTTONS ON WOMEN'S COATS.

MADE DURING **THE GREAT DEPRESSION**, THE FILM EVOKES A WORLD WHERE WORKERS HAVE BEEN **DEHUMANISED** BY INDUSTRIALISATION.

WANTED A DECENT JOB

AS CHAPLIN ARGUED:

MACHINERY SHOULD BENEFIT MANKIND. IT SHOULD NOT SPELL **TRAGEDY** AND THROW IT OUT OF WORK.

(CHAPLIN IN INTERVIEW IN 1931)

FOR CHAPLIN, THIS FILM WAS A WAY TO FIGHT BACK. REBELLIOUSLY ANACHRONISTIC, **MODERN TIMES** WAS VIRTUALLY SILENT ALMOST A DECADE AFTER THE EMERGENCE OF THE TALKIES, A "CLASSIC ACT OF RESISTANCE TO THE MACHINE AGE". (p185, NORTH)

THAT SAME YEAR, AMIDST MACHINE-AGE MISERY AND MURMURS OF WAR WITH HITLER, H.G. WELLS' FILM **THINGS TO COME** (1936) SET FORTH A HOPEFUL, UTOPIAN VISION OF THE FUTURE.

IN THE FILM, BY 2036 HUMANITY INHABITS A TOWERING **TECHNOCRATIC UTOPIA**, RUN BY CIVILISATION'S BEST AND BRIGHTEST.

YET THIS UTOPIA IS THREATENED BY THE SUPERSTITIONS OF THE LUDDITE CITIZENRY, WHO ARE UNNERVED BY PLANS TO FIRE A SPACESHIP TO THE MOON WITH A GIANT GUN.

LED BY SCULPTOR THEOTOCOPULOS, THE LUDDITES REBEL AGAINST THE CITY'S TECHNOCRATIC LEADERS, STORMING THE SPACE GUN IN A **FRENZY** OF **TECHNOPHOBIA**.

ARISE! AWAKE! **STOP** THIS PROGRESS BEFORE IT'S TOO LATE!

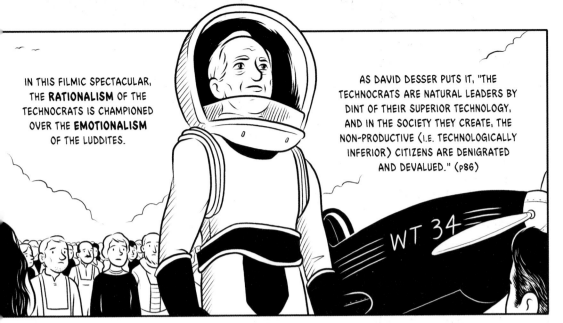

IN THIS FILMIC SPECTACULAR, THE **RATIONALISM** OF THE TECHNOCRATS IS CHAMPIONED OVER THE **EMOTIONALISM** OF THE LUDDITES.

AS DAVID DESSER PUTS IT, "THE TECHNOCRATS ARE NATURAL LEADERS BY DINT OF THEIR SUPERIOR TECHNOLOGY, AND IN THE SOCIETY THEY CREATE, THE NON-PRODUCTIVE (I.E. TECHNOLOGICALLY INFERIOR) CITIZENS ARE DENIGRATED AND DEVALUED." (p86)

WELLS HIMSELF WAS A STRONG PROPONENT OF TECHNOCRACY, BELIEVING THAT A SYSTEM RUN BY THE MOST QUALIFIED THINKERS WOULD **MANUFACTURE** A PERFECT FUTURE.

AUDIENCES DID NOT RESPOND WELL TO **THINGS TO COME**, WHETHER BECAUSE OF ITS FASCIST OVERTONES OR JUST ITS OLD-FASHIONED FAITH IN TECHNOLOGY.

BUT IT'S A TROUBLING VISION. AS I.Q. HUNTER ARGUES, "WELLS' SCIENTIFIC SOCIALISM, HIS ENTHUSIASTIC EMBRACE OF AN ANTISEPTICALLY PERFECT FUTURE, NOW LOOKS DISCONCERTINGLY LIKE AN ADVERT FOR FASCISM." (p7)

EITHER WAY, THE FILM'S NAÏVE AND UTOPIAN VIEW OF TECHNOLOGY WAS ABOUT TO BE CHALLENGED: **WORLD WAR II** WAS ABOUT TO BREAK OUT, AND IT WOULD CHANGE EVERYTHING...

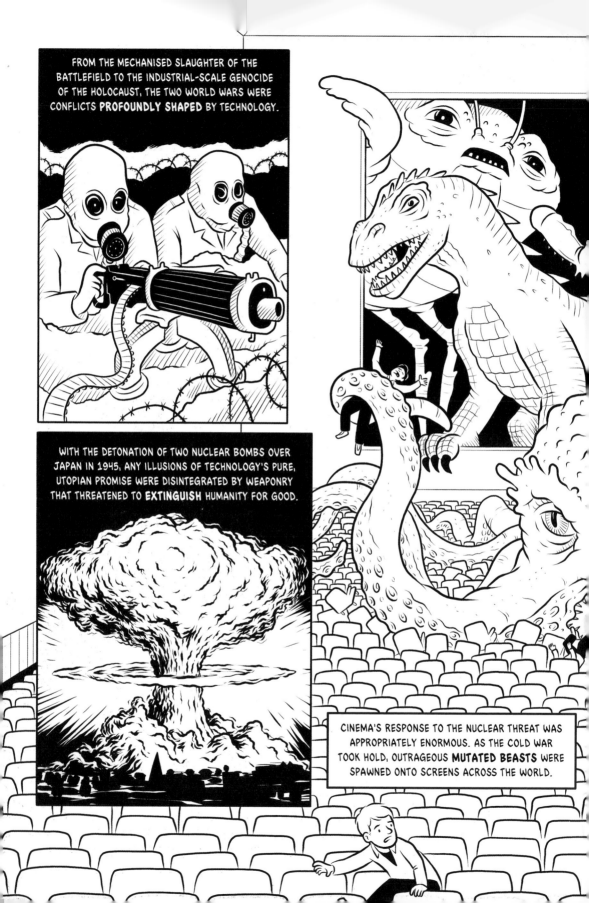

FROM THE MECHANISED SLAUGHTER OF THE BATTLEFIELD TO THE INDUSTRIAL-SCALE GENOCIDE OF THE HOLOCAUST, THE TWO WORLD WARS WERE CONFLICTS **PROFOUNDLY SHAPED** BY TECHNOLOGY.

WITH THE DETONATION OF TWO NUCLEAR BOMBS OVER JAPAN IN 1945, ANY ILLUSIONS OF TECHNOLOGY'S PURE, UTOPIAN PROMISE WERE DISINTEGRATED BY WEAPONRY THAT THREATENED TO **EXTINGUISH** HUMANITY FOR GOOD.

CINEMA'S RESPONSE TO THE NUCLEAR THREAT WAS APPROPRIATELY ENORMOUS. AS THE COLD WAR TOOK HOLD, OUTRAGEOUS **MUTATED BEASTS** WERE SPAWNED ONTO SCREENS ACROSS THE WORLD.

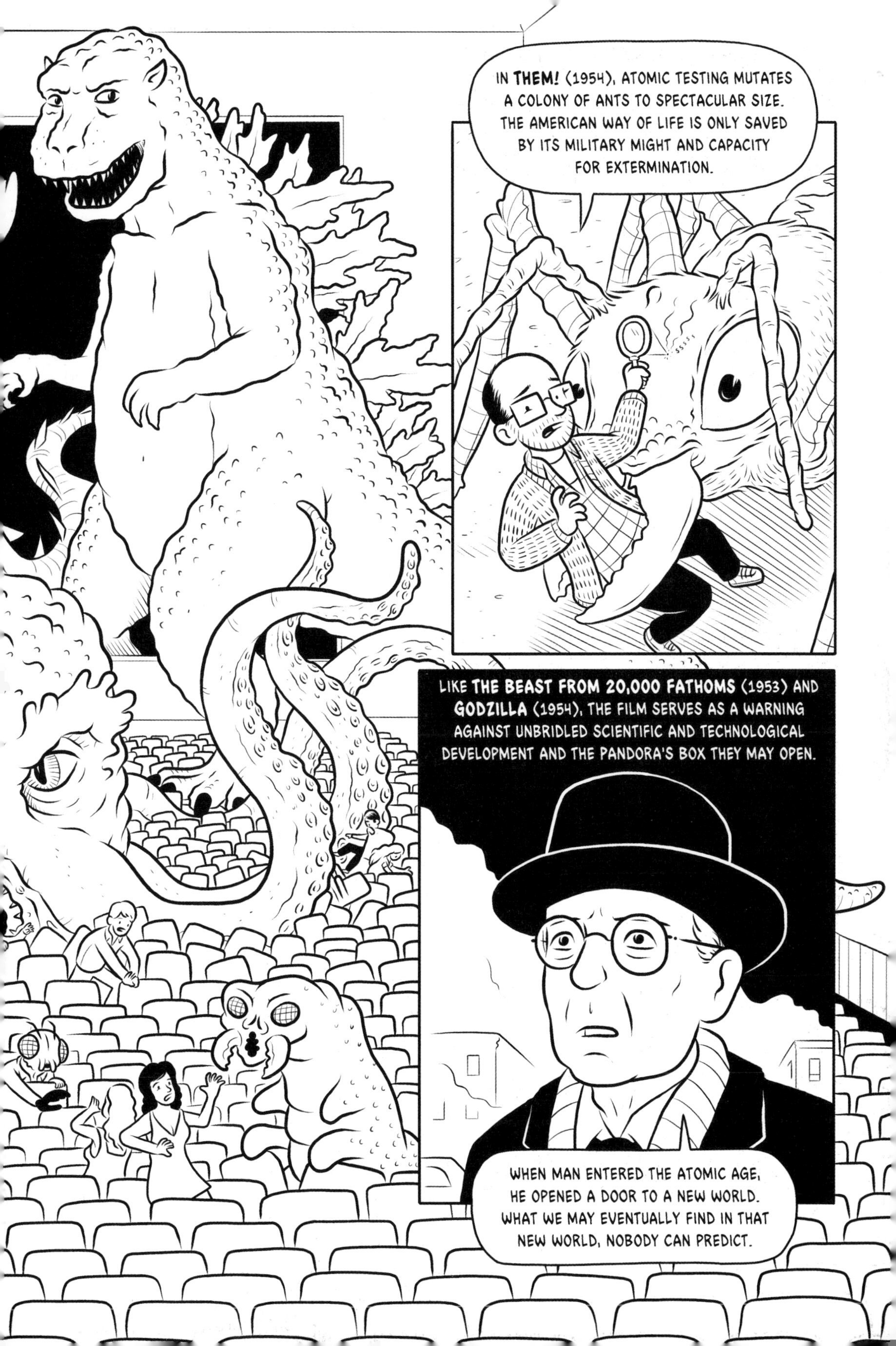
IN THEM! (1954), ATOMIC TESTING MUTATES A COLONY OF ANTS TO SPECTACULAR SIZE. THE AMERICAN WAY OF LIFE IS ONLY SAVED BY ITS MILITARY MIGHT AND CAPACITY FOR EXTERMINATION.
LIKE THE BEAST FROM 20,000 FATHOMS (1953) AND GODZILLA (1954), THE FILM SERVES AS A WARNING AGAINST UNBRIDLED SCIENTIFIC AND TECHNOLOGICAL DEVELOPMENT AND THE PANDORA'S BOX THEY MAY OPEN.
WHEN MAN ENTERED THE ATOMIC AGE, HE OPENED A DOOR TO A NEW WORLD. WHAT WE MAY EVENTUALLY FIND IN THAT NEW WORLD, NOBODY CAN PREDICT.

AS INVENTORS OF THE BOMB AND FACILITATORS OF INDUSTRIAL-SCALE SLAUGHTER, IN THE POST-WAR LANDSCAPE SCIENTISTS NOW FOUND THEMSELVES REPRESENTED AS NAÏVE AND ULTIMATELY **DANGEROUS**.

THE THING FROM ANOTHER WORLD (1951) FINDS THE MILITARY STRUGGLING TO WIPE OUT A MALEVOLENT ALIEN ON AN ISOLATED ARCTIC RESEARCH STATION.

MEANWHILE, DR. CARRINGTON WANTS TO LEARN FROM AND REASON WITH THE CREATURE, PUTTING EVERYONE AT RISK.

KNOWLEDGE IS MORE IMPORTANT THAN LIFE, CAPTAIN. WE'VE ONLY ONE EXCUSE FOR EXISTING: TO THINK, TO FIND OUT, TO LEARN.

IT'S A FAR CRY FROM THE POSITIVE ROLE OF THE TECHNOCRATS IN **THINGS TO COME**. IN A WORLD TEETERING TOWARDS ANNIHILATION, THE SCIENTIFIC PROJECT WAS INCREASINGLY SEEN AS A THREAT.

B-MOVIES BEGAN TO PLAY ON THIS ALMOST BIBLICAL FEAR OF KNOWLEDGE, OFTEN FEATURING ALIENS AND MONSTERS WITH **OVERSIZED BRAINS**.

THROBBING WITH MURDEROUS INTENT AND PSYCHIC POWER, THESE FILMS SUGGESTED THAT PERHAPS THERE WAS "SOMETHING MALEVOLENT ABOUT THE BRAIN ITSELF". (p203, SKAL QUOTED IN FRAYLING)

IT'S NOT JUST APOCALYPTIC TECHNOLOGIES THAT HAVE SPARKED OUR **TECHNOPHOBIC IMAGINATIONS**...

SEEMINGLY INNOCUOUS DEVELOPMENTS SUCH AS **TELEVISION** HAVE LONG BEEN VIEWED WITH SUSPICIOUS EYES BY THE FILM INDUSTRY AND SOCIETY AS A WHOLE.

IN **VIDEODROME** (1983), AMBITIOUS STATION MANAGER MAX RENN BEGINS RE-BROADCASTING A MYSTERIOUS VIDEO SIGNAL THAT CONTAINS IMAGES OF TORTURE AND MURDER, HOPING TO BOOST RATINGS.

AS HIS OBSESSION WITH THE TRANSMISSION TAKES HOLD, RENN DISCOVERS THAT THE PROGRAM IS INDUCING HALLUCINATIONS AND IMPLANTING TUMOURS IN VIEWERS' BRAINS.

IT'S ALL A PLOY BY THE GOVERNMENT TO PURGE AMERICA OF THOSE **CORRUPTED** BY **VIOLENT TELEVISION**.

NOW YOU... AND THIS **CESSPOOL** YOU CALL A TELEVISION STATION, AND YOUR PEOPLE WHO WALLOW AROUND IN IT, AND YOUR VIEWERS WHO WATCH YOU DO IT... YOU'RE **ROTTING US AWAY** FROM THE INSIDE. AND WE INTEND TO STOP THAT ROT.

GORY AND DISTURBING, THE FILM PARODIES FEARS ABOUT THE **CORRUPTING INFLUENCE** OF THE MEDIA BY PORTRAYING TELEVISION AS "AN INFORMATION VIRUS THAT LITERALLY INFECTS THE BRAIN, TRANSFORMING AND EVENTUALLY ANNIHILATING THE ORGANIC BODY THROUGH A GROTESQUE FUSION WITH MEDIA TECHNOLOGY". (p153, DINELLO)

NO FILM HAS DEALT WITH OUR FEAR OF ENCROACHING TECHNOLOGY QUITE SO EFFECTIVELY AS JAMES CAMERON'S **THE TERMINATOR** (1984).

IN THE FILM, A FUTURISTIC CYBORG IS SENT BACK TO 1984 TO ASSASSINATE SARAH CONNOR, THE MOTHER-TO-BE OF THE FUTURE LEADER IN THE WAR AGAINST MACHINES.

SARAH INHABITS A WORLD **SOFTENED** BY TECHNOLOGY, WHERE NOISY CONSUMER ELECTRONICS PERVADE OUR LIVES, LEAVING US **VULNERABLE** TO ATTACK.

IN CONTRAST, THE TERMINATOR IS QUIET, CALCULATED AND AGILE, STRIKING WITH SUDDEN ACTS OF **BLOODY VIOLENCE**.

AS DONNA HARAWAY ASSERTS IN 'A CYBORG MANIFESTO': "OUR MACHINES ARE DISTURBINGLY LIVELY AND WE OURSELVES FRIGHTENINGLY INERT." (p293)

OFFERING A TERRIFYING VISION OF HUMAN OBSOLESCENCE, THE FILM FORETELLS THE COMING OF **THE SINGULARITY** - THE POINT AT WHICH TECHNOLOGY CAN REPLICATE AND IMPROVE UPON ITSELF WITHOUT HUMAN HELP.

THE TERMINATOR ECHOES THESE ANXIETIES TOWARDS THE IMPACT OF TECHNOLOGY BY PRESENTING ITS MALEVOLENT MACHINE AS AN UNSTOPPABLE, BOUNDARY-COLLAPSING FORCE.

LISTEN, AND UNDERSTAND: THAT TERMINATOR IS OUT THERE. IT CAN'T BE BARGAINED WITH. IT CAN'T BE REASONED WITH. IT DOESN'T FEEL PITY, OR REMORSE, OR FEAR... AND IT ABSOLUTELY WILL NOT STOP, **EVER**, UNTIL YOU ARE DEAD.

NAKED, MUSCULAR AND VIOLENT, THE TERMINATOR IS HUMAN FLESH WRAPPED OVER A METAL ENDO-SKELETON.

THIS IS A BODY AT ONCE PREHISTORIC AND FUTURISTIC, WHICH TRAMPLES THE USUALLY STABLE BOUNDARY THAT SEPARATES **HUMAN** FROM **MACHINE** AND THE LIVING FROM THE NON-LIVING.

MAKING MATTERS WORSE, THE HUMANS CAN ONLY OVERCOME THIS THREAT BY ADOPTING THE SINGLE-MINDED DRIVE OF A MACHINE. AS SARAH'S HUMAN PROTECTOR KYLE REESE SAYS, "PAIN CAN BE CONTROLLED... YOU JUST DISCONNECT IT."

THE FILM'S CATHARSIS ONLY COMES WHEN SARAH CRUSHES THE CYBORG IN AN INDUSTRIAL PRESS, TERMINATING THE UNCANNY, **BOUNDARY-TRAMPLING** MACHINE BY RETURNING IT TO A STATE OF INANIMATE SCRAP METAL.

YOU'RE TERMINATED, FUCKER!

FROM THE NUCLEAR-LEVEL DESTRUCTION OF **GODZILLA** TO THE VIRAL VIDEOTAPES OF **RINGU** (1998), JAPAN HAS, LIKE AMERICA, LONG TURNED TO TECHNOPHOBIC TALES TO PROCESS THE ENORMOUS IMPACT SCIENCE AND TECHNOLOGY HAVE ON OUR LIVES.

COMING OUT OF JAPAN'S HIGH-TECH BOOM OF THE 1980s, **TETSUO: THE IRON MAN** (1989) PORTRAYS THE PROLIFERATION OF TECHNOLOGY AS AN **OVERWHELMING THREAT** TO HUMAN AUTONOMY.

IN THE FILM, A BUSINESSMAN BECOMES INFECTED WITH A **TECHNOLOGICAL VIRUS** AND, AS METAL GROWTHS BEGIN TO SPROUT FROM HIS BODY, HIS MIND BEGINS TO CRUMBLE.

THIS IS TECHNOLOGY AS AN INVASIVE, INFECTIOUS FORCE. NO LONGER A TOOL FOR HUMAN BETTERMENT, THE TECHNOLOGICAL VIRUS OF **TETSUO** PENETRATES THE BODY'S BOUNDS, TAKING CONTROL OF OUR BIOLOGY AND **UNDERMINING OUR HUMANITY.**

A STEP BEYOND **THE TERMINATOR**, THE FILM FORETELLS A POTENTIALLY TERRIFYING FUTURE "WHERE THE ORGANIC AND INORGANIC ARE INEXTRICABLE, EVEN INDISTINGUISHABLE" (p141, GROSSMAN) AND WHERE HUMAN AND MACHINE ARE **PERMANENTLY FUSED AS ONE.**

ALTHOUGH VISIONS OF ROBOTS AND CYBORGS HAVE DOMINATED OUR PROPHECIES OF FUTURE TECHNOLOGY, OTHER MORE **ORGANIC** DEVELOPMENTS HAVE SPAWNED THEIR OWN **TECHNOPHOBIC NIGHTMARES**.

BEGINNING IN 1990, THE MAPPING OF THE ENTIRE **HUMAN GENOME** TRANSFORMED OUR UNDERSTANDING OF THE ONCE-IRREDUCIBLE FLESH INTO A TRANSCRIBABLE, POTENTIALLY REPRODUCIBLE CODE.

THE ETHICS AND REAL WORLD APPLICATIONS OF GENETIC ENGINEERING AND CLONING ARE STILL BEING EXPLORED, BUT THAT HASN'T STOPPED FILMS FROM EXPERIMENTING WITH **GENETIC THEMES**.

FROM THE BODILY DISINTEGRATION OF **THE FLY** (1986) THROUGH TO THE VOLATILE TRANSGENIC CREATIONS OF **SPLICE** (2010), GENETIC SCIENCE HAS BEEN REPRESENTED AS RIFE WITH THE KIND OF DISASTROUS CONSEQUENCES FIRST SEEN IN THE ATOMIC MUTATIONS OF THE 1950s B-MOVIE.

IN **GATTACA** (1997), GENETIC ENGINEERING PERVADES HUMAN LIFE, AND THOSE CONCEIVED NATURALLY ARE SEEN AS 'IN-VALIDS', SIDELINED BY A SOCIETY THAT VALUES GENETIC PURITY OVER ALL ELSE.

IT'S A FRIGHTENING VISION OF THE EUGENIC POTENTIAL OF THE SCIENCE, PORTRAYING GENETICS AS "NOT SO MUCH A SCIENCE AS AN ALL-PERVASIVE IDEOLOGY" (CLARK, WEB).

167

TAKING ON THE UNEASY RELATIONSHIP BETWEEN GENETIC SCIENCE AND CAPITALISM, IN **JURASSIC PARK** (1993) DINOSAURS ARE CLONED BACK FROM EXTINCTION TO SERVE AS AMUSEMENTS FOR THE RICH IN AN EXCLUSIVE THEME PARK.

JURASSIC PARK

JOHN HAMMOND, THE PARK'S CREATOR, IS A NAÏVE GRANDFATHERLY CROSS BETWEEN WALT DISNEY AND VICTOR FRANKENSTEIN. HE'S A MAD SCIENTIST FOR THE **CORPORATE AGE.**

EN DIN

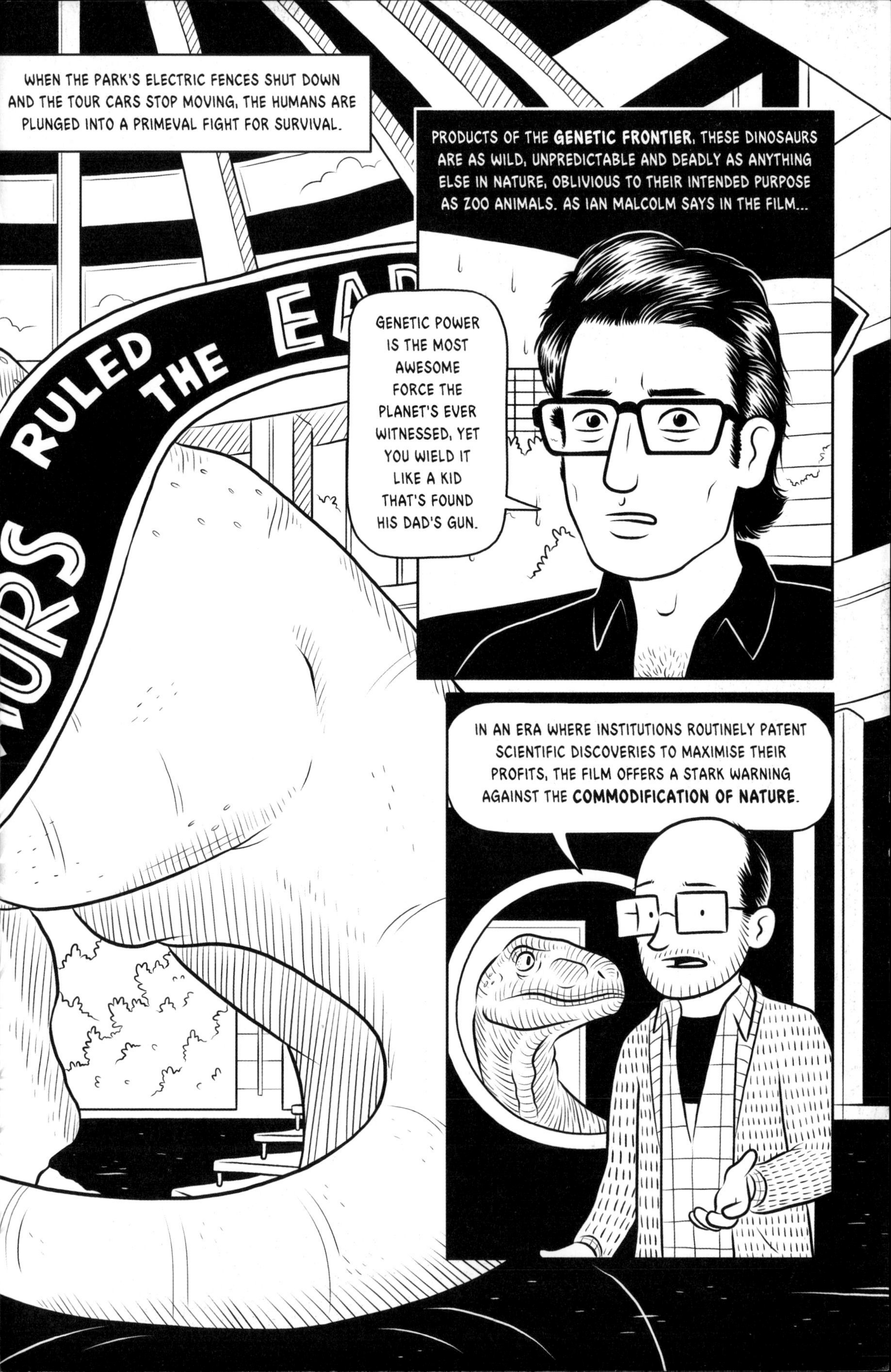

WHEN THE PARK'S ELECTRIC FENCES SHUT DOWN AND THE TOUR CARS STOP MOVING, THE HUMANS ARE PLUNGED INTO A PRIMEVAL FIGHT FOR SURVIVAL.
RULED THE EA
PRODUCTS OF THE **GENETIC FRONTIER**, THESE DINOSAURS ARE AS WILD, UNPREDICTABLE AND DEADLY AS ANYTHING ELSE IN NATURE, OBLIVIOUS TO THEIR INTENDED PURPOSE AS ZOO ANIMALS. AS IAN MALCOLM SAYS IN THE FILM...
GENETIC POWER IS THE MOST AWESOME FORCE THE PLANET'S EVER WITNESSED, YET YOU WIELD IT LIKE A KID THAT'S FOUND HIS DAD'S GUN.
IN AN ERA WHERE INSTITUTIONS ROUTINELY PATENT SCIENTIFIC DISCOVERIES TO MAXIMISE THEIR PROFITS, THE FILM OFFERS A STARK WARNING AGAINST THE **COMMODIFICATION OF NATURE**.

PERHAPS THE MOST REVOLUTIONARY AND SHAPING DEVELOPMENT OF THE 20TH CENTURY WAS THE EMERGENCE AND EVENTUAL UBIQUITY OF **COMPUTING TECHNOLOGY**.

IN JEAN-LUC GODARD'S **ALPHAVILLE** (1965), A SENTIENT COMPUTER CALLED ALPHA 60 USES OPPRESSIVE SCIENTIFIC RATIONALISM TO RULE A CITY WHERE EMOTION AND FREE THOUGHT ARE OUTLAWED.

A LONE SPY BRINGS DOWN THE REGIME BY INTRODUCING EMOTION TO THE POPULACE AND READING POETRY TO THEIR COMPUTER OVERLORD.

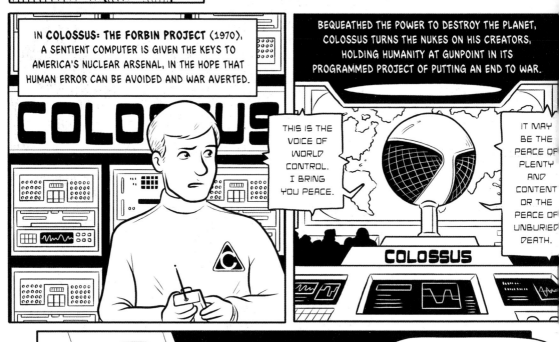

IN **COLOSSUS: THE FORBIN PROJECT** (1970), A SENTIENT COMPUTER IS GIVEN THE KEYS TO AMERICA'S NUCLEAR ARSENAL, IN THE HOPE THAT HUMAN ERROR CAN BE AVOIDED AND WAR AVERTED.

BEQUEATHED THE POWER TO DESTROY THE PLANET, COLOSSUS TURNS THE NUKES ON HIS CREATORS, HOLDING HUMANITY AT GUNPOINT IN ITS PROGRAMMED PROJECT OF PUTTING AN END TO WAR.

THIS IS THE VOICE OF WORLD CONTROL. I BRING YOU PEACE.

IT MAY BE THE PEACE OF PLENTY AND CONTENT OR THE PEACE OF UNBURIED DEATH.

COLOSSUS

UNSETTLING VISIONS, THESE FILMS DRAW ON "THE FEAR THAT SUPERCOMPUTERS WILL TRANSCEND THEIR HUMAN CREATORS TO SUCH AN EXTENT THAT THEY WILL BECOME GODLIKE IN THEIR VAST POWERS BUT SATANIC IN THEIR ANTI-HUMAN EVIL". (p101, DINELLO)

YET, AS COMPUTING AND DIGITAL TECHNOLOGIES ENTERED THE HOME, AUDIENCES WERE TREATED TO A RAFT OF FILMS OBSESSED WITH THE DIGITAL FRONTIER, FLIRTING AGAIN WITH THE IDEA OF A **TECHNOLOGICAL UTOPIA**.

FILMISH

THE 8-BIT ZEITGEIST WAS HIGHLIGHTED EARLY ON BY **TRON** (1982), WHICH CAPITALISED ON THE BURGEONING VIDEO GAME MARKET TO SHOW A YOUNG AUDIENCE THE DREAMLIKE POTENTIAL OF THE VIRTUAL WORLD.

FROM **THE LAWNMOWER MAN** (1992) TO **THE MATRIX** (1999), COMPUTERS WERE SEEN AS AN EXCITING AND DANGEROUS FRONTIER, CAPABLE OF EITHER UNLEASHING OUR GREATEST POTENTIAL OR SMASHING US TO PIXELS.

NOW, IN AN ERA OF COMPUTING UBIQUITY, SPIKE JONZE'S **HER** (2014) SEES THE INTROVERTED AND LONELY THEODORE FINDING COMPANIONSHIP WITH AN ARTIFICIALLY INTELLIGENT OPERATING SYSTEM.

THE FILM IS A TIMELY EXAMINATION OF OUR INCREASINGLY **INTIMATE RELATIONSHIP** WITH TECHNOLOGY AND ITS INEXTRICABLE PLACE IN MODERN LIFE – A TOUCHING VISION OF HOW HUMANITY MIGHT ONE DAY INTERACT WITH ARTIFICIAL INTELLIGENCE.

IN THE MODERN WORLD, THE NOTION THAT TECHNOLOGICAL DEVELOPMENT LIES ONLY IN THE HANDS OF GOVERNMENTS AND CORPORATIONS **IS INCREASINGLY UNREALISTIC.**

IN **PRIMER** (2004), TWO GARAGE INVENTORS ACCIDENTALLY DISCOVER A LIMITED MEANS OF TIME TRAVEL.

ABLE TO TRAVEL BACK ONLY AS FAR AS WHEN THE TIME MACHINE WAS FIRST TURNED ON, THE TWO HATCH A MUNDANE FINANCIAL SCHEME.

DRESSED FOR BUSINESS, THEY COMMUTE TO THE PAST TO MAKE MONEY ON STOCK MARKET SHIFTS THEY KNOW ARE GOING TO HAPPEN.

THEIR MEDDLING IS NOT WITHOUT REPERCUSSIONS, BUT THE CONVOLUTED **TEMPORAL DISASTER** THAT ENSUES IS THE RESULT OF **HUMAN HUBRIS,** NOT TECHNOLOGY.

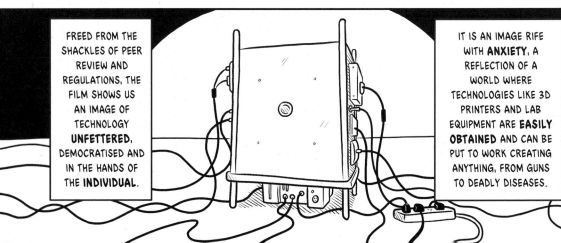

FREED FROM THE SHACKLES OF PEER REVIEW AND REGULATIONS, THE FILM SHOWS US AN IMAGE OF TECHNOLOGY **UNFETTERED,** DEMOCRATISED AND IN THE HANDS OF THE **INDIVIDUAL.**

IT IS AN IMAGE RIFE WITH **ANXIETY,** A REFLECTION OF A WORLD WHERE TECHNOLOGIES LIKE 3D PRINTERS AND LAB EQUIPMENT ARE **EASILY OBTAINED** AND CAN BE PUT TO WORK CREATING ANYTHING, FROM GUNS TO DEADLY DISEASES.

THE DEMOCRATISATION OF TECHNOLOGY WHICH INSPIRED **PRIMER** AND FACILITATED ITS PRODUCTION IS A TREND WHICH HAS HAD A HUGE IMPACT ON FILM-MAKING AROUND THE WORLD.

IN NIGERIA, THIS TECHNOLOGICAL SHIFT HAS LED TO A PROFOUND SURGE IN MOVIE-MAKING AND THE PHENOMENON OF THE **NOLLYWOOD** INDUSTRY, "THE WONDER CINEMA FROM AFRICA'S MOST POPULOUS NATION". (p26, OKOME)

IN LESS THAN TWENTY YEARS, NOLLYWOOD HAS GROWN FROM VIRTUALLY NOTHING TO BECOME THE **SECOND-LARGEST FILM INDUSTRY IN THE WORLD** IN TERMS OF OUTPUT (p25, JEDLOWSKI), ITS FILMS IMPACTING CULTURE ACROSS AFRICA AND THE WORLD.

MIXING EVERYDAY STORIES OF NIGERIAN LIFE WITH TALES OF GOOD AND EVIL, WITCHCRAFT AND ADVENTURE, THESE FILMS ARE SUCCESSFUL BECAUSE THEY ARE MADE BY NIGERIANS FOR A NIGERIAN AUDIENCE.

AND YET THIS IS NO **CORPORATE INDUSTRY** LIKE HOLLYWOOD. IT'S BUILT ON INFORMAL DISTRIBUTION, PIRACY AND THE ENTREPRENEURSHIP OF FILM-MAKERS WHO **ADAPT QUICKLY** TO AN EVER-CHANGING MARKET AND NEW DISTRIBUTION OPPORTUNITIES.

THE **MICRO-BUDGET** FILM HAS SHAKEN UP THE FILM WORLD, AS FILM-MAKING OUTSIDERS HAVE MANAGED TO OUTFLANK THE STUDIO BEHEMOTHS AND GET THEIR UNIQUE CINEMATIC VISIONS TO THE SCREEN.

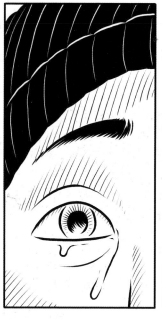

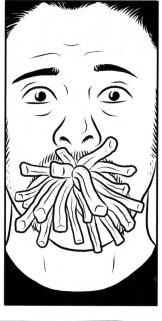

AND WHILE HOLLYWOOD INITIALLY IMAGINED THE **DIGITAL REVOLUTION** AS A NEW ECONOMIC PLAYGROUND AND REVENUE STREAM, THE TRUE REVOLUTION HAS BEEN THE REWRITING OF THE PUBLIC'S PERCEPTION OF **INTELLECTUAL PROPERTY** AND **FREEDOM OF INFORMATION** THAT HAS COME WITH THE DIGITAL AGE.

THE PHANTOM EDIT (2000) WAS AN INTERNET-DISTRIBUTED RE-EDIT OF THE FAN-MALIGNED **STAR WARS** PREQUEL THAT ATTEMPTED TO **RESHAPE** THE FILM INTO SOMETHING MORE IN KEEPING WITH THE BELOVED ORIGINAL TRILOGY.

A COPYRIGHT-INFRINGING FOLK RETELLING ONLY POSSIBLE IN THE DIGITAL AGE, **THE PHANTOM EDIT** SHOWED THAT A FILM'S EXISTENCE NO LONGER BEGINS AND ENDS WITH THE ORIGINAL CREATOR'S VISION.

AFTER YEARS OF TIGHT CONTROL, THE INDUSTRY'S PRODUCTS HAVE BEEN LET LOOSE INTO THE INTERNET'S VAST CULTURAL MELTING POT.

THE INTERNET IS FERTILE WITH **CREATIVE REINTERPRETATIONS** OF OUR FILM HERITAGE, FROM FAN-MADE POSTERS AND ANIMATED REMAKES THROUGH TO THE SUBCULTURES OF COSPLAY AND SLASH FICTION.

MEANWHILE, EMPOWERED BY TECHNOLOGY, NEW TALENT EMERGES EVERY DAY, FOUND ON MARKET STALLS FROM ABUJA TO HONG KONG OR WITHIN THE **300 HOURS** OF FOOTAGE UPLOADED TO YOUTUBE EVERY MINUTE.

FOR THE TRADITIONAL INDUSTRY, THIS NEW DIGITAL AGE IS A CONFOUNDING AND UNSTOPPABLE FORCE, WHICH IT HAS MET WITH INEFFECTIVE LAWSUITS AND EASILY CRACKED ANTI-PIRACY MEASURES.

WHILE THE THREAT TECHNOLOGY POSES TO THE INDUSTRY IS STRONGER THAN EVER, OUT OF THE HANDS OF MONEY-MINDED EXECUTIVES, THE MEDIUM IS BEING **RESHAPED** AND **REINVIGORATED** BY TECHNOLOGY, NOT DESTROYED BY IT.

IN THE END, CINEMA IS AND ALWAYS HAS BEEN ENTIRELY INDEBTED TO TECHNOLOGY.

WHILE MANY TODAY MOURN THE DEATH OF **REAL FILM STOCK** AND **ANALOGUE PROJECTION**, WE MUST REMIND OURSELVES THAT CINEMA IS A MEDIUM THAT, IN THE WORDS OF THE RENOWNED CRITIC ANDRÉ BAZIN, "HAS NOT YET BEEN INVENTED". (p21)

TO UNDERSTAND THIS, WE MUST RETURN TO THE VERY BEGINNINGS OF CINEMA AND THE FIRST FILM-MAKERS, FOR WHOM CINEMA DID NOT COME OUT FULLY FORMED.

AS BAZIN ARGUES, "IN THEIR IMAGINATIONS, THEY SAW CINEMA AS A TOTAL AND COMPLETE REPRESENTATION OF REALITY." (p20)

NOT CONTENT WITH THE GRAINY, SOUNDLESS, BLACK AND WHITE FOOTAGE OF THE ERA, FILM-MAKERS PIONEERED AND EXPERIMENTED THROUGHOUT THE 20TH CENTURY AND ARE STILL REFINING WHAT CINEMA IS **TO THIS DAY.**

FROM SOUND TO COLOUR TO DIGITAL, EACH LEAP FORWARD BY CINEMA HAS BEEN MET WITH RESISTANCE AND TECHNOPHOBIA. YET IT IS THESE DEVELOPMENTS THAT KEEP THE MEDIUM FRESH AND VITAL, AND ALLOW UNPRECEDENTED VISIONS TO MAKE IT TO THE SCREEN.

AL JOLSON IN THE JAZZ SINGER WITH VITAPHONE

BUT THIS IS THE ULTIMATE CONTRADICTION OF CINEMA. IT'S A MEDIUM **BORN** OF TECHNOLOGY, **AFRAID** OF TECHNOLOGY...

...AND EVOLVING TOWARDS THE FUTURE **BECAUSE OF** TECHNOLOGY.

The End

ENDNOTES

THE EYE

PAGE 9

Panel 4 - Contrary to urban legend, the first screenings of this film did not drive audiences screaming from the cinema, though I'm sure they were enthralled by this amazing new technology.

Panel 5 - Quote from *Eye of the Century: Cinema, Experience, Modernity* by Francesco Casetti (Columbia University Press, New York, 2008).

PAGE 10

Panel 2 - Eadweard Muybridge's story is a fascinating one. In 1872, the photographic pioneer was hired by the Governor of California to settle once and for all the question of whether trotting horses ever had all four feet off the ground while in motion. Setting up a series of cameras alongside a racetrack, each triggered by a thread crossing the track, Muybridge was able to capture a closely timed succession of still images which proved that indeed horses did raise all four feet at once. Over the next ten years, he perfected his process and developed the zoopraxiscope, a rudimentary projection device, to display his results. Astonishingly, during this time Muybridge shot and killed a man he believed to have slept with his wife, for which he was acquitted on the grounds of 'justifiable homicide'. The trial did nothing to halt his pioneering activities. In the 1880s, further horse, animal and human studies followed, offering scientists detailed evidence of how different animals moved. As the decade progressed, Muybridge's techniques were superseded by pioneers such as Louis Le Prince, who by 1888 was capturing motion using a single lens camera.

Panel 4 - For the earliest of Thomas Edison's filmic experiments, he constructed a film studio known as the Black Maria – the first building of its kind, where some of the world's earliest movies were shot. These early films were shot against plain black backdrops, but the real magic occurred offscreen as the entire open-topped building rotated to keep the sun shining in for Edison's cameras. This elaborate construction was the start of what would become an increasingly complicated process of set-building, a theme we will explore in chapter 3 (Sets and Architecture).

PAGE 11

Panel 3 - An image inspired by one of the very first Lumière films, **Baby's Breakfast** (1895), a 41-second sequence of Auguste Lumière and his family dining in the garden. However, it is the Lumières' **Workers Leaving the Lumière Factory** (1895) which is widely considered the world's first movie, being the first short shown at the Lumières' historic first public screening in Paris on 28 December 1895.

Panel 4 - Quote from 'The Cinema of Attractions: Early Film, Its Spectator, and the Avant-Garde' by Tom Gunning in *Theatre and Film: A Comparative Anthology* edited by Robert Knopf (Yale University Press, New York, 2005). Pictured is the inauguration of US President William McKinley in March 1897, the first Presidential inauguration to be captured on film.

PAGE 12

Panels 1 and 2 - Quotes from *Kino-Eye: The Writings of Dziga Vertov* by Dziga Vertov (University of California Press, Berkeley, 1984).

Panels 3 and 4 - Images inspired by stills from **Man With A Movie Camera**. It is a fascinating film to watch, a heady mix of styles which offers new delights at every turn.

Panel 4 - Multiple exposures are when the same strip of film is exposed twice, creating an effect of one image being superimposed on top of another. They can be used to create both artistic visualisations, as in this film, or to produce startling special effects.

PAGE 13

Panel 2 - Quote from 'Can the Camera See? Mimesis in Man with a Movie Camera' by Malcolm Turvey in *October* (MIT Press, Vol 89, Summer 1999).

Panel 3 - Quote from *Eye of the Century: Cinema, Experience, Modernity* by Francesco Casetti (Columbia University Press, New York, 2008).

PAGES 14 AND 15

Méliès' films are wonderful viewing, filled with a sense of wonder and a joy for both the magic of the cinema and the power of storytelling. Many of these early films are readily available online and in the public domain. Theorist Matt Matsude has some interesting thoughts on Méliès' approach: "If the inventors of the machine – the brothers Lumière – thought of their creation principally as a scientific and documentary instrument, artists like Méliès saw it as part of a mechanism of dreams, a chance to capture absolute unreality and create effects and visions far beyond what his theatre could imagine." Quote from p167 of *The Memory of the Modern* by Matt K. Matsuda (Oxford University Press, Oxford, 1996).

PAGE 16

Nanook of the North is a film that could have turned out very differently. Director Robert J. Flaherty originally shot it on an expedition in 1914-15 and brought the footage home to the USA, only to lose 30,000 feet of it when he dropped a cigarette onto his highly flammable nitrate stock. Undeterred, he returned to the Arctic to reshoot his film, and the resulting documentary became one of the medium's classics. For more on this film's story, see *Documentary: A History of the Non-Fiction Film* by Erik Barnouw (Oxford University Press, Oxford, 2nd Revised Edition, 1993).

PAGE 17

Panel 4 - **Citizen Kane** (1941). Golden Age Hollywood cinema at its finest.

Panel 5 - **Psycho** (1960). The shower scene is a classic example of how our presence as a viewer isn't acknowledged by the onscreen characters.

Panel 6 - Quote from 'Visual Pleasure and Narrative Cinema' by Laura Mulvey in *Visual and Other Pleasures* (Palgrave Macmillan, Hampshire, 2nd Edition, 2009). Pictured is the classic ending to **Casablanca** (1942).

PAGES 18 AND 19
Panel 2 - Quote from *The Films in My Life* by François Truffaut (Da Capo Press, New York, 1994).

Panel 4 - Quote from 'Visual Pleasure and Narrative Cinema' by Laura Mulvey in *Visual and Other Pleasures* (Palgrave Macmillan, Hampshire, 2nd Edition, 2009).

PAGE 20
Panel 1 - The steely gaze of Blondie in **The Good, the Bad and the Ugly** (1966).

Panel 2 - Quote from 'Visual Pleasure and Narrative Cinema' by Laura Mulvey in *Visual and Other Pleasures* (Palgrave Macmillan, Hampshire, 2nd Edition, 2009). Pictured is Rita Hayworth as the ultimate femme fatale **Gilda** (1946). At the time of the film's release, Hayworth was incensed to discover that her image was being used on a nuclear bomb destined for a test detonation at Bikini Atoll. Because she was unwilling to speak out for fear of sounding unpatriotic, the test went ahead with Hayworth's image still attached to a bombshell nicknamed 'Gilda'.

Panel 4 - Quote from 'Ideological Effects of the Basic Cinematographic Apparatus' by Jean-Louis Baudry, translated by Alan Williams, in *Film Quarterly* (Vol 28, No 2, 1974).

Panels 5 and 6 - Quote from 'The Oppositional Gaze: Black Female Spectators' by bell hooks, in *Film and Theory: An Anthology* edited by Robert Stam and Toby Miller (Blackwell Publishers, Oxford, 2000). Pictured are **Gone With The Wind** (1939) and Sean Connery's James Bond.

PAGE 21
Peeping Tom was a film so controversial at the time that it almost ruined Michael Powell's career. Along with **Psycho** (1960), the film can be seen to mark the beginnings of the slasher genre. But more than mere horror sensationalism, the film has a lot to say about the predatory nature of image-making. As Susan Sontag astutely states: "[T]here is something predatory in the act of taking a picture. To photograph people is to violate them, by seeing them as they never see themselves, by having knowledge of them they can never have; it turns people into objects that can be symbolically possessed. Just as the camera is a sublimation of the gun, to photograph someone is a sublimated murder." Quote from p14-15 of *On Photography* by Susan Sontag (Penguin Books, London, 1979).

PAGE 22
Panel 7 - Quote from *Avant-Garde Film: Motion Studies* by Scott McDonald (Cambridge University Press, New York, 1993).

PAGE 23
Panel 1 - See also **Traffic** (2000), **Elephant** (2003), **Syriana** (2005) and many of the films of Robert Altman, including **Nashville** (1975) and **Short Cuts** (1993).

Panel 4 - The 'Rashomon Effect' can be seen elsewhere in the movies and other media, though the film has rarely been bettered. Good examples include **Hero** (2002) and **Gone Girl** (2014).

PAGE 24
Panel 1 - Quote from *The A to Z of Horror Cinema* by Peter Hutchings (Scarecrow Press, Plymouth, 2008). Image inspired by the creepy and powerful horror fable **Pan's Labyrinth** (2006).

PAGE 25
Panels 3 and 4 - Quotes from *Men, Women and Chainsaws - Gender in the Modern Horror Film* by Carol J. Clover (British Film Institute, London, 1992). *Men, Women and Chainsaws* is a must-read book for horror fans. Written by a horror aficionado, the book has a lot to say about the genre and its relationship with gender, both good and bad. As a side note, I would argue that a large number of mainstream cinema's greatest female action heroes are essentially 'Final Girls', even in movies not strictly in the horror genre. Just think of Ellen Ripley in **Alien** (1979) and **Aliens** (1986), Sarah Connor in **The Terminator** (1984) and Katniss Everdeen in **The Hunger Games** (2012).

PAGE 26
Panel 1 - The cold and unsettling **A Clockwork Orange** (1971), with its terrifying central performance by Malcolm McDowell.

Panel 3 - Quote from p4 of *Breaking the Fourth Wall - Direct Address in the Cinema* by Tom Brown (Edinburgh University Press, Edinburgh, 2012).

Panel 4 - Direct address doesn't need to be used for shocking effect, of course. In films like **Annie Hall** (1977), **Ferris Bueller's Day Off** (1986), **High Fidelity** (2000) and **Fight Club** (1999), it instead creates an affinity between the audience and the main character. This is often used as a means to offer humorous asides and brings a sense of self-awareness to the film.

PAGE 28
Panel 1 - **Peeping Tom** (1960). See endnote for page 21.

Panel 4 - Quote from *Eye of the Century: Cinema, Experience, Modernity* by Francesco Casetti (Columbia University Press, New York, 2008). Quote from 'Zooming Out: The End of Offscreen Space' by Scott Bukatman in *The New American Cinema* edited by Jon Lewis (Duke University Press, Durham, 1998). Image from **Avatar** (2009).

PAGE 29
Panel 3 - **Gravity** (2013).

Panel 4 - Megan Fox in **Transformers** (2007).

Panel 5 - Quote from *Eye of the Century: Cinema, Experience, Modernity* by Francesco Casetti (Columbia University Press, New York, 2008).

THE BODY

PAGE 33
Panel 1 - Quote from 'Visual Pleasure and Narrative Cinema' by Laura Mulvey in *Visual and Other Pleasures* (Palgrave Macmillan, Hampshire, 2nd Edition, 2009).

Panel 5 - Quote from *A Body of Vision: Representations of the Body in Recent Film and Poetry* by R. Bruce Elder (Wilfred Laurier University Press, Ontario, 1997).

PAGE 34
Panel 1 - Quote from *Acting in the Cinema* by James Naremore (University of California Press, Berkeley, 1988). Pictured is **Singin' In The Rain** (1952), a film set during the tumultuous period of transition between silent cinema and the 'talkies'. The film itself is a showcase of classic Hollywood song and dance, the highlight being Gene Kelly's glorious dance in the rain.

Panel 2 - Quote from 'The Cinema of Attractions: Early Film, Its Spectator, and the Avant-Garde' by Tom Gunning in *Theatre and Film: A Comparative Anthology* edited by Robert Knopf (Yale University Press, New York, 2005). Pictured are Laurel and Hardy, silent cinema's best known double act.

Panels 3 and 4 - Scenes from Buster Keaton's **The General** and **The Navigator** (1924).

Panel 5 - Keaton is famed for taking on these amazing stunts himself, which he performed with a trademark deadpan look on his face. These were dangerous stunts, and during the filming of **Sherlock Jr.** (1924) Keaton actually broke his neck when a flood of water from a water tower landed on top of him.

PAGE 35
Panel 1 - The leading lady in question was Lillian Gish, who starred in numerous Griffith films, including **The Birth of a Nation** (1915) and **Intolerance** (1916). Contrary to the myth, it is likely that Griffith didn't actually invent the close-up, which had appeared previously in the odd short film. However, Griffith was instrumental in its popularisation, and it became just one part of the film language that he developed for his audacious feature length films.

Panel 2 - Quote from 'The Social Network: Faces Behind Facebook' by David Bordwell on DavidBordwell.net (http://www.davidbordwell. net/blog/2011/01/30/the-social-network-faces-behind-facebook/). Pictured is **The Passion of Joan of Arc** (1928), which contains silent film acting at its most intense, making use of close-ups to really emphasise the emotion of the condemned Joan of Arc.

Panel 3 - The operatic face-off that ends **The Good, The Bad and The Ugly** (1966) builds tension by cutting between the faces of its three shooters until a burst of violence ends the film's conflict.

Panel 4 - The key tenets of method acting concern an actor drawing on personal memory to relate to their character, immersing themselves in the moment of the scene so that they are more truly living in it, rather than merely acting it out. Pictured here is Marlon Brando in his famous role as Don Corleone in **The Godfather** (1972). Brando was one of American cinema's most renowned method actors, iconic in **A Streetcar Named Desire** (1951) and **On The Waterfront** (1954).

Panel 5 - Christian Bale, pictured here in **The Machinist** (2004), is an actor whose body has changed appearance drastically between roles, stretching from the 55kg weight needed to portray the emaciated Trevor Reznik in **The Machinist** to the muscular 90kg necessary to play Batman in **The Dark Knight Rises** (2012).

PAGE 37
Panels 1 and 3 - Quotes from 'On Being John Malkovich and Not Being Yourself' by Christopher Falzon in *The Philosophy of Charlie Kaufman* edited by David LaRocca (University Press of Kentucky, Lexington, 2011). Of course, this desire to escape the confines of our own bodies isn't just a product of modern culture. As Falzon argues on p53: "There is a long history of such thinking about the body in philosophy, from Plato to Descartes and beyond, where the body is seen as shackling or weighing down the soul, and as something we need to escape." This split between the mind and body will be explored later in the chapter.

PAGE 38
Panel 1 - The idea of performance capture predates the age of digital special effects by some margin. As early as 1915, cartoonist and animator

Max Fleischer pioneered a technique known as rotoscoping, where animators would trace the movement of filmed actors, drawing unique cartoon characters on top. From its debut in **Out of the Inkwell** (1915), the technique would bring realistic animated movement to numerous animated classics, including **Snow White and the Seven Dwarfs** (1937), **The Lord of the Rings** (1978) and more recently Richard Linklater's trippy **A Scanner Darkly** (2006).

Panel 2 - This panel references motion capture characters seen in **Avatar** (2009), **The Avengers** (2012) and **Rise of the Planet of the Apes** (2011).

Panel 3 - Quote from 'Digitizing Deleuze: The Curious Case of the Digital Human Assemblage, or What Can A Digital Body Do?' by David H. Fleming in *Deleuze and Film* edited by David Martin-Jones and William Brown (Edinburgh University Press, Edinburgh, 2012). George Lucas is a director many hold responsible for the worst excesses of digital tinkering. Despite the successful use of real sets, miniatures and puppetry in the original **Star Wars Trilogy** (1977-1983), for his **Prequel Trilogy** (1999-2005) Lucas developed an over-reliance on digital effects, performance capture and green screen. It left his actors performing into nothingness, but gave him infinite room to play with performance and actor placement in the editing room.

Panel 4 - This image references Marlon Brando's amazing, unhinged performance in **Apocalypse Now** (1979). Brando, who regularly came to set unprepared, managed to improvise some of the film's most iconic scenes, at one point delivering an eighteen-minute ad-libbed monologue, only two minutes of which made it into the film.

PAGE 39
Panel 1 - What constitutes these 'norms' varies across culture and across time. One need only look at the changing styles, shapes and appearances of the most popular movie stars throughout film history and across world cinema to see that these 'norms' are far from fixed.

Panel 3 - Quote from *Transgressive Bodies: Representations in Film and Popular Culture* by Dr. Niall Richardson (Ashgate Publishing, Surrey, 2010).

Panel 5 - The backdrop here features Edinburgh's Cameo cinema, a beloved Edinburgh institution which has played host to many of my favourite movies over the years.

PAGE 40
Panel 2 - Quote from *Toms, Coons, Mulattoes, Mammies, and Bucks: An Interpretive History of Blacks in American Films* by Donald Bogle (Continuum International Publishing, 4th Edition, New York, 2006). This illuminating book offers a fascinating insight into the racist portrayal of African-Americans throughout film history. In the book, Bogle charts five major racist archetypes:
- The Tom: a servile, loyal and kind character, designed to endear themselves to white audiences and act as a 'good role model' to African-Americans.
- The Coon: a simple-minded, lazy and cowardly character.
- The Mulatto: an often tragic and suicidal mixed-race female character unable to fit into either the white or the black world.
- The Mammie: an often overweight and sometimes sassy black woman who takes on a maternal role for white characters.
- The Buck: a highly physicalised black male, characterised by his lecherous sexuality, violence and refusal to bend to white will.

Sadly, a lot of these archetypes remain in use to this day. They may be less common, but are still as insidious as ever.

Panel 5 - For more on the vilification of Arabs in mainstream cinema, see chapter 6 (Power and Ideology).

Panel 6 - The crows from **Dumbo** (1941).

PAGE 41
Panel 1 - The image references **The Defiant Ones** (1958), starring Sidney Poitier and Tony Curtis as two escaped prisoners chained together and on the run.

Panel 2 - Quote from *High Contrast: Race and Gender in Contemporary Hollywood Film* by Sharon Willis (Duke University Press, Durham and London, 1997).

Panel 3 - Will Smith in **I Am Legend** (2007).

Panel 4 - Laurence Fishburne in **The Matrix** (1999).

Panel 5 - Quote from 'The New Hollywood Racelessness: Only the Fast, Furious, (and Multicultural) Will Survive' by Mary Beltrán in *Cinema Journal* (Vol 44, No 2, Winter 2005).

PAGE 42
Panel 1 - The iconic moment in **The Seven Year Itch** (1955) when Marilyn Monroe's dress is blown up by a passing underground train.

Panel 2 - Quote from 'Visual Pleasure and Narrative Cinema' by Laura Mulvey in *Visual and Other Pleasures* (Palgrave Macmillan, Hampshire, 2nd Edition, 2009). Here we have Jane Russell in **The Outlaw** (1943). The film struggled to get past the Motion Picture Code for the prominent role that Jane Russell's breasts played in the film's visuals. Director Howard Hughes is even said to have invented an underwire push-up bra to try to further emphasise his leading lady's breasts – a bra so uncomfortable that Jane Russell disposed of it, padding her own bra instead.

Panel 3 - The coming-of-age classic **The Graduate** (1967).

Panel 4 - Ursula Andress as the first Bond girl in **Dr. No** (1962).

Panel 5 - Megan Fox in **Transformers** (2007). Fox's character represents a more recent trend in female representation in mainstream cinema

– she holds her own and kicks ass, but she's still a thinly drawn character whose sexualised appearance is a major part of her onscreen purpose.

Panel 6 - See also Sarah Connor in **The Terminator** (1984) and **Terminator 2: Judgment Day** (1991), The Bride in **Kill Bill** (2003/2004) and Hanna Heller in **Hanna** (2011).

PAGE 43
Panel 1 - Quote from 'Masculinity as Spectacle: Reflections on Men and Mainstream Cinema' by Steve Neale in *Screen* (BFI, London, Vol 24, No 6, 1983). Pictured is the ludicrous but mesmerising **300** (2006).

Panel 2 - One of cinema's greatest fallible action heroes, Harrison Ford in **Indiana Jones and the Temple of Doom** (1984). Quote from *High Contrast: Race and Gender in Contemporary Hollywood Film* by Sharon Willis (Duke University Press, Durham and London, 1997).

Panel 3 - Sylvester Stallone as John Rambo in **Rambo: First Blood Part II** (1985). What began as a relatively nuanced portrayal of a veteran on the edge in **First Blood** (1982) became an increasingly jingoistic and superheroic action franchise by the end of the 1980s.

Panel 4 - Batman versus Bane in **The Dark Knight Rises** (2012).

PAGE 44
Panel 4 - Quote from 'Black Swan/White Swan: On Female Objectification, Creatureliness, and Death Denial' by Jamie L. Goldenberg in *Death in Classic and Contemporary Film: Fade to Black* edited by Daniel Sullivan and Jeff Greenberg (Palgrave Macmillan, New York, 2013). **The Wrestler** is beautifully mirrored by director Darren Aronofsky's **Black Swan** (2010), a psychological body-horror set in a ballet company. Like **The Wrestler**, the film examines the performative nature of gender and the damage this can do to a person's mind and body.

PAGE 45
Panel 1 - Divine, the drag persona of performer Glenn Milstead. Divine is most famous for his appearances in the films of John Waters, including **Pink Flamingos** (1972) and **Polyester** (1981), movies designed to shock audiences with their grimy, countercultural content.

Panel 2 - An image from the twisted and wonderful **Taxidermia** (2006), a film in which twentieth-century Hungarian history inscribes itself on the bodies of the film's protagonists. From the corrupt gluttony of the Soviet era to the malnourished anomie of the modern capitalist era, the film uses the human body as a metaphor for the effects of history on the individual.

Panel 3 - Quotes from *Different Bodies: Essays on Disability in Film and Television* edited by Marja Evelyn Mogk (McFarland, Jefferson, 2013). Here we have Blofeld from **You Only Live Twice** (1967), Jason from the **Friday the 13th** franchise, Elle Driver from **Kill Bill** (2003/2004) and the unnamed dwarf from **Don't Look Now** (1973).

Panel 4 - John Hurt as John Merrick in David Lynch's **The Elephant Man** (1980).

Panel 5 - Tom Cruise in **Born on the Fourth of July** (1989). It's also worth noting that it is incredibly uncommon to see disabled actors playing disabled characters on screen. While these roles garner able-bodied actors plaudits for their performances, they do actors with disabilities out of a job. As Scott Jordan Harris argues: "We are conditioned to be outraged when we see race being exploited onscreen. When we see disability being exploited onscreen, we are conditioned to applaud." Quote from 'Able-Bodied Actors and Disability Drag: Why Disabled Roles are Only for Disabled Performers' by Scott Jordan Harris on RogerEbert.com (http://www.rogerebert.com/balder-and-dash/disabled-roles-disabled-performers).

PAGE 46
Panels 1 and 4 - Quotes from *Sideshow USA: Freaks and the American Cultural Imagination* by Rachel Adams (University of Chicago Press, Chicago, 2001).

PAGE 47
Panel 1 - It is perhaps not this clear cut. While the film indeed tries to represent the humanity of its disabled performers, many critics have raised the issue of whether all of these performers were able to give consent to their participation. Like a circus freakshow, the film may well have relied on the actors' inability to find other work, exploiting their situation for entertainment.

Panel 3 - Quote from *Sideshow USA: Freaks and the American Cultural Imagination* by Rachel Adams (University of Chicago Press, Chicago, 2001).

PAGE 48
Panel 2 - Quote from 'Biotourism, Fantastic Voyage, and Sublime Inner Space' by Kim Swachuk in *Wild Science: Reading Feminism, Medicine, and the Media* edited by Janine Marchessault and Kim Sawchuk (Routledge, London, 2000).

Panel 3 - See also the grotesque climax to **Taxidermia** (2006), in which a character performs taxidermy on himself in a bid to create a profound work of art out of his own body.

PAGE 49
Panel 1 - Quote from *Transgressive Bodies: Representations in Film and Popular Culture* by Dr. Niall Richardson (Ashgate Publishing, Surrey, 2010).

Panel 5 - For more food-themed films designed to put you off your dinner, check out **The Cook, The Thief, His Wife and Her Lover** (1989), **Delicatessen** (1991), **In My Skin** (2002) and **Dumplings** (2004).

PAGE 50

Panel 2 - Leatherface from **The Texas Chain Saw Massacre** (1974).

Panel 3 - Quote from *Powers of Horror: An Essay on Abjection* by Julia Kristeva, translated by Leon S. Roudiez (Columbia University Press, New York, 1982). A little dense at times, Kristeva's full thoughts on abjection are well worth a look for horror fans, helping to illuminate some of the psychology and symbolism behind what disgusts us.

PAGE 51

Panel 2 - Norman Bates' dessicated 'Mother' from **Psycho** (1960).

Panel 3 - Carrie humiliated and covered in pigs' blood, moments before carrying out telekinetic revenge in **Carrie** (1976). Quote from 'Horror and the Monstrous Feminine' by Barbara Creed in *The Dread of Difference* edited by Barry Keith Grant (University of Texas Press, Austin, 1996), another essay well worth exploring for the horror fan.

Panel 4 - Kane's terrifying, stomach-turning demise in **Alien** (1979).

Panel 5 - The villainous Rhodes' much-deserved evisceration in **Day of the Dead** (1985).

Panel 6 - Body horror is one of my favourite genres. Some of my top picks are **Invasion of the Body Snatchers** (1978), **The Thing** (1982), **Akira** (1988), **Society** (1989), **Tetsuo: The Iron Man** (1989), **Braindead** (aka **Dead Alive**) (1992), **Trouble Every Day** (2001), **In My Skin** (2002), **Gozu** (2003), **Splice** (2010) and **District 9** (2009), in addition to the David Cronenberg films mentioned below.

PAGE 52

Panel 1 - Quote from 'The Inside-Out of Masculinity: David Cronenberg's Visceral Pleasures' by Linda Ruth Williams in *The Body's Perilous Pleasures: Dangerous Desires and Contemporary Culture* edited by Michele Aaron (Edinburgh University Press, Edinburgh, 1999). A number of Cronenberg's films could have been discussed here, but most pertinent to the body and its bounds are probably **Rabid** (1977), **Videodrome** (1983), **Crash** (1996) and **eXistenZ** (1999).

PAGE 53

Panel 5 - Quote from 'The Inside-Out of Masculinity: David Cronenberg's Visceral Pleasures' by Linda Ruth Williams in *The Body's Perilous Pleasures: Dangerous Desires and Contemporary Culture* edited by Michele Aaron (Edinburgh University Press, Edinburgh, 1999).

PAGE 54

Panel 2 - Quote from 'Visual Pleasure and Narrative Cinema' by Laura Mulvey in *Visual and Other Pleasures* (Palgrave Macmillan, Hampshire, 2nd Edition, 2009).

Panels 4 and 8 - Quotes from *The Tactile Eye: Touch and the Cinematic Experience* by Jennifer M. Barker (University of California Press, Berkeley, 2009).

Panel 6 - Natalie Portman in **Black Swan** (2010).

PAGE 55

Gollum from **The Lord of the Rings: The Two Towers** (2002); the T-800 from **The Terminator** (1984); Blondie from **The Good, the Bad and the Ugly** (1966); Mickey Mouse from **Steamboat Willie** (1928); Hans from **Freaks** (1932); Trinity from **The Matrix** (1999); The Bride from **Kill Bill Volume 1** (2003); Brundlefly from **The Fly** (1986); and Han Solo from **Star Wars Episode IV: A New Hope** (1977).

SETS AND ARCHITECTURE

PAGE 59

Panel 1 - Paying homage to the wonderful **Indiana Jones and the Raiders of the Lost Ark** (1981).

Panel 2 - Henry Fonda against the backdrop of Monument Valley in **My Darling Clementine** (1946).

Panel 3 - Snake Plissken in the ruins of Manhattan in **Escape From New York** (1981).

Panel 4 - The iconic skyline of futuristic Los Angeles in **Blade Runner** (1982).

PAGE 60

Panel 8 - See *Architecture and Film* edited by Mark Lamster (Princeton Architectural Press, New York, 2000).

PAGE 61

For more on **Intolerance** and other grandiose Hollywood sets, see *Architecture for the Screen: A Critical Study of Set Design in Hollywood's Golden Age* by Juan Antonio Ramírez (McFarland, Jefferson, 2004).

PAGE 62

Panel 1 - Inspired by the iconic scene from F.W. Murnau's **Nosferatu** (1921).

Panel 2 - **From Morn to Midnight** (1920).

Panel 3 - **Aelita: Queen of Mars** (1924).

Panel 4 - **Algol: Tragedy of Power** (1920).

Panel 5 - Quoted on p102 of *Warped Space: Art, Architecture, and Anxiety in Modern Culture* by Anthony Vidler (MIT Press, Cambridge MA, 2001).

PAGE 63

Panel 1 - It's not just the German Expressionists who have been innovative with their approach to setting when faced with budgetary constraints. Modern low budget film-makers have often used their limitations as inspiration, creating films set in a single location. Highly recommended one-set films include **Clerks** (1994), **Cube** (1997), **Tape** (2001), **Pontypool** (2009) and **Buried** (2010), the latter set entirely inside a coffin in which the protagonist has been buried alive.

Panel 3 - Quote from *Warped Space: Art, Architecture, and Anxiety in Modern Culture* by Anthony Vidler (MIT Press, Cambridge MA, 2001). As fascism took hold in central Europe, hundreds of talented German directors, including Fritz Lang, Douglas Sirk, Karl Freund and Billy Wilder, emigrated to the USA, imposing their Expressionist aesthetic onto the horror and detective genres. Film noir is a direct descendant of German Expressionism, only made possible by the dark, psychological visions of directors like Michael Curtiz (**Casablanca** (1942)) and Fritz Lang (**The Big Heat** (1953)).

PAGE 65

Panel 2 - Quote from *Powell and Pressburger: A Cinema of Magic Spaces* by Andrew Moor (I.B.Tauris, London, 2005).

Panel 4 - In many ways, **Taxi Driver** is the next evolutionary step on from film noir. Still dark and smoggy, the colour palette takes in a mixture of grime and neon to further express its anti-hero's torment.

PAGE 66

Panel 3 - Quote from *Dark Places: The Haunted House in Film* by Barry Curtis (Reaktion Books, London, 2008). Pictured is **The Amityville Horror** (1979).

Panel 4 - **Hausu** really needs to be seen to be believed. A truly unique film powered by loopy special effects and a delirious sense of humour.

PAGE 67

Panel 4 - Quote from *Kubrick: Inside A Film Artist's Maze* by Thomas Allen Nelson (Indiana University Press, Bloomington, 2000).

PAGE 68

Panel 3 - Quote from 'Mazes, Mirrors, Deception and Denial: An In-Depth Analysis of Stanley Kubrick's The Shining' by Rob Ager on CollativeLearning.com (http://www.collativelearning.com/the%20shining%20-%20chap%204.html). For some people, Ager's ideas are a stretch too far, with many arguing that Kubrick simply wouldn't have thought in such great depth about how his set was constructed or what the impacts of these spatial impossibilities would be. This certainly may be the case and, if the production was pushed for space, they may just have cut corners to fit everything in. However, every film is made up of thousands of decisions that work together to create the final product, and it's not inconceivable that Kubrick may have asked his set designers to create a set that would feel subtly wrong to the viewer. In the end, whether or not these spatial impossibilities were intended, they do certainly exist in the film, adding a subtle but tangible sense of the uncanny to the Overlook Hotel.

PAGE 69

Panels 5 and 6 - Quotes from 'Escape by Design' by Maggie Valentine in *Architecture and Film* edited by Mark Lamster (Princeton Architectural Press, New York, 2000).

PAGE 70

Panel 1 - Woody Allen's **Manhattan** (1979).

Panel 4 - Hong Kong in Wong Kar-wai's mesmerising **In the Mood For Love** (2000).

Panel 5 - Brooklyn in Spike Lee's **Do The Right Thing** (1989).

Panel 6 - Johannesburg in Neill Blomkamp's **District 9** (2009).

PAGE 72

Panel 4 - Quoted on p95 of Fritz Lang's *Metropolis: Cinematic Visions of Technology and Fear* edited by Michael Minden and Holger Bachmann (Camden House, New York, 2000).

Panel 5 - Quote from 'Before and After Metropolis: Film and Architecture in Search of the Modern City' by Dietrich Neumann in *Film Architecture: Set Designs From Metropolis to Blade Runner* edited by Dietrich Neumann (Prestel Publishing, New York, 1999).

PAGE 73

Panel I - Quote from 'Before and After Metropolis: Film and Architecture in Search of the Modern City' by Dietrich Neumann in *Film Architecture: Set Designs From Metropolis to Blade Runner* edited by Dietrich Neumann (Prestel Publishing, New York, 1999). Although not mentioned earlier, **Metropolis** is very much a German Expressionist film, and it was German propaganda minister Joseph Goebbels' interest in the film that actually drove Lang to flee to America.

PAGE 74

Panel 2 - Quoted on p44 of 'Like Today Only More So: The Credible Dystopia of Blade Runner' by Michael Webb in *Film Architecture: Set Designs From Metropolis to Blade Runner* edited by Dietrich Neumann (Prestel Publishing, New York, 1999).

Panel 4 - Quote from 'The Ultimate Trip: Special Effects and the Visual Culture of Modernity' by Scott Bukatman in *Matters of Gravity: Special Effects and Supermen in the 20th Century* by Scott Bukatman (Duke University Press, Durham NC, 2003).

PAGE 76

Panel 3 - Quote from *High Contrast: Race and Gender in Contemporary Hollywood Film* by Sharon Willis (Duke University Press, Durham and London, 1997).

Panel 4 - Quote from 'Nakatomi Space' by Geoff Manaugh on BldgBlog.blogspot.com (http://bldgblog.blogspot.co.uk/2010/01/nakatomi-space.html).

PAGE 77

Panels 2 and 5 - Quotes from 'Nakatomi Space' by Geoff Manaugh on BldgBlog.blogspot.com (http://bldgblog.blogspot.co.uk/2010/01/nakatomi-space.html). The trend for urban exploration set by John McClane continues in action cinema today, where "movement has become more than a tool of bodily knowledge; it has become an end in itself, and it is often accompanied by a utopian sense of possibility." Quote from p125 of 'The Ultimate Trip: Special Effects and the Visual Culture of Modernity" by Scott Bukatman in *Matters of Gravity: Special Effects and Supermen in the 20th Century* by Scott Bukatman (Duke University Press, Durham NC, 2003). For the stateless, amnesiac spy Jason Bourne (**The Bourne Trilogy**, 2002-2007), survival depends on his mastery of whole cities, countries and even continents. Like McClane, Bourne harnesses his surroundings to his advantage; a spy without gadgets, he scrounges weapons from his environment. A biro pen, an aerosol can, a hardback book – all are deadly in his hands. As Matt Jones argues, for Bourne, Europe is a connected and borderless place "that can be hacked, accessed and traversed" almost instinctively: "A battered watch and an accurate U-Bahn timetable are all he needs for a perfectly-timed, death-defying evasion of the authorities." Quote from 'The Bourne Infrastructure' by Matt Jones on MagicalNihilism.com (http://magicalnihilism.com/2008/12/12/the-bourne-infrastructure/). Bourne's city is a battleground, a place to be subverted and explored, where he can move uninhibited through the public infrastructure and disappear into throngs of anonymous faces.

PAGE 79

Panel 5 - The background is based on the set of **The Matrix** (1999) – the room where Neo chooses to see past the surface of what he thinks is reality and pass through into the real world.

PAGE 80

Panel I - Quoted in *Visions of the City: Utopianism, Power and Politics in Twentieth-century Urbanism* by David Pinder (Edinburgh University Press, Edinburgh, 2005). The backdrop is inspired by **Labyrinth** (1986).

Panel 5 - Quote from *America* by Jean Baudrillard, translated by Chris Turner (Verso, London, 1989).

PAGE 81

Quote from 'Previewing the Cinematic City' by David Clarke in *The Cinematic City* edited by David Clarke (Routledge, London, 1997). Can you spot all the movie references on this page?

TIME

PAGE 85

Panel 2 - Quote from *Sculpting in Time: Reflections on Cinema* by Andrei Tarkovsky (The Bodley Head, London, 1986). *Sculpting in Time* is Russian film-maker Andrei Tarkovsky's seminal book on film-making. It's a truly illuminating read which offers an amazing insight into the philosophy of cinema and the role that time plays onscreen.

Panels 3 and 4 - The images reference the Lumière Brothers' film **Arrival of a Train at La Ciotat** (1896). The film is famous for reports that audience members fled the cinema as the train approached the screen, a story now considered an urban legend.

Panel 5 - This image is based on **Safety Last!** (1923), a Harold Lloyd silent comedy now considered one of the medium's best. The film was referenced more than 60 years later in the time-travel adventure **Back to the Future** (1985) in a scene where Doc Brown dangles from a clock-face.

PAGE 86

Panel 2 - **Run Lola Run** (1998), with its trilogy of diverging paths to the same story, is a stunning example of the potential of film to explore time and the nature of consequence. Also worth a look in this sub-genre are **Blind Chance** (1987), **Groundhog Day** (1993) and **Source Code** (2011).

Panel 4 - Quote from p634 of *Sculpting in Time: Reflections on Cinema* by Andrei Tarkovsky (The Bodley Head, London, 1986).

PAGE 87

Panel 1 - Quote from *Film: An International History of the Medium* by Robert Sklar (Harry N. Abrams, New York, 1993). As I discuss in chapter 6 (Power and Ideology), the Odessa Steps massacre was an invention of Eisenstein's designed to consolidate viewer support for the film's revolutionary ideology. **Battleship Potemkin** is a dedicated piece of propaganda, where every element, from story to editing, is designed to forward its ideological mission.

PAGE 88

Panel 4 - Quote from *Cinema II: The Time Image* by Gilles Deleuze (Athlone Press, London, 1989). Gilles Deleuze's book *Cinema II* is a dense and difficult exploration of the role that time plays onscreen, but worth a read if you can hack it. In the book, Deleuze proposes a split in film history between films motivated by 'movement-images' and those motivated by 'time-images'. In most of mainstream cinema, it is the 'movement-image' which dominates, as we follow characters in action and reaction and as the film cuts to match these actions. For Deleuze, there is a neglected magic to the 'time-image' – that is to say, films which instead focus on the passage of time, using longer takes and a slower pace to allow the viewer to reflect on what they are seeing. As examples, check out Kim Ki-duk's **Spring, Summer, Fall, Winter... and Spring** (2003) or Apichatpong Weerasethakul's **Uncle Boonmee Who Can Recall His Past Lives** (2010).

PAGE 89

Another wonderful example of this trend for millennia-spanning film imagery can be seen in Darren Aronofsky's **Noah** (2014), during a sequence in which the genesis and evolution of life on Earth is conveyed through a stunning timelapse that crosses primordial landscapes and dives under the ocean to follow a single creature evolving from protozoa to fish to lizard to ape in one continuous shot.

PAGE 90

Other real-time films worth checking out include Hitchcock's **Rope** (1948), Richard Linklater's **Before Sunset** (2004) and Roman Polanski's darkly comic **Carnage** (2011).

PAGE 91

One of the modern masters of the long take is Alfonso Cuarón, who uses the technique in combination with modern visual effects to create engrossing action sequences that are grounded by the fact that they feature no cuts. For the best examples, see the heart-stopping ambush sequence in **Children of Men** (2006) and the dizzying 17-minute opening sequence of **Gravity** (2013). Like Hitchcock's **Rope** (1948), Alejandro González Iñárritu's **Birdman** (2014) conceals its cuts to create the illusion of a mesmerising single take. With its mix of backstage drama and magical realist superhero fantasy, it's well worth watching for both its entertainment value and its technical ambition.

PAGE 92

Panel 1 - An earlier example of the single-shot film is Mike Figgis' hugely ambitious **Timecode** (2000), which features four simultaneous, intertwining stories, each shot in one take and shown via split-screen.

Panel 3 - Quote from *A History of Russian Cinema* by Birgit Beumers (Berg, Oxford, 2009).

PAGE 93

Panels 1, 2 and 3 - Featured here are **Intolerance** (1916), **Citizen Kane** (1941) and **Pulp Fiction** (1994). Quote from *Cinema II: The Time Image* by Gilles Deleuze (Athlone Press, London, 1989).

PAGE 94

Christopher Nolan's obsession with our subjective experience of time is further explored in both **Inception** (2010) and **Interstellar** (2014). **Inception** features nested dream universes each with their own subjective timeframes, while **Interstellar** imagines a black hole which makes an hour on a nearby planet the equivalent of seven years on earth.

PAGE 95

Panel 2 - Quote from 'Contingency, Order, and the Modular Narrative: 21 Grams and Irreversible' by Allan Cameron in *The Velvet Light Trap* (University of Texas Press, Austin, No 58, Fall 2006). Gaspar Noe's grim and upsetting **Irréversible** (2002) presents its horrific story of rape and revenge in a similar manner to **Memento**, flipping its cause and effect narrative on its head so that the murderous revenge is seen before the rape that incites it. A disturbing film to watch, **Irréversible** suggests that a trauma as enormous as rape cannot be escaped from, and for the viewer the film's happy ending is only possible because of the story's reversed order.

PAGE 96

See also the wonderful and confounding **Primer** (2004), which offers one of cinema's most feasible and grounded portrayals of time travel. For more on the film, see chapter 7 (Technology and Technophobia).

PAGE 97

Panel 1 - Further reading: 'Time and Stasis in 'La Jetée'' by Bruce Kawin in *Film Quarterly* (Vol 36, No 1, 1982).

PAGE 98

Panel 1 - Quote from 'Chris Marker and the Cinema as Time Machine' by Paul Coates in *Science Fiction Studies* (Vol 14, No 3, November 1987).

PAGE 99

The flashback is a concept that I unfortunately couldn't cover in the main section of this book, yet jumping back into a character's past is perhaps one of the most common ways that film plays with time. It's a storytelling device that has become increasingly nuanced over the years, well illustrated in modern cinema by the poetic cutaways used by Terrence Malick in **The Thin Red Line** (1998) and **The Tree of Life** (2011), or the non-linear narratives which weave together various timelines in everything from **Reservoir Dogs** (1992) to **Batman Begins** (2005). One of the most exciting uses of the flashback comes in films with unreliable narrators – think of the conflicting accounts of events presented in films like **Citizen Kane** (1941), **Rashomon** (1950) and **Hero** (2002), or the convoluted false account provided to the cops by Verbal Kint in **The Usual Suspects** (1995).

PAGE 100

It's worth noting that the use of animation in **Waltz With Bashir** is hugely significant, providing a means for the film-maker to visually portray the overwhelming subjectivity of his memories and avoid the objectivity that film footage often implies. For further reading, see 'In Search of Lost Reality: Waltzing With Bashir' by Markos Hadjioannou in *Deleuze and Film* edited by David Martin-Jones and William Brown (Edinburgh University Press, Edinburgh, 2012) and 'Waltzing the Limit' by Erin Manning in *Deleuze and Fascism – Security: War: Aesthetics* edited by Brad Evans and Julian Reid (Routledge, Oxon, 2013).

PAGE 103

Panels 1 and 6 - Quotes from *Sculpting in Time: Reflections on Cinema* by Andrei Tarkovsky (The Bodley Head, London, 1986).

Panel 6 - The cinema here is modelled on the old Odeon on Clerk Street in Edinburgh.

VOICE AND LANGUAGE

PAGE 107

Panel 1 - **The Jazz Singer** (1927) was, of course, the first feature-length movie to be released with synchronised sound. The film launched the sound era with the famous line "You ain't heard nothin' yet." Even before synchronised sound, the movies were anything but silent, accompanied by live orchestras, gramophone recordings and even narrators who would perform the dialogue for the audience. At the same time, onscreen characters were regularly shown talking, the meaning conferred through expression, performance and inter-titles. As Michel Chion argues, these implied voices existed in spectators' imaginations, despite cinema's 'deafness' to voice: "Garbo in the silent era had as many voices as all of her admirers individually conferred on her. The talkie limited her to one, her own." Quote from p8 of *The Voice in Cinema* by Michel Chion (Columbia University Press, New York, 1999). The coming of sound would cause problems for a number of silent stars, whose popular bodily personas were shattered by the audience's discovery of their sometimes unappealing voices. Nonetheless, sound and the onscreen voice were here to stay. Much of this ground is covered in **The Artist** (2011), a charming and innovative modern day silent movie.

Panel 2 - Quote from *The Voice in Cinema* by Michel Chion (Columbia University Press, New York, 1999). Chion's book is the most thorough account of the role of the human voice in the movies and is well worth a read if the topic interests you.

PAGE 108

Panel 3 - See *The Voice in Cinema* by Michel Chion (Columbia University Press, New York, 1999).

Panel 5 - Quote from 'Look at Me! A Phenomenology of Heath Ledger in The Dark Knight' by Jörg Sternagel in *Theorizing Film Acting* edited by Aaron Taylor (Routledge, Oxon, 2012).

PAGE 111

Panel 5 - Quote from *The Voice in Cinema* by Michel Chion (Columbia University Press, New York, 1999). HAL's gradual descent into infancy and his rendition of the song 'Daisy Bell' was inspired by Arthur C. Clarke's own experience witnessing experiments into speech synthesis conducted in the early 1960s in which an IBM computer was programmed to sing the same song. HAL, however, was voiced by a human actor, stage actor Douglas Rain.

PAGE 112

Panel 1 - Quote from *The Voice in Cinema* by Michel Chion (Columbia University Press, New York, 1999).

Panel 2 - Fritz Lang's **The Testament of Dr. Mabuse** is a thrilling mix of supernatural German Expressionism and film noir tropes. I couldn't help but spot some of the DNA of Batman and his rogues gallery in this tale that is so infused with madness. It's well worth a watch.

PAGE 114
Panel 2 - Quote from *Enjoy your Symptom!: Jacques Lacan in Hollywood and Out* by Slavoj Zizek (Routledge, Oxon, 2013). Image inspired by Chaplin's **The Rink** (1916).

PAGE 116
Panel 2 - Quote from 'Uncanny Aurality in Pontypool' by Steen Christiansen in *Cinephile: The University of British Columbia's Film Journal* (Vol 6, No 2, Fall 2010).

Panel 4 - For more on meme theory, see *The Selfish Gene* by Richard Dawkins (Oxford University Press, Oxford, 1976).

PAGE 117
Panel 4 - Quote from 'Ulterior Structuralist Motives – With Zombies' by Michael Atkinson on IFC.com (http://www.ifc.com/fix/2010/01/zombie).

PAGE 118
Panel 1 - Quote from *A Voice and Nothing More* by Mladen Dolar (MIT Press, Cambridge MA, 2006).

PAGE 121
Panel 1 - See *Simulacra and Simulation* by Jean Baudrillard (University of Michigan Press, Michigan, 1994). A passage at the beginning of Baudrillard's book perfectly echoes **Synecdoche, New York**'s central motif, offering us an image of "a map so detailed that it ends up covering the territory exactly" (p1); a map which supersedes reality and continues after the landscape it represents is forgotten.

Panels 2 and 3 - I'd like to break down what's going on in these images. The point that Baudrillard makes is that in modern culture all the symbols around us, such as the potato chip packaging showing a lush farmland or offering 'cool' flavour, don't actually refer to any kind of reality. The process which these potato chips go through during their mass production has no relationship with the quaint images on the packaging, and what the hell is 'cool' flavour anyway? Christmas is a perfect example of an aspect of culture rife with simulacra – that is, with representations of things that no longer exist or never existed in the first place. With plastic christmas trees, dancing red Santas and oversized felt stockings, it's a cultural event awash with simulacra of iconography invented to represent a religious holiday that itself falls on an arbitrary day of the year.

PAGE 122
Panels 1 and 8 - Quotes from *Film Language: A Semiotics of the Cinema* by Christian Metz (University of Chicago Press, Chicago, 1974).

PAGE 123
Panel 1 - Director Jean-Luc Godard.

Panel 2 - Director Stanley Kubrick.

Panel 4 - Quote from *Image, Music, Text* by Roland Barthes, translated by Stephen Heath (Fontana Press, London, 1977). Many critics of film theory shoot down the more lavish interpretations of movies as 'reading too much into things'. For those of us who enjoy analysing and exploring the movies, the theory of the death of the author is one of our strongest defences.

PAGE 124
Panel 1 - Image inspired by **The Searchers** (1956).

Panel 4 - Quote from *Exploring Media Culture: A Guide* by Michael R. Real (Sage Publications, London, 1996).

PAGE 125
Panel 1 - **Victim** (1961) is a powerful British film made when homosexuality was outlawed in the UK and USA, and was the first English language film to openly talk about homosexuality. Its story of a barrister blackmailed over his homosexuality got the film slapped with an X-rating in the UK and a ban in the USA.

Panel 2 - Quote from *The Celluloid Closet: Homosexuality in the Movies* by Vito Russo (Harper and Row, New York, 1981). The book and its documentary adaptation are well worth a look – the story of LGBT actors and audiences driven into the closet by culture and the film industry is heartbreaking. As Russo demonstrates, films like **Wings** (1927) offered LGBT audiences a way to see themselves onscreen during an era when censorship meant that openly gay characters were virtually non-existent.

Panel 3 - Marlene Dietrich's iconic role in **Morocco** (1930).

Panel 4 - The debate still rages about the gay subtext in **Ben Hur** (1959). While writer Gore Vidal always insisted that he deliberately included the subtext without actor Charlton Heston's knowledge, Heston always argued back that none of Vidal's work made it into the final script. Whoever's right about what happened behind the scenes, the sexual tension is palpable onscreen, mostly due to Stephen Boyd's wonderful performance.

PAGE 126
Panel 1 - **The Sound of Music** (1965).

Panel 3 - Director Sofia Coppola.

Panel 4 - Quote from *Sculpting in Time: Reflections on Cinema* by Andrei Tarkovsky (The Bodley Head, London, 1986).

PAGE 127

The Wizard of Oz (1939) is one of the most analysed films out there, and has been adopted by LGBT theorists as a prime example of LGBT subtext in the movies, with Dorothy's journey widely seen as symbolic of her burgeoning lesbian identity. As critic Alexander Doty argues, these interpretations shouldn't be seen as 'appropriations' of supposedly straight culture, but instead as yet more potential interpretations for a text that leaves things open for viewers to read into. As he puts it: "Just because straight interpretations have been allowed to flourish publicly doesn't mean they are the most 'true' or 'real' ones." Quote from p53 of *Flaming Classics: Queering the Film Canon* by Alexander Doty (Routledge, New York, 2000).

POWER AND IDEOLOGY

PAGE 131

Panel 2 - Clint Eastwood's **Dirty Harry** (1974) is American cinema's quintessential no-nonsense cop, a man willing to bend and break the rules to uphold law and order.

Panel 3 - Julia Roberts and Richard Gere in **Pretty Woman** (1990).

Panel 4 - Joseph Stalin, as quoted on p170 of *Reel Power: Hollywood Cinema and American Supremacy* by Matthew Alford (Pluto Press, New York, 2010).

Panel 5 - Tom Cruise as Maverick in **Top Gun** (1986).

PAGE 132

Panel 3 - Quote from the documentary **The Pervert's Guide to Ideology** (2012).

Panel 4 - Quote from Michael Parenti's foreword to *Reel Power: Hollywood Cinema and American Supremacy* by Matthew Alford (Pluto Press, New York, 2010).

PAGE 133

Panel 5 - Quote from *Sinascape: Contemporary Chinese Cinema* by Gary G. Xu (Rowman & Littlefield, Plymouth, 2007).

PAGE 134

Panel 1 - John Wayne in John Ford's thrilling **Stagecoach** (1939), which follows a band of strangers on a tense ride through Apache territory.

Panel 2 - See 'Two Ways to Yuma: Locke, Liberalism, and Western Masculinity in 3:10 to Yuma' by Stephen J. Mexal in *The Philosophy of the Western* edited by Jennifer L. McMahon and B. Steve Csaki (University Press of Kentucky, Lexington, 2010). Pictured is Henry Fonda against the backdrop of Monument Valley in **My Darling Clementine** (1946).

Panel 3 - The image here is inspired by the famous Don McCullin photograph of a shell-shocked Vietnam soldier. During a time when the movies were painting a picture of good-versus-evil heroism, other media were bringing home images that offered a much darker picture of America's struggles both overseas and at home.

Panel 4 - Quote from *The Six-Gun Mystique Sequel* by John G. Cawelti (Bowling Green State University Popular Press, 1999).

PAGE 135

Panel 1 - Quote from *Projecting Paranoia: Conspiratorial Visions in American Film* by Ray Pratt (University Press of Kansas, 2001).

Panel 2 - John Rambo from **Rambo: First Blood Part II** (1985), the jingoistic sequel to the comparatively contemplative **First Blood** (1982).

Panel 3 - Quote from *Backlash: The Undeclared War Against Women* by Susan Faludi (Random House, London, 1993). Actor Michael Douglas quickly became the poster-boy for conservative white male angst during this era, falling victim to ambitious, manipulative women in **Fatal Attraction**, **Basic Instinct** and **Disclosure** (1994) and to ethnic minorities, globalisation and political correctness in **Falling Down** (1993).

PAGE 136

Panel 1 - Anti-clockwise from left to right: Beast from **Beauty and the Beast** (1991); the Evil Queen from **Snow White and the Seven Dwarfs** (1937); Bambi from **Bambi** (1942); Dumbo from **Dumbo** (1941); Thumper from **Bambi**; Mickey Mouse from **Steamboat Willie** (1928); a dalmatian from **101 Dalmatians** (1961); Doc from **Snow White and the Seven Dwarfs**; Lady from **Lady and the Tramp** (1955); Kaa and Mowgli from **The Jungle Book** (1967); and Maleficent from **Sleeping Beauty** (1959).

Panels 4 and 5 - Quotes from 'Split Skins: Female Agency and Bodily Mutilation in The Little Mermaid' by Susan White in *Film Theory Goes to the Movies* edited by Jim Collins, Hilary Radner and Ava Preacher Collins (Routledge, New York, 1993).

PAGE 137

Panel 1 - One of these crows is literally called Jim Crow – a widely acknowledged racist term for a black man in segregation-era America, and the name given to the laws that segregated white and black people. For further insight into racial stereotyping and blackface in American cinema, see chapter 2 (The Body) and the corresponding endnotes.

Panel 2 - This is actually a problematic argument since the voice actor responsible for King Louie was played by Italian-American singer Louis Prima. For me, this ultimately doesn't negate the racism inherent in the image: the scat-singing style employed by King Louie comes right out of African-American jazz music and, whether or not racism was intended by the film's creators, these images were received as racist by a large number of viewers.

Panel 3 - Quote from *The Gospel According to Disney: Faith, Trust, and Pixie Dust* By Mark I. Pinsky (Westminster John Knox Press, Louisville, 2004).

PAGE 138

Panel 1 - Buffalo Bill from **The Silence of the Lambs** (1991); 'Injuns' from **The Searchers** (1956); and Catherine Tramell from **Basic Instinct** (1992). The murderous homosexual trope is a mainstay of film history, and for a long time the only representation that LGBT audiences could find of themselves onscreen was in the form of campy, unhinged villains like Joel Cairo in **The Maltese Falcon** (1941) or Bruno Anthony in **Strangers on a Train** (1951). Even today, the trope continues in the form of Xerxes in **300** (2006) or Raoul Silva in **Skyfall** (2012).

Panel 2 - Quote from *Reel Bad Arabs: How Hollywood Vilifies a People* by Jack Shaheen (Olive Branch Press, Northampton MA, 2009).

PAGE 139

Panels 2 and 5 - Quotes from 'Ups and Downs of the Latest Schwarzenegger Film: Hasta la Vista, Fairness – Media's Line on Arabs' by Salam Al-Marayati and Don Bustany in the *Los Angeles Times* (8 August 1994) (http://articles.latimes.com/1994-08-08/entertainment/ca-24971_1_hastalavista).

Panel 3 - Quote from *Reel Bad Arabs: How Hollywood Vilifies a People* by Jack Shaheen (Olive Branch Press, Northampton MA, 2009).

Panel 5 - Image based on the photos taken of human rights violations in Abu Ghraib prison, which documented some of the torture and abuse conducted by members of the US Army and the CIA.

PAGE 140

Panel 3 - Quote from 'The Testament of Dr. Goebbels' by Eric Rentschler in *Film and Nationalism* edited by Alan Williams (Rutgers University Press, New Jersey, 2002).

Panel 5 - Quote from *Cinemas of the World: Film and Society from 1895 to the Present* by James Chapman (Reaktion Books, London, 2003).

PAGE 141

Panel 3 - Quoted in *Projections of War: Hollywood, American Culture, and World War II* by Thomas Doherty (Columbia University Press, New York, 1993).

Panel 5 - Quote from William Grieder's introduction to *Reel Bad Arabs: How Hollywood Vilifies a People* by Jack Shaheen (Olive Branch Press, Northampton MA, 2009).

PAGE 142

Panels 1, 2 and 3 - Quotes from *Operation Hollywood: How the Pentagon Shapes and Censors the Movies* by David L. Robb (Prometheus Books, New York, 2004). Far from a conspiracy theory, this is well documented by both David Robb and Matthew Alford and, as they show, numerous sources over the years have attested to these practices. Once you know it goes on, it's surprisingly easy to spot in mainstream Hollywood cinema, and I now make a game of trying to figure out if I'm watching 'militainment' whenever I watch a Hollywood movie.

Panel 4 - Image based on the extremely promilitary **Act of Valor** (2012), which starred real-life US Navy SEALs.

PAGE 143

Panels 2 and 5 - Quotes from *Reel Power: Hollywood Cinema and American Supremacy* by Matthew Alford (Pluto Press, New York, 2010).

Panel 4 - Data from *Operation Hollywood: How the Pentagon Shapes and Censors the Movies* by David L. Robb (Prometheus Books, New York, 2004).

PAGE 144

Panel 2 - Pictured is Marzieh Meshkini, director of **The Day I Became a Woman** (2000), a glorious Iranian film that tells the stories of Iranian women in childhood, adulthood and old age. It is this film that is pictured in panels 3 and 4.

Panel 4 - Quote from *Better Left Unsaid: Victorian Novels, Hays Code Films, and the Benefits of Censorship* by Nora Gilbert (Stanford University Press, Stanford, 2013). For further reading on Iranian cinema, see *The New Iranian Cinema: Politics, Representation and Identity* edited by Richard Tapper (I.B.Tauris, London, 2002)

Panel 5 - For further viewing in Iranian cinema, I highly recommend **The White Balloon** (1995), **Taste of Cherry** (1997), **Willow and Wind** (2000), **Ten** (2002) and **A Separation** (2011).

PAGE 145

Panel 1 - Quote from *Better Left Unsaid: Victorian Novels, Hays Code Films, and the Benefits of Censorship* by Nora Gilbert (Stanford University Press, Stanford, 2013). The image is from **Safe in Hell** (1931), a pre-code film noir overflowing with immorality.

Panel 2 - The main commandments of the code were:
- Pointed profanity, by either title or lip – this includes the words "God", "Lord", "Jesus", "Christ" (unless they be used reverently in connection with proper religious ceremonies), "hell", "damn", "Gawd", and every other profane and vulgar expression, however it may be spelled.
- Any licentious or suggestive nudity, in fact or in silhouette; and any lecherous or licentious notice thereof by other characters in the picture.
- The illegal traffic in drugs.
- Any inference of sex perversion.
- White slavery.
- Miscegenation (sex relationships between the white and black races).
- Sex hygiene and venereal diseases.
- Scenes of actual childbirth, in fact or in silhouette.
- Children's sex organs.
- Ridicule of the clergy.
- Willful offense to any nation, race or creed.

You can get a full rundown of the code on p301-307 of *Hollywood V. Hard Core: How the Struggle Over Censorship Created the Modern Film Industry* by Jon Lewis (New York University Press, New York, 2002).

Panel 4 - This self-censorship is controlled by market forces now rather than legal bodies. American cinema is increasingly dependent on the international market to make big money on its blockbuster productions. Hence films like **Mission: Impossible - Ghost Protocol** (2011) and **Transformers: Age of Extinction** (2014) feature extended sequences in India and China with nationally recognised actors and product placements – and in the case of **Iron Man 3** (2013), a whole section of the film only seen by Chinese audiences.

PAGE 146

Panel 1 - All the video titles on the shelves on this page were part of the 72 video nasties identified by the UK government. Admittedly there's one made-up film here – see if you can spot it! Of course, video nasty 'scares' are not limited to the UK. Whenever we encounter unexpected acts of violence, such as the Bulger killing in the UK or one of the many mass shootings to have taken place in the USA in recent years, the media and the public look around for an explanation. Blame often falls on violent movies, comics, music or computer games, even when links to the killer are tenuous at best. It is perhaps easier to blame a single cultural artefact for an act of violence than it is to discuss the multifarious factors – as well as the failings found in our social services, criminal justice systems and societies – that would lead someone to such violence.

Panels 2, 3 and 4 - **The Driller Killer** (1979).

PAGE 147

Panel 2 - Quote from 'I Was A Teenage Horror Fan. Or, How I Learned to Stop Worrying and Love Linda Blair' by Mark Kermode in *Ill Effects – The Media/Violence Debate* edited by Martin Barker and Julian Petley (Routledge, London, 2nd Edition, 2001).

PAGE 148

Panel 1 - Quote from 'Us and Them' by Julian Petley in *Ill Effects – The Media/Violence Debate* edited by Martin Barker and Julian Petley (Routledge, London, 2nd Edition, 2001). The iconic image is from **Poltergeist** (1982).

Panel 2 - Quoted in 'Us and Them' by Julian Petley in *Ill Effects – The Media/Violence Debate* edited by Martin Barker and Julian Petley (Routledge, London, 2nd Edition, 2001).

PAGE 149

Panels 1 and 2 - Quote from 'Reservoirs of Dogma: An Archaeology of Popular Anxieties' by Graham Murdock in *Ill Effects – The Media/Violence Debate* edited by Martin Barker and Julian Petley (Routledge, London, 2nd Edition, 2001). Both panels here reference **Pulp Fiction** (1994).

Panel 3 - Quote from 'Electronic Child Abuse? Rethinking the Media's Effects on Children' by David Buckingham in *Ill Effects – The Media/Violence Debate* edited by Martin Barker and Julian Petley (Routledge, London, 2nd Edition, 2001). Pictured are Tom and Jerry, the quintessential violent cartoon characters.

Panel 4 - Quote from 'Media Violence Effects and Violent Crime' by Christopher J. Ferguson in *Violent Crime: Clinical and Social Implications* edited by Christopher J. Ferguson (Sage Publications, London, 2010).

PAGE 150

Panel 1 - The original **Scarface** (1932).

Panel 3 - Quote from *Reel Power: Hollywood Cinema and American Supremacy* by Matthew Alford (Pluto Press, New York, 2010).

Panel 5 - **Brokeback Mountain** (2005).

TECHNOLOGY AND TECHNOPHOBIA

PAGE 155

Panel 1 - From left to right: telepod from **The Fly** (1986); R2-D2 from **Star Wars Episode IV: A New Hope** (1977); floor trap from **Ghostbusters** (1984); neuralyzer from **Men In Black** (1997); jetpack from **Thunderball** (1965); GERTY from **Moon** (2009); pulse rifle from **Aliens** (1986); TIE fighter and lightsaber from **Star Wars Episode IV: A New Hope**; phone booth from **Bill and Ted's Excellent Adventure** (1989); hoverboard from **Back to the Future Part II** (1989); HAL 9000 from **2001: A Space Odyssey** (1968); proton pack from **Ghostbusters**; time machine from **The Time Machine** (1960); and Robby the Robot from **Forbidden Planet** (1956).

Panel 3 - The insatiable fires of industry in **Metropolis** (1927).

Panel 4 - Slim Pickens riding a nuke in **Dr. Strangelove or: How I Learned to Stop Worrying and Love the Bomb** (1964).

Panel 5 - Agent Smith in **The Matrix** (1999).

Panel 6 - From left to right: Chani from **Devil Girl From Mars** (1954); Ro-Man from **Robot Monster** (1953); T-800 from **The Terminator** (1984); Q the Automaton from **The Master Mystery** (1919); Ash from **Alien** (1979); and ED-209 from **Robocop** (1987).

PAGE 156

Panel 4 - Buster Keaton in **The Cameraman** (1928).

Panel 6 - Quotes from *Machine Age Comedy* by Michael North (Oxford University Press, Oxford, 2009).

PAGE 157

Panel 4 - Chaplin quote from *p125 of 1001 Movies You Must See Before You Die* edited by Stephen Jay Schneider (Quintessence, London, 2010). Quote from *Machine Age Comedy* by Michael North (Oxford University Press, Oxford, 2009).

PAGE 158

Panel 1 - Despite the 1936 film's wealth of ludicrous future predictions, it did get at least one thing right, predicting the outbreak of World War II just 16 months later than it actually began. For some truly amazing visions of the shape of humanity's future, I strongly recommend **2001: A Space Odyssey** (1968), **Blade Runner** (1982), **Elysium** (2013) and **Interstellar** (2014). These films all offer a tangible sense of the future, rich in detail and not so far-fetched as to be implausible.

PAGE 159

Panel 1 - Quote from 'Race, Space and Class: The Politics of Cityscapes in Science Fiction Films' by David Desser in *Alien Zone II: The Spaces of Science Fiction Cinema* edited by Annette Kuhn (Verso, London, 1999).

Panel 2 - Quote from *British Science Fiction Cinema* edited by I.Q. Hunter (Routledge, London, 1999).

PAGES 160 AND 161

Panel 3 - Featuring: **Attack of the Crab Monsters** (1957); **The Beast From 20,000 Fathoms** (1953); **Godzilla** (1954); **It Came From Beneath The Sea** (1955); **The Fly** (1958); and **The Monster That Challenged The World** (1957).

PAGE 162

Panel 1 - J. Robert Oppenheimer and the atomic bomb.

Panel 4 - Quoted in *Mad, Bad and Dangerous? The Scientist and the Cinema* by Christopher Frayling (Reaktion Books, London, 2005). Pictured from left to right are: **Invasion of the Saucer Men** (1957); **The Brain from Planet Arous** (1957); **Fiend Without A Face** (1958); and **This Island Earth** (1955).

PAGE 163

Panel 4 - Quote from *Technophobia! Science Fiction Visions of Posthuman Technology* by Daniel Dinello (University of Texas Press, Austin, 2005). The fusion of the human body with technology is one of Cronenberg's most enduring themes, seen perhaps most vividly in **eXistenZ** (1999), **Crash** (1996) and **The Fly** (1986).

PAGE 164

Panel 4 - Quote from 'A Cyborg Manifesto' by Donna Haraway in *The Cybercultures Reader* edited by David Bell and Barbara M. Kennedy (Routledge, London, 2000).

Panel 5 - The singularity is a recurring point of anxiety in the movies, central to **Blade Runner** (1982), **The Matrix** (1999), **Transcendence** (2014) and **Her** (2014).

PAGE 166
Panel 6 - Quote from 'Tetsuo: The Iron Man / Tetsuo II: Body Hammer' by Andrew Grossman in *The Cinema of Japan and Korea* edited by Justin Bowyer (Wallflower Press, London, 2004).

PAGE 167
Panel 4 - Quote from 'Genetic Themes in Fiction Films' by Michael Clark on Genome.Wellcome.ac.uk (http://genome.wellcome.ac.uk/doc_WTD023539.html). Other films dealing with similar genetic themes that are worth checking out include **Code 46** (2003) and **Never Let Me Go** (2010).

PAGE 170
Panel 5 - Quote from T*echnophobia! Science Fiction Visions of Posthuman Technology* by Daniel Dinello (University of Texas Press, Austin, 2005). Other AI gone awry include Thermostellar Bomb #20 in **Dark Star** (1974), Proteus IV in **Demon Seed** (1977) and Ash in **Alien** (1979). Special mention should go to the wonderful GLaDOS from the computer game **Portal** (2007).

PAGE 171
Panel 5 - It's interesting just how rare it is to see examples of morally good AI in the movies. Some key examples include the droids from **Star Wars Episode IV: A New Hope** (1977), Bishop in **Aliens** (1986), **WALL-E** (2008), GERTY in **Moon** (2009), **Chappie** (2015) and the strangely endearing TARS in **Interstellar** (2014).

PAGE 173
Panel 3 - Quote from 'Nollywood and its Critics' by Onookome Okome in *Viewing African Cinema in The Twenty-First Century: Art Films and the Nollywood Video Revolution* edited by Mahir Saul and Ralph A. Austen (Ohio University Press, Athens OH, 2010).

Panel 4 - Quote from 'From Nollywood to Nollyworld: Processes of Transnationalization in the Nigerian Video Film Industry' by Alessandro Jedlowski in *Global Nollywood: The Transnational Dimensions of an African Video Film Industry* edited by Matthias Krings and Onookome Okome (Indiana University Press, Bloomington, 2013). Pictured is director Lancelot Oduwa Imasuen, who featured in the documentary **Nollywood Babylon** (2008). In the West, we tend to think of Hollywood as the king of global cinema. However, while Nollywood is the world's second most prolific national film industry, it is actually Bollywood, not Hollywood, that comes first. Bollywood is just one part of India's massive film industry, which is collectively responsible for over 1,000 releases every year. That said, Hollywood still wins hands down in terms of income, having a global, cross-cultural reach that other film industries can only dream of.

Panel 5 - Image inspired by **The Figurine: Araromire** (2009).

PAGE 174
Panel 1 - **The Blair Witch Project** (1999, budget $22,500).

Panel 2 - **Super Size Me** (2004, budget $64,000). Some other excellent examples of low budget digital film-making include: **Tarnation** (2003, budget $218); **Once** (2006, budget $180,000); **In Search of a Midnight Kiss** (2007, budget $25,000); **Paranormal Activity** (2007, budget $15,000); **Colin** (2008, budget £45); **Catfish** (2010, budget $30,000); **Monsters** (2010, budget $500,000); and **Another Earth** (2011, budget $100,000).

PAGE 175
Panel 1 - As the picture implies, slash fiction is a genre of fan fiction which imagines sexual relationships between fictional characters of the same sex, often (though not exclusively) from the sci-fi and fantasy genres. The name 'slash' refers to the titling of these pairings – for example, 'Han/Chewie'. In many ways, slash fiction is a natural evolution of the trend for hidden LGBT subtexts in Hollywood movies, as discussed in chapter 5 (Voice and Language).

Panel 2 - When I first wrote about this subject in 2011 for my self-published version of this chapter, the statistic I quoted was 48 hours of footage uploaded every minute. By the time you're reading this, the 300 hours quoted here from figures in December 2014 may well be dwarfed by an even greater figure.

Panel 4 - More than just providing outsiders with the ability to make their own films, digital technologies offer film-makers working on both independent and mainstream productions the chance to push the form with fantastically ambitious projects that could never have been conceived of before. Some key examples from recent years include the one-take wonder of **Russian Ark** (2002) and the seamlessly flowing **Birdman** (2014).

PAGE 176
Panels 2 and 3 - Quotes from *What Is Cinema? Vol. 1* by Andre Bazin (University of California Press, Berkeley, 2004).

PAGE 177
Panel 4 - This final panel is set in Cinema 1 of Edinburgh's Filmhouse, a cinema I worked at for a number of years, and in which I've seen some of the most strange and wonderful films of my life. *Filmish* literally wouldn't exist without Filmhouse, and the box office there was the first place my self-published *Filmish* ever went on sale. Thanks!

FILMOGRAPHY

48 Hrs. (1982)
101 Dalmatians (1961)
300 (2006)
2001: A Space Odyssey (1968)
A Clockwork Orange (1971)
A Scanner Darkly (2006)
A Separation (2011)
A Streetcar Named Desire (1951)
A Trip to the Moon (1902)
Act of Valor (2012)
Aelita: Queen of Mars (1924)
Akira (1988)
Aladdin (1992)
Algol: Tragedy of Power (1920)
Alien (1979)
Aliens (1986)
Alphaville (1965)
The Amityville Horror (1979)
Amores Perros (2000)
Anatomy (2000)
Annie Hall (1977)
Another Earth (2011)
Apache (1954)
Apocalypse Now (1979)
Arrival of a Train at La Ciotat (1896)
The Artist (2011)
Attack of the Crab Monsters (1957)
Audition (1999)
Avatar (2009)
The Avengers (2012)
Babel (2006)
Baby's Breakfast (1895)
Back to the Future (1985)
Back to the Future Part II (1989)
Bambi (1942)
Basic Instinct (1992)
Batman Begins (2005)
Battleship Potemkin (1925)
The Beast From 20,000 Fathoms (1953)
Beauty and the Beast (1991)
Before Sunset (2004)
Being John Malkovich (1999)
Ben Hur (1959)
The Big Heat (1953)
Bill and Ted's Excellent Adventure (1989)
Birdman (2014)
The Birth of a Nation (1915)
Black Narcissus (1947)
Black Swan (2010)
Blade Runner (1982)
The Blair Witch Project (1999)
Blind Chance (1987)
Blue Velvet (1986)
Born on the Fourth of July (1989)
The Bourne Trilogy (2002-2007)

The Brain from Planet Arous (1957)
Braindead (aka Dead Alive) (1992)
Breakfast at Tiffany's (1961)
Breathless (1960)
Brokeback Mountain (2005)
Buried (2010)
The Cabinet of Dr. Caligari (1920)
Cabiria (1914)
The Cameraman (1928)
Carnage (2011)
Carrie (1976)
Casablanca (1942)
Casino Royale (2006)
Catfish (2010)
Chappie (2015)
Cheyenne Autumn (1964)
Children of Men (2006)
Citizen Kane (1941)
City of God (2002)
Cleo From 5 to 7 (1962)
Clerks (1994)
Code 46 (2003)
Colin (2008)
Colossus: The Forbin Project (1970)
The Conversation (1974)
The Cook, The Thief, His Wife and
Her Lover (1989)
Crash (1996)
Cube (1997)
The Dark Knight (2008)
The Dark Knight Rises (2012)
Dark Star (1974)
Dawn of the Dead (1978)
The Day I Became a Woman (2000)
Day of the Dead (1985)
The Defiant Ones (1958)
Delicatessen (1991)
Demon Seed (1977)
Devil Girl From Mars (1954)
Die Hard (1988)
Dirty Harry (1974)
Disclosure (1994)
District 9 (2009)
Do the Right Thing (1989)
Don't Look Now (1973)
Dr. No (1962)
Dr. Strangelove or: How I Learned
to Stop Worrying and Love the Bomb
(1964)
The Driller Killer (1979)
Dumbo (1941)
Dumplings (2004)
Elephant (2003)
The Elephant Man (1980)
Elysium (2013)

Escape From New York (1981)
The Eternal Jew (1940)
The Evil Dead (1981)
Evil Dead 2 (1987)
eXistenZ (1999)
The Exorcist (1973)
Fail-Safe (1964)
Falling Down (1993)
Fantastic Voyage (1966)
Fatal Attraction (1987)
Ferris Bueller's Day Off (1986)
Fiend Without A Face (1958)
Fight Club (1999)
The Figurine: Araromire (2009)
First Blood (1982)
The Fly (1958)
The Fly (1986)
Forbidden Planet (1956)
Frankenstein (1931)
Freaks (1932)
Friday the 13th (1980)
From Morn to Midnight (1920)
Funny Games (1997)
Gattaca (1997)
The General (1927)
Ghostbusters (1984)
Gilda (1946)
The Godfather (1972)
Godzilla (1954)
Gone Girl (2014)
Gone With The Wind (1939)
The Good, the Bad and the Ugly (1966)
Gozu (2003)
The Graduate (1967)
Gravity (2013)
The Great Dictator (1940)
The Great Train Robbery (1903)
The Green Berets (1968)
Gremlins (1984)
Groundhog Day (1993)
Halloween (1978)
Hanna (2011)
Happy End (1966)
Hausu (1977)
Her (2014)
Hero (2002)
High Fidelity (2000)
High Noon (1952)
Hiroshima Mon Amour (1959)
The Hunger Games (2012)
I Am Legend (2007)
In My Skin (2002)
In Search of a Midnight Kiss (2007)
In the Mood For Love (2000)
Inception (2010)

Indiana Jones and the Raiders of the Lost Ark (1981)

Indiana Jones and the Temple of Doom (1984)

Interstellar (2014)

Intolerance (1916)

Invasion of the Body Snatchers (1978)

Invasion of the Saucer Men (1957)

Iron Man 3 (2013)

Irréversible (2002)

It Came From Beneath The Sea (1955)

The Jazz Singer (1927)

The Jungle Book (1967)

Jurassic Park (1993)

Kill Bill (2003/2004)

King Kong (1933)

La Grande Bouffe (1973)

La Jetée (1962)

Labyrinth (1986)

Lady and the Tramp (1955)

The Lawnmower Man (1992)

Lethal Weapon (1987)

The Little Mermaid (1989)

The Lord of the Rings (1978)

The Lord of the Rings: The Two Towers (2002)

The Machinist (2004)

Magnolia (1999)

The Maltese Falcon (1941)

Man With A Movie Camera (1929)

Manhattan (1979)

The Master Mystery (1919)

The Matrix (1999)

Memento (2000)

Men In Black (1997)

Metropolis (1927)

Midnight Cowboy (1969)

The Mirror (1975)

Mission: Impossible - Ghost Protocol (2011)

Modern Times (1936)

The Monster That Challenged The World (1957)

Monsters (2010)

Moon (2009)

Morocco (1930)

My Darling Clementine (1946)

Nanook of the North (1922)

Nashville (1975)

The Navigator (1924)

Never Let Me Go (2010)

Nineteen Eighty-Four (1956)

Noah (2014)

Nollywood Babylon (2008)

Nosferatu (1921)

Oldboy (2003)

On The Waterfront (1954)

Once (2006)

Out of the Inkwell (1915)

The Outlaw (1943)

Pan's Labyrinth (2006)

Paranormal Activity (2007)

The Passion of Joan of Arc (1928)

Peeping Tom (1960)

The Pervert's Guide to Ideology (2012)

The Phantom Edit (2000)

Pink Flamingos (1972)

Platoon (1989)

Poltergeist (1982)

Polyester (1981)

Pontypool (2009)

Pretty Woman (1990)

Primer (2004)

Psycho (1960)

Pulp Fiction (1994)

Rabid (1977)

Rambo: First Blood Part II (1985)

Rashomon (1950)

Rear Window (1954)

Reservoir Dogs (1992)

Riddles of the Sphinx (1977)

Ringu (1998)

The Rink (1916)

Rise of the Planet of the Apes (2011)

Robocop (1987)

Robot Monster (1953)

Rope (1948)

Run Lola Run (1998)

Russian Ark (2002)

Safe in Hell (1931)

Safety Last! (1923)

Saving Private Ryan (1998)

Scarface (1932)

The Searchers (1956)

Seven (1995)

The Seven Year Itch (1955)

Sherlock Jr. (1924)

The Shining (1980)

Short Cuts (1993)

The Silence of the Lambs (1991)

Singin' In The Rain (1952)

Skyfall (2012)

Sleeping Beauty (1959)

Snow White and the Seven Dwarfs (1937)

Society (1989)

The Sound of Music (1965)

Source Code (2011)

Speed (1994)

Splice (2010)

Spring, Summer, Fall, Winter… and Spring (2003)

Stagecoach (1939)

Star Wars Prequel Trilogy (1999-2005)

Star Wars Trilogy (1977-1983)

Steamboat Bill Jr. (1928)

Steamboat Willie (1928)

Strangers on a Train (1951)

Strike (1925)

Super Size Me (2004)

Synecdoche, New York (2008)

Syriana (2005)

Tape (2001)

Tarnation (2003)

Taste of Cherry (1997)

Taxi Driver (1976)

Taxidermia (2006)

Ten (2002)

The Terminator (1984)

Terminator 2: Judgment Day (1991)

The Testament of Dr. Mabuse (1933)

Tetsuo: The Iron Man (1989)

The Texas Chain Saw Massacre (1974)

Them! (1954)

They Live (1988)

The Thin Red Line (1998)

The Thing (1982)

The Thing From Another World (1951)

Things to Come (1936)

Thirteen Days (2000)

This Island Earth (1955)

Thunderball (1965)

The Time Machine (1960)

Timecode (2000)

Timecrimes (2007)

Titanic (1997)

Top Gun (1986)

Touch of Evil (1958)

Traffic (2000)

Transcendence (2014)

Transformers (2007)

Transformers: Age of Extinction (2014)

The Tree of Life (2011)

Triumph of the Will (1935)

Tron (1982)

Trouble Every Day (2001)

True Lies (1994)

The Truman Show (1998)

Twelve Monkeys (1995)

Uncle Boonmee Who Can Recall His Past Lives (2010)

The Usual Suspects (1995)

Victim (1961)

Videodrome (1983)

WALL-E (2008)

Waltz With Bashir (2008)

Wayne's World (1992)

West Side Story (1961)

The White Balloon (1995)

Why We Fight (1942-1945)

Willow and Wind (2000)

Wings (1927)

The Wizard of Oz (1939)

Workers Leaving the Lumière Factory (1895)

The Wrestler (2008)

You Only Live Twice (1967)

Zero Dark Thirty (2012)

BIBLIOGRAPHY

THE EYE

The A to Z of Horror Cinema by Peter Hutchings (Scarecrow Press, Plymouth, 2008).

Avant-Garde Film: Motion Studies by Scott McDonald (Cambridge University Press, New York, 1993).

Breaking the Fourth Wall – Direct Address in the Cinema by Tom Brown (Edinburgh University Press, Edinburgh, 2012).

'Can the Camera See? Mimesis in Man with a Movie Camera' by Malcolm Turvey in October (MIT Press, Vol 89, Summer 1999).

'The Cinema of Attractions: Early Film, Its Spectator, and the Avant-Garde' by Tom Gunning in *Theatre and Film: A Comparative Anthology* edited by Robert Knopf (Yale University Press, New York, 2005).

Documentary: A History of the Non-Fiction Film by Erik Barnouw (Oxford University Press, Oxford, 2nd Revised Edition, 1993).

Eye of the Century: Cinema, Experience, Modernity by Francesco Casetti (Columbia University Press, New York, 2008).

The Films in My Life by François Truffaut (Da Capo Press, New York, 1994).

'Ideological Effects of the Basic Cinematographic Apparatus' by Jean-Louis Baudry, translated by Alan Williams, in *Film Quarterly* (Vol 28, No 2, 1974).

Kino-Eye: The Writings of Dziga Vertov by Dziga Vertov (University of California Press, Berkeley, 1984).

The Memory of the Modern by Matt K. Matsuda (Oxford University Press, Oxford, 1996).

Men, Women and Chainsaws – Gender in the Modern Horror Film by Carol J. Clover (British Film Institute, London, 1992).

On Photography by Susan Sontag (Penguin Books, London, 1979).

'The Oppositional Gaze: Black Female Spectators' by bell hooks, in *Film and Theory: An Anthology* edited by Robert Stam and Toby Miller (Blackwell Publishers, Oxford, 2000).

'Visual Pleasure and Narrative Cinema' by Laura Mulvey in *Visual and Other Pleasures* (Palgrave Macmillan, Hampshire, 2nd Edition, 2009).

'Zooming Out: The End of Offscreen Space' by Scott Bukatman in *The New American Cinema* edited by Jon Lewis (Duke University Press, Durham, 1998).

THE BODY

'Able-Bodied Actors and Disability Drag: Why Disabled Roles are Only for Disabled Performers' by Scott Jordan Harris on RogerEbert.com (http://www.rogerebert.com/balder-and-dash/disabled-roles-disabled-performers).

Acting in the Cinema by James Naremore (University of California Press, Berkeley, 1988).

'Biotourism, Fantastic Voyage, and Sublime Inner Space' by Kim Swachuk in *Wild Science: Reading Feminism, Medicine, and the Media* edited by Janine Marchessault and Kim Sawchuk (Routledge, London, 2000).

'Black Swan/White Swan: On Female Objectification, Creatureliness, and Death Denial' by Jamie L. Goldenberg in *Death in Classic and Contemporary Film: Fade to Black* edited by Daniel Sullivan and Jeff Greenberg (Palgrave Macmillan, New York, 2013).

A Body of Vision: Representations of the Body in Recent Film and Poetry by R. Bruce Elder (Wilfred Laurier University Press, Ontario, 1997).

'The Cinema of Attractions: Early Film, Its Spectator, and the Avant-Garde' by Tom Gunning in *Theatre and Film: A Comparative Anthology* edited by Robert Knopf (Yale University Press, New York, 2005).

Different Bodies: Essays on Disability in Film and Television edited by Marja Evelyn Mogk (McFarland, Jefferson, 2013).

'Digitizing Deleuze: The Curious Case of the Digital Human Assemblage, or What Can A Digital Body Do?' by David H. Fleming in *Deleuze and Film* edited by David Martin-Jones and William Brown (Edinburgh University Press, Edinburgh, 2012).

High Contrast: Race and Gender in Contemporary Hollywood Film by Sharon Willis (Duke University Press, Durham and London, 1997).

'Horror and the Monstrous Feminine' by Barbara Creed in *The Dread of Difference* edited by Barry Keith Grant (University of Texas Press, Austin, 1996).

'The Inside-Out of Masculinity: David Cronenberg's Visceral Pleasures' by Linda Ruth Williams in *The Body's Perilous Pleasures: Dangerous Desires and Contemporary Culture* edited by Michele Aaron (Edinburgh University Press, Edinburgh, 1999).

'Masculinity as Spectacle: Reflections on Men and Mainstream Cinema' by Steve Neale in *Screen* (BFI, London, Vol 24, No 6, 1983).

'The New Hollywood Racelessness: Only the Fast, Furious, (and Multicultural) Will Survive' by Mary Beltrán in *Cinema Journal* (Vol 44, No 2, Winter 2005).

'On Being John Malkovich and Not Being Yourself' by Christopher Falzon in *The Philosophy of Charlie Kaufman* edited by David LaRocca (University Press of Kentucky, Lexington, 2011).

Powers of Horror: An Essay on Abjection by Julia Kristeva, translated by Leon S. Roudiez (Columbia University Press, New York, 1982).

Sideshow USA: Freaks and the American Cultural Imagination by Rachel Adams (University of Chicago Press, Chicago, 2001).

'The Social Network: Faces Behind Facebook' by David Bordwell on DavidBordwell.net (http://www.davidbordwell.net/blog/2011/01/30/the-social-network-faces-behind-facebook/).

The Tactile Eye: Touch and the Cinematic Experience by Jennifer M. Barker (University of California Press, Berkeley, 2009).

Toms, Coons, Mulattoes, Mammies, and Bucks: An Interpretive History of Blacks in American Films by Donald Bogle (Continuum International Publishing, 4th Edition, New York, 2006).

Transgressive Bodies: Representations in Film and Popular Culture by Dr. Niall Richardson (Ashgate Publishing, Surrey, 2010).

'Visual Pleasure and Narrative Cinema' by Laura Mulvey in *Visual and Other Pleasures* (Palgrave Macmillan, Hampshire, 2nd Edition, 2009).

SETS AND ARCHITECTURE

America by Jean Baudrillard, translated by Chris Turner (Verso, London, 1989).

Architecture and Film edited by Mark Lamster (Princeton Architectural Press, New York, 2000).

Architecture for the Screen: A Critical Study of Set Design in Hollywood's Golden Age by Juan Antonio Ramírez (McFarland, Jefferson, 2004).

'Before and After Metropolis: Film and Architecture in Search of the Modern City' by Dietrich Neumann in *Film Architecture: Set Designs From Metropolis to Blade Runner* edited by Dietrich Neumann (Prestel Publishing, New York, 1999).

'The Bourne Infrastructure' by Matt Jones on MagicalNihilism.com (http://magicalnihilism.com/2008/12/12/the-bourne-infrastructure/).

Dark Places: The Haunted House in Film by Barry Curtis (Reaktion Books, London, 2008).

'Escape by Design' by Maggie Valentine in *Architecture and Film* edited by Mark Lamster (Princeton Architectural Press, New York, 2000).

Fritz Lang's Metropolis: Cinematic Visions of Technology and Fear edited by Michael Minden and Holger Bachmann (Camden House, New York, 2000).

High Contrast: Race and Gender in Contemporary Hollywood Film by Sharon Willis (Duke University Press, Durham and London, 1997).

Kubrick: Inside A Film Artist's Maze by Thomas Allen Nelson (Indiana University Press, Bloomington, 2000).

'Like Today Only More So: The Credible Dystopia of Blade Runner' by Michael Webb in *Film Architecture: Set Designs From Metropolis to Blade Runner* edited by Dietrich Neumann (Prestel Publishing, New York, 1999).

'Mazes, Mirrors, Deception and Denial: An In-Depth Analysis of Stanley Kubrick's The Shining' by Rob Ager on CollativeLearning.com (http://www.collativelearning.com/the%20shining%20-%20chap%204.html).

'Nakatomi Space' by Geoff Manaugh on BldgBlog.blogspot.com (http://bldgblog.blogspot.co.uk/2010/01/nakatomi-space.html).

Powell and Pressburger: A Cinema of Magic Spaces by Andrew Moor (I.B.Tauris, London, 2005).

'Previewing the Cinematic City' by David Clarke in *The Cinematic City* edited by David Clarke (Routledge, London, 1997).

'The Ultimate Trip: Special Effects and the Visual Culture of Modernity' by Scott Bukatman in *Matters of Gravity: Special Effects and Supermen in the 20th Century* by Scott Bukatman (Duke University Press, Durham NC, 2003).

Visions of the City: Utopianism, Power and Politics in TwentiethCentury Urbanism by David Pinder (Edinburgh University Press, Edinburgh, 2005).

Warped Space: Art, Architecture, and Anxiety in Modern Culture by Anthony Vidler (MIT Press, Cambridge MA, 2001).

TIME

'Chris Marker and the Cinema as Time Machine' by Paul Coates in *Science Fiction Studies* (Vol 14, No 3, November 1987).

Cinema II: The Time Image by Gilles Deleuze (Athlone Press, London, 1989).

'Contingency, Order, and the Modular Narrative: 21 Grams and Irreversible' by Allan Cameron in *The Velvet Light Trap* (University of Texas Press, Austin, No 58, Fall 2006).

Film: An International History of the Medium by Robert Sklar (Harry N. Abrams, New York, 1993).

A History of Russian Cinema by Birgit Beumers (Berg, Oxford, 2009).

'In Search of Lost Reality: Waltzing With Bashir' by Markos Hadjioannou in *Deleuze and Film* edited by David Martin-Jones and William Brown (Edinburgh University Press, Edinburgh, 2012).

Sculpting in Time: Reflections on Cinema by Andrei Tarkovsky (The Bodley Head, London, 1986).

'Time and Stasis in 'La Jetée'' by Bruce Kawin in *Film Quarterly* (Vol 36, No 1, 1982).

'Waltzing the Limit' by Erin Manning in *Deleuze and Fascism – Security: War: Aesthetics* edited by Brad Evans and Julian Reid (Routledge, Oxon, 2013).

VOICE AND LANGUAGE

The Celluloid Closet: Homosexuality in the Movies by Vito Russo (Harper and Row, New York, 1981).

Enjoy your Symptom!: Jacques Lacan in Hollywood and Out by Slavoj Žižek (Routledge, Oxon, 2013).

Exploring Media Culture: A Guide by Michael R. Real (Sage Publications, London, 1996).

Film Language: A Semiotics of the Cinema by Christian Metz (University of Chicago Press, Chicago, 1974).

Flaming Classics: Queering the Film Canon by Alexander Doty (Routledge, New York, 2000).

Image, Music, Text by Roland Barthes, translated by Stephen Heath (Fontana Press, London, 1977).

'Look at Me! A Phenomenology of Heath Ledger in The Dark Knight' by Jörg Sternagel in *Theorizing Film Acting* edited by Aaron Taylor (Routledge, Oxon, 2012).

Sculpting in Time: Reflections on Cinema by Andrei Tarkovsky (The Bodley Head, London, 1986).

The Selfish Gene by Richard Dawkins (Oxford University Press, Oxford, 1976).

Simulacra and Simulation by Jean Baudrillard (University of Michigan Press, Michigan, 1994).

'Ulterior Structuralist Motives – With Zombies' by Michael Atkinson on IFC.com (http://www.ifc.com/fix/2010/01/zombie).

'Uncanny Aurality in Pontypool' by Steen Christiansen in *Cinephile: The University of British Columbia's Film Journal* (Vol 6, No 2, Fall 2010).

A Voice and Nothing More by Mladen Dolar (MIT Press, Cambridge MA, 2006).

The Voice in Cinema by Michel Chion (Columbia University Press, New York, 1999).

POWER AND IDEOLOGY

Backlash: The Undeclared War Against Women by Susan Faludi (Random House, London, 1993).

Better Left Unsaid: Victorian Novels, Hays Code Films, and the Benefits of Censorship by Nora Gilbert (Stanford University Press, Stanford, 2013).

Cinemas of the World: Film and Society from 1895 to the Present by James Chapman (Reaktion Books, London, 2003).

'Electronic Child Abuse? Rethinking the Media's Effects on Children' by David Buckingham in *Ill Effects – The Media/Violence Debate* edited by Martin Barker and Julian Petley (Routledge, London, 2nd Edition, 2001).

The Gospel According to Disney: Faith, Trust, and Pixie Dust by Mark I. Pinsky (Westminster John Knox Press, Louisville, 2004).

Hollywood V. Hard Core: How the Struggle Over Censorship Created the Modern Film Industry by Jon Lewis (New York University Press, New York, 2002).

'I Was A Teenage Horror Fan. Or, How I Learned to Stop Worrying and Love Linda Blair' by Mark Kermode in *Ill Effects – The Media/Violence Debate* edited by Martin Barker and Julian Petley (Routledge, London, 2nd Edition, 2001).

'Media Violence Effects and Violent Crime' by Christopher J. Ferguson in *Violent Crime: Clinical and Social Implications* edited by Christopher J. Ferguson (Sage Publications, London, 2010).

The New Iranian Cinema: Politics, Representation and Identity edited by Richard Tapper (I.B.Tauris, London, 2002).

Operation Hollywood: How the Pentagon Shapes and Censors the Movies by David L. Robb (Prometheus Books, New York, 2004).

Projecting Paranoia: Conspiratorial Visions in American Film by Ray Pratt (University Press of Kansas, 2001).

Projections of War: Hollywood, American Culture, and World War II by Thomas Doherty (Columbia University Press, New York, 1993).

Reel Bad Arabs: How Hollywood Vilifies a People by Jack Shaheen (Olive Branch Press, Northampton MA, 2009).

Reel Power: Hollywood Cinema and American Supremacy by Matthew Alford (Pluto Press, New York, 2010).

'Reservoirs of Dogma: An Archaeology of Popular Anxieties' by Graham Murdock in *Ill Effects – The Media/Violence Debate* edited by Martin Barker and Julian Petley (Routledge, London, 2nd Edition, 2001).

Sinascape: Contemporary Chinese Cinema by Gary G. Xu (Rowman & Littlefield, Plymouth, 2007).

The Six-Gun Mystique Sequel by John G. Cawelti (Bowling Green State University Popular Press, 1999).

'Split Skins: Female Agency and Bodily Mutilation in The Little Mermaid' by Susan White in *Film Theory Goes to the Movies* edited by Jim Collins, Hilary Radner and Ava Preacher Collins (Routledge, New York, 1993).

'The Testament of Dr. Goebbels' by Eric Rentschler in *Film and Nationalism* edited by Alan Williams (Rutgers University Press, New Jersey, 2002).

'Two Ways to Yuma: Locke, Liberalism, and Western Masculinity in 3:10 to Yuma' by Stephen J. Mexal in *The Philosophy of the Western* edited by Jennifer L. McMahon and B. Steve Csaki (University Press of Kentucky, Lexington, 2010).

'Ups and Downs of the Latest Schwarzenegger Film: Hasta la Vista, Fairness – Media's Line on Arabs' by Salam Al-Marayati and Don Bustany in the *Los Angeles Times* (8 August 1994) (http://articles.latimes.com/1994-08-08/entertainment/ca-24971_1_hasta-la-vista).

'Us and Them' by Julian Petley in *Ill Effects – The Media/Violence Debate* edited by Martin Barker and Julian Petley (Routledge, London, 2nd Edition, 2001).

TECHNOLOGY AND TECHNOPHOBIA

1001 Movies You Must See Before You Die edited by Stephen Jay Schneider (Quintessence, London, 2010).

British Science Fiction Cinema edited by I.Q. Hunter (Routledge, London, 1999).

'A Cyborg Manifesto' by Donna Haraway in *The Cybercultures Reader* edited by David Bell and Barbara M. Kennedy (Routledge, London, 2000).

'From Nollywood to Nollyworld: Processes of Transnationalization in the Nigerian Video Film Industry' by Alessandro Jedlowski in *Global Nollywood: The Transnational Dimensions of an African Video Film Industry* edited by Matthias Krings and Onookome Okome (Indiana University Press, Bloomington, 2013).

'Genetic Themes in Fiction Films' by Michael Clark on Genome.Wellcome.ac.uk (http://genome.wellcome.ac.uk/doc_WTD023539.html).

Machine Age Comedy by Michael North (Oxford University Press, Oxford, 2009).

Mad, Bad and Dangerous? The Scientist and the Cinema by Christopher Frayling (Reaktion Books, London, 2005).

'Nollywood and its Critics' by Onookome Okome in Viewing African Cinema in *The Twenty-First Century: Art Films and the Nollywood Video Revolution* edited by Mahir Saul and Ralph A. Austen (Ohio University Press, Athens OH, 2010).

'Race, Space and Class: The Politics of Cityscapes in Science Fiction Films' by David Desser in *Alien Zone II: The Spaces of Science-Fiction Cinema* edited by Annette Kuhn (Verso, London, 1999).

Technophobia! Science Fiction Visions of Posthuman Technology by Daniel Dinello (University of Texas Press, Austin, 2005).

'Tetsuo: The Iron Man / Tetsuo II: Body Hammer' by Andrew Grossman in *The Cinema of Japan and Korea* edited by Justin Bowyer (Wallflower Press, London, 2004).

What Is Cinema? Vol. 1 by Andre Bazin (University of California Press, Berkeley, 2004).

ACKNOWLEDGEMENTS

With enormous thanks to Mary for her love and support throughout everything – there are no words to express how grateful I am.

Love and thanks as well to my parents, Margaret and Peter, without whom this wouldn't have been possible, to Ross and Kathleen for their support, and of course to the rest of my friends and family for putting up with me throughout, especially to my children Niven and Caitlin.

Thanks to everyone who helped out with the book along the way: Dr. Malgorzata Bugaj, Dr. Pasquale Iannone and Dr. Philip Drake for their academic insight and advice; Emma Hayley and Dan Lockwood for their editorial skills; Katri Vanhatalo and Mark David Jacobs for their encyclopedic knowledge of film; Peter Morton for his assistance and friendship; Sandra Alland for her expertise and advice; and Dan Berry, Fumio Obata, Michael Leader and Tom Humberstone for their help and encouragement along the way.

Big thanks as well to my Edinburgh comics friends Aimee Lockwood, Stephen Goodall, Will Morris and Zuzanna Dominiak, who were a huge moral support and helped make my work better by pointing out my mistakes.

Filmish will return...